THE ANDES OF SOUTHERN PERU

GEOGRAPHICAL RECONNAISSANCE ALONG THE SEVENTY-THIRD MERIDIAN

BY

ISAIAH BOWMAN

Director of the American Geographical Society

GREENWOOD PRESS, PUBLISHERS
NEW YORK   1968

Printed in the United States of America

PREFACE

THE geographic work of the Yale Peruvian Expedition of 1911 was essentially a reconnaissance of the Peruvian Andes along the 73rd meridian. The route led from the tropical plains of the lower Urubamba southward over lofty snow-covered passes to the desert coast at Camaná. The strong climatic and topographic contrasts and the varied human life which the region contains are of geographic interest chiefly because they present so many and such clear cases of environmental control within short distances. Though we speak of "isolated" mountain communities in the Andes, it is only in a relative sense. The extreme isolation felt in some of the world's great deserts is here unknown. It is therefore all the more remarkable when we come upon differences of customs and character in Peru to find them strongly developed in spite of the small distances that separate unlike groups of people.

My division of the Expedition undertook to make a contour map of the two-hundred-mile stretch of mountain country between Abancay and the Pacific coast, and a great deal of detailed geographic and physiographic work had to be sacrificed to insure the completion of the survey. Camp sites, forage, water, and, above all, strong beasts for the topographer's difficult and excessively lofty stations brought daily problems that were always serious and sometimes critical. I was so deeply interested in the progress of the topographic map that whenever it came to a choice of plans the map and not the geography was first considered. The effect upon my work was to distribute it with little regard to the demands of the problems, but I cannot regret this in view of the great value of the maps. Mr. Kai Hendriksen did splendid work in putting through two hundred miles of plane-tabling in two months under conditions of extreme difficulty. Many of his triangulation stations ranged in elevation from 14,000 to nearly

18,000 feet, and the cold and storms—especially the hailstorms of mid-afternoon—were at times most severe.

It is also a pleasure to say that Mr. Paul Baxter Lanius, my assistant on the lower Urubamba journey, rendered an invaluable service in securing continuous weather records at Yavero and elsewhere, and in getting food and men to the river party at a critical time. Dr. W. G. Erving, surgeon of the Expedition, accompanied me on a canoe journey through the lower gorge of the Urubamba between Rosalina and the mouth of the Timpia, and again by pack train from Santa Ana to Cotahuasi. For a time he assisted the topographer. It is due to his prompt surgical assistance to various members of the party that the field work was uninterrupted. He was especially useful when two of our river Indians from Pongo de Mainique were accidentally shot. I have since been informed by their *patrón* that they were at work within a few months.

It is difficult to express the gratitude I feel toward Professor Hiram Bingham, Director of the Expedition, first for the executive care he displayed in the organization of the expedition's plans, which left the various members largely care-free, and second, for generously supplying the time of various assistants in the preparation of results. I have enjoyed so many facilities for the completion of the work that at least a year's time has been saved thereby. Professor Bingham's enthusiasm for pioneer field work was in the highest degree stimulating to every member of the party. Furthermore, it led to a determination to complete at all hazards the original plans.

Finally, I wish gratefully to acknowledge the expert assistance of Miss Gladys M. Wrigley, of the editorial staff of the American Geographical Society, who prepared the climatic tables, many of the miscellaneous data related thereto, and all of the curves in Chapter X. Miss Wrigley also assisted in the revision of Chapters IX and X and in the correction of the proof. Her eager and in the highest degree faithful assistance in these tasks bespeaks a true scientific spirit.

Isaiah Bowman.

SPECIAL ACKNOWLEDGMENTS FOR ILLUSTRATIONS

Fig. 28. Photograph by H. L. Tucker, Engineer, Yale Peruvian Expedition of 1911.

Fig. 43. Photograph by H. L. Tucker.

Fig. 44. Photograph by Professor Hiram Bingham.

Figs. 136, 139, 140. Data for hachured sketch maps, chiefly from topographic sheets by A. H. Bumstead, Topographer to Professor Bingham's Peruvian Expeditions of 1912 and 1914.

CONTENTS

PART I

HUMAN GEOGRAPHY

xi

PART I

HUMAN GEOGRAPHY

CHAPTER I

THE REGIONS OF PERU

LET four Peruvians begin this book by telling what manner of country they live in. Their ideas are provincial and they have a fondness for exaggerated description: but, for all that, they will reveal much that is true because they will at least reveal themselves. Their opinions reflect both the spirit of the toiler on the land and the outlook of the merchant in the town in relation to geography and national problems. Their names do not matter; let them stand for the four human regions of Peru, for they are in many respects typical men.

THE FOREST DWELLER

One of them I met at a rubber station on the lower Urubamba River.[1] He helped secure my canoe, escorted me hospitably to his hut, set food and drink before me, and talked of the tropical forest, the rubber business, the Indians, the rivers, and the trails. In his opinion Peru was a land of great forest resources. Moreover, the fertile plains along the river margins might become the sites of rich plantations. The rivers had many fish and his garden needed only a little cultivation to produce an abundance of food. Fruit trees grew on every hand. He had recently married the daughter of an Indian chief.

Formerly he had been a missionary at a rubber station on the Madre de Dios, where the life was hard and narrow, and he doubted if there were any real converts. Himself the son of an Englishman and a Chilean woman, he found, so he said, that a missionary's life in the rubber forest was intolerable for more than a few

---

[1] For all locations mentioned see maps accompanying the text or Appendix C.

years. Yet he had no fault to find with the religious system of which he had once formed a part; in fact he had still a certain curious mixed loyalty to it. Before I left he gave me a photograph of himself and said with little pride and more sadness that perhaps I would remember him as a man that had done some good in the world along with much that might have been better.

We shall understand our interpreter better if we know who his associates were. He lived with a Frenchman who had spent several years in Africa as a soldier in the "Foreign Legion." If you do not know what that means, you have yet all the pleasure of an interesting discovery. The Frenchman had reached the station the year before quite destitute and clad only in a shirt and a pair of trousers. A day's journey north lived a young half-breed—son of a drunken father and a Machiganga woman, who cheated me so badly when I engaged Indian paddlers that I should almost have preferred that he had robbed me. Yet in a sense he had my life in his hands and I submitted. A German and a native Peruvian ran a rubber station on a tributary two days' journey from the first. It will be observed that the company was mixed. They were all Peruvians, but of a sort not found in such relative abundance elsewhere. The defeated and the outcast, as well as the pioneer, go down eventually to the hot forested lands where men are forgotten.

While he saw gold in every square mile of his forested region, my clerical friend saw misery also. The brutal treatment of the Indians by the whites of the Madre de Dios country he could speak of only as a man reviving a painful memory. The Indians at the station loved him devotedly. There was only justice and kindness in all his dealings. Because he had large interests to look after, he knew all the members of the tribe, and his word was law in no hackneyed sense. A kindlier man never lived in the rubber forest. His influence as a high-souled man of business was vastly greater than as a missionary in this frontier society. He could daily illustrate by practical example what he had formerly been able only to preach.

He thought the life of the Peruvian cities debasing. The

Fig. 1.

Fig. 2.

Fig. 1—Tropical vegetation, clearing on the river bank and rubber station at Pongo de Mainique. The pronounced scarp on the northeastern border of the Andes is seen in the right background.

Fig. 2—Pushing a heavy dugout against the current in the rapids below Pongo de Mainique. The Indian boy and his father in the canoe had been accidentally shot.

Fig. 3—From ice to sugar cane, Urubamba Valley, at Colpani. On the north-eastern border of the Cordillera Vilcapampa looking upstream. In the extreme background and thirteen sixteenths of an inch from the top of the picture is the sharp peak of Salcantay. Only the lower end of the more open portion of the Canyon of Torontoy is here shown. There is a field of sugar cane in the foreground and the valley trail is shown on the opposite side of the river.

coastal valleys were small and dry and the men who lived there were crowded and poor (sic). The plateau was inhabited by Indians little better than brutes. Surely I could not think that the fine forest Indian was lower than the so-called civilized Indian of the plateau. There was plenty of room in the forest; and there was wealth if you knew how to get at it. Above all you were far from the annoying officials of the government, and therefore could do much as you pleased so long as you paid your duties on rubber and did not wantonly kill too many Indians.

For all his kindly tolerance of men and conditions he yet found fault with the government. "They" neglected to build roads, to encourage colonization, and to lower taxes on the forest products, which were always won at great risk. Nature had done her part well—it was only government that hindered. Moreover, the forested region was the land of the future. If Peru was to be a great nation her people would have to live largely upon the eastern plains. Though others spoke of "going in" and "coming out" of the rubber country as one might speak of entering and leaving a dungeon, he always spoke of it as home. Though he now lived in the wilderness he hoped to see the day when plantations covered the plains. A greater Peru and the forest were inseparable ideas to him.

THE EASTERN VALLEY PLANTER

My second friend lived in one of the beautiful mountain valleys of the eastern Andes. We walked through his clean cacao orchards and cane fields. Like the man in the forest, he believed in the thorough inefficiency of the government; otherwise why were there no railways for the cheaper transportation of the valley products, no dams for the generation of power and the storage of irrigation water, not even roads for mule carts? Had the government been stable and efficient there would now be a dense population in the eastern valleys. Revolutions were the curse of these remote sections of the country. The ne'er-do-wells became generals. The loafer you dismissed today might demand ten thousand dollars tomorrow or threaten to destroy your plantation.

The government troops might come to help you, but they were always too late.

For this one paid most burdensome taxes. Lima profited thereby, not the valley planters. The coast people were the favored of Peru anyhow. They had railroads, good steamer service, public improvements at government expense, and comparatively light taxes. If the government were impartial the eastern valleys also would have railways and a dense population. Who could tell? Perhaps the capital city might be here. Certainly it was better to have Lima here than on the coast where the Chileans might at any time take it again. The blessings of the valleys were both rich and manifold. Here was neither a cold plateau nor the hot plains, but fertile valleys with a vernal climate.

We talked of much else, but our conversation had always the pioneer flavor. And though an old man he saw always the future Peru growing wonderfully rich and powerful as men came to recognize and use the resources of the eastern valleys. This too was the optimism of the pioneer. Once started on that subject he grew eloquent. He was provincial but he was also intensely patriotic. He never missed an opportunity to impress upon his guests that a great state would arise when people and rulers at last recognized the wealth of eastern Peru.

The Highland Shepherd

The people who live in the lofty highlands and mountains of Peru have several months of real winter weather despite their tropical latitude. In the midst of a snowstorm in the Maritime Cordillera I met a solitary traveler bound for Cotahuasi on the floor of a deep canyon a day's journey toward the east. It was noon and we halted our pack trains in the lee of a huge rock shelter to escape the bitter wind that blew down from the snow-clad peaks of Solimana. Men who follow the same trails are fraternal. In a moment we had food from our saddle-bags spread on the snow under the corner of a *poncho* and had exchanged the best in each other's collection as naturally as friends exchange greetings. By the time I had told him whence and why in response to his inevitable questions we had finished the food and had gathered a heap of *tola* bushes for a fire. The *arriero* (muleteer) brought water from a spring in the hollow below us. Though the snow thickened, the wind fell. We were comfortable, even at 16,000 feet, and called the place "The Salamanca Club." Then I questioned him, and this is what he said:

"I live in the deep valley of Cotahuasi, but my lands lie chiefly up here on the plateau. My family has held title to this *puna* ever since the Wars of Liberation, except for a few years after one of our early revolutions. I travel about a great deal looking after my flocks. Only Indians live up here. Away off yonder beyond that dark gorge is a group of their huts, and on the bright days of summer you may see their sheep, llamas, and alpacas up here, for on the floors of the watered valleys that girdle these volcanoes there are more tender grasses than grow on this *despoblado*. I give them corn and barley from my irrigated fields in the valley; they give me wool and meat. The alpaca wool is most valuable. It is hard to get, for the alpaca requires short grasses and plenty of water, and you see there is only coarse tufted *ichu* grass about us, and there are no streams. It is all right for llamas, but alpacas require better forage.

"No one can imagine the poverty and ignorance of these mountain shepherds. They are filthier than beasts. I have to watch them constantly or they would sell parts of the flocks, which do not belong to them, or try to exchange the valuable alpaca wool for coca leaves in distant towns. They are frequently drunk."

"But where do they get the drink?" I asked. "And what do you pay them?"

"Oh, the drink is chiefly imported alcohol, and also *chicha* made from corn. They insist on having it, and do better when I bring them a little now and then. They get much more from the dealers in the towns. As for pay, I do not pay them anything in money except when they bring meat to the valley. Then I give them a few *reales* apiece for the sheep and a little more for the llamas. The flocks all belong to me really, but of course the poor Indian must have a little money. Besides, I let him have a part of the yearly increase. It is not much, but he has always lived this way and I suppose that he is contented after a fashion.''

Then he became eager to tell what wealth the mountains contained in soil and climate if only the right grasses were introduced by the government.

''Here, before us, are vast *punas* almost without habitations. If the officials would bring in hardy Siberian grasses these lava-covered plateaus might be carpeted with pasture. There would be villages here and there. The native Indians easily stand the altitude. This whole Cordillera might have ten times as many people. Why does the government bother about concessions in the rubber forests and roads to the eastern valleys when there are these vast tracts only requiring new seeds to develop into rich pastures? The government could thus greatly increase its revenues because there is a heavy tax on exported wool.''

Thus he talked about the bleak Cordillera until we forgot the pounding of our hearts and our frequent gasps for breath on account of the altitude. His rosy picture of a well-populated highland seemed to bring us down nearer sea level where normal folks lived. To the Indians the altitude is nothing. It has an effect, but it is slight; at any rate they manage to reproduce their kind at elevations that would kill a white mother. If alcohol were abolished and better grasses introduced, these lofty pastures might indeed support a much larger population. The sheep pastures of the world are rapidly disappearing before the march of the farmer. Here, well above the limit of cultivation, is a permanent range, one of the great as well as permanent assets of Peru.

THE COASTAL PLANTER

The man from the deep Majes Valley in the coastal desert rode out with me through cotton fields as rich and clean as those of a Texas plantation. He was tall, straight-limbed, and clear-eyed—one of the energetic younger generation, yet with the blood of a proud old family. We forded the river and rode on through vine-yards and fig orchards loaded with fruit. His manner became deeply earnest as he pictured the future of Peru, when her people

Fig. 4.

Fig. 5.

FIG. 4—Large ground moss—so-called *yareta*—used for fuel. It occurs in the zone of Alpine vegetation and is best developed in regions where the snowline is highest. The photograph represents a typical occurrence between Cotahuasi and Salamanca, elevation 16,000 feet (4,880 m.). The snowline is here at 17,500 feet (5,333 m.). In the foreground is the most widely distributed *tola* bush, also used for fuel.

FIG. 5—Expedition's camp near Lambrama, 15,500 feet (4,720 m.), after a snowstorm. The location is midway in the pasture zone.

Fig. 6.

Fig. 7.

Fig. 6—Irrigated Chili Valley on the outskirts of Arequipa. The lower slopes of El Misti are in the left background. The *Alto de los Huesos* or Plateau of Bones lies on the farther side of the valley.

Fig. 7—Crossing the highest pass (Chuquito) in the Cordillera Vilcapampa, 14,500 feet (4,420 m.). Grazing is here carried on up to the snowline.

would take advantage of scientific methods and use labor-saving machinery. He said that the methods now in use were medieval, and he pointed to a score of concrete illustrations. Also, here was water running to waste, yet the desert was on either hand. There should be dams and canals. Every drop of water was needed. The population of the valley could be easily doubled.

Capital was lacking but there was also lacking energy among the people. Slipshod methods brought them a bare living and they were too easily contented. Their standards of life should be elevated. Education was still for the few, and it should be universal. A new spirit of progress was slowly developing—a more general interest in public affairs, a desire to advance with the more progressive nations of South America,—and when it had reached its culmination there would be no happier land than coastal Peru, already the seat of the densest populations and the most highly cultivated fields.

These four men have portrayed the four great regions of Peru —the lowland plains, the eastern mountain valleys, the lofty plateaus, and the valley oases of the coast. This is not all of Peru. The mountain basins have their own peculiar qualities and the valley heads of the coastal zone are unlike the lower valleys and the plateau on either hand. Yet the chief characteristics of the country are set forth with reasonable fidelity in these individual accounts. Moreover the spirit of the Peruvians is better shown thereby than their material resources. If this is not Peru, it is what the Peruvians think is Peru, and to a high degree a man's country is what he thinks it is—at least it is little more to him.

CHAPTER II

THE RAPIDS AND CANYONS OF THE URUBAMBA

AMONG the scientifically unexplored regions of Peru there is no other so alluring to the geographer as the vast forested realm on the eastern border of the Andes. Thus it happened that within two weeks of our arrival at Cuzco we followed the northern trail to the great canyon of the Urubamba (Fig. 8), the gateway to the eastern valleys and the lowland plains of the Amazon. It is here that the adventurous river, reënforced by hundreds of mountain-born tributaries, finally cuts its defiant way through the last of its great topographic barriers. More than seventy rapids interrupt its course; one of them, at the mouth of the Sirialo, is at least a half-mile in length, and long before one reaches its head he hears its roaring from beyond the forest-clad mountain spurs.

The great bend of the Urubamba in which the line of rapids occurs is one of the most curious hydrographic features in Peru. The river suddenly changes its general northward course and striking south of west flows nearly fifty miles toward the axis of the mountains, where, turning almost in a complete circle, it makes a final assault upon the eastern mountain ranges. Fifty miles farther on it breaks through the long sharp-crested chain of the Front Range of the Andes in a splendid gorge more than a half-mile deep, the famous *Pongo de Mainique* (Fig. 9).

Our chief object in descending the line of rapids was to study the canyon of the Urubamba below Rosalina and to make a topographic sketch map of it. We also wished to know what secrets might be gathered in this hitherto unexplored stretch of country, what people dwelt along its banks, and if the vague tales of deserted towns and fugitive tribes had any basis in fact.

We could gather almost no information as to the nature of the river except from the report of Major Kerbey, an American, who, in 1897, descended the last twenty miles of the one hundred we proposed to navigate. He pronounced the journey more hazard-

8

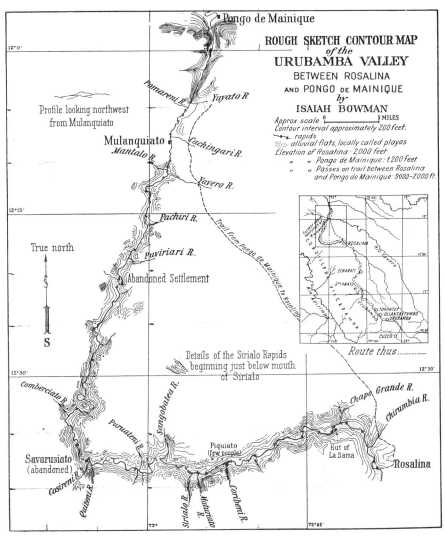

FIG. 8—Sketch map showing the route of the Yale-Peruvian Expedition of 1911 down the Urubamba Valley, together with the area of the main map and the changes in the delineation of the bend of the Urubamba resulting from the surveys of the Expedition. Based on the "Mapa que comprende las ultimas exploraciones y estudios verificados desde 1900 hasta 1906," 1:1,000,000, Bol. Soc. Geogr. Lima, Vol. 25, No. 3, 1909. For details of the trail from Rosalina to Pongo de Mainique see "Plano de las Secciones y Afluentes del Rio Urubamba: 1902-1904, scale 1:150,000 by Luis M. Robledo in Bol. Soc. Geogr. Lima, Vol. 25, No. 4, 1909. Only the lower slopes of the long mountain spurs can be seen from the river; hence only in a few places could observations be made on the topography of distant ranges. Paced distances of a half mile at irregular intervals were used for the estimation of longer distances. Directions were taken by compass corrected for magnetic deviation as determined on the seventy-third meridian (See Appendix A). The position of Rosalina on Robledo's map was taken as a base.

ous than Major Powell's famous descent of the Grand Canyon in 1867—an obvious exaggeration. He lost his canoe in a treacherous rapid, was deserted by his Indian guides, and only after a painful march through an all but impassable jungle was he finally able to escape on an abandoned raft. Less than a dozen have ventured down since Major Kerbey's day. A Peruvian mining engineer descended the river a few years ago, and four Italian traders a year later floated down in rafts and canoes, losing almost all of their cargo. For nearly two months they were marooned upon a sand-bar waiting for the river to subside. At last they succeeded in reaching Mulanquiato, an Indian settlement and plantation owned by Pereira, near the entrance to the last canyon. Their attempted passage of the worst stretch of rapids resulted in the loss of all their rubber cargo, the work of a year. Among the half dozen others who have made the journey—Indians and slave traders from down-river rubber posts—there is no record of a single descent without the loss of at least one canoe.

To reach the head of canoe navigation we made a two weeks' muleback journey north of Cuzco through the steep-walled granite Canyon of Torontoy, and to the sugar and cacao plantations of the middle Urubamba, or Santa Ana Valley, where we outfitted. At Echarati, thirty miles farther on, where the heat becomes more intense and the first patches of real tropical forest begin, we were obliged to exchange our beasts for ten fresh animals accustomed to forest work and its privations. Three days later we pitched our tent on the river bank at Rosalina, the last outpost of the valley settlements. As we dropped down the steep mountain slope before striking the river flood plain, we passed two half-naked Machiganga Indians perched on the limbs of a tree beside the trail, our first sight of members of a tribe whose territory we had now entered. Later in the day they crossed the river in a dugout, landed on the sand-bar above us, and gathered brush for the nightly fire, around which they lie wrapped in a single shirt woven from the fiber of the wild cotton.

Rosalina is hardly more than a name on the map and a camp site on the river bank. Some distance back from the left bank of

FIG. 10—The lower half of a two-thousand-foot cliff, granite Canyon of Torontoy, Urubamba Valley. The wall is developed almost entirely along joint planes. It is here that the Urubamba River crosses the granite axis of the Cordillera Vilcapampa, the easternmost system of the Andes of southern Peru. Compare also Figs. 144 and 145.

FIG. 9—The upper entrance to the Pongo de Mainique, where the Urubamba crosses the Front Range of the Andes in a splendid gateway 4,000 feet deep. The river is broken by an almost continuous line of rapids.

Fig. 11.

Fig. 12.

Fig. 11—A temporary shelter-hut on a sand-bar near the great bend of the Urubamba (see map, Fig. 8). The Machiganga Indians use these cane shelters during the
fishing season, when the river is low.

Fig. 12—Thirty-foot canoe in a rapid above Pongo de Mainique.

the river is a sugar plantation, whose owner lives in the cooler mountains, a day's journey away; on the right bank is a small clearing planted to sugar cane and yuca, and on the edge of it is a reed hut sheltering three inhabitants, the total population of Rosalina. The owner asked our destination, and to our reply that we should start in a few days for Pongo de Mainique he offered two serious objections. No one thought of arranging so difficult a journey in less than a month, for canoe and Indians were difficult to find, and the river trip was dangerous. Clearly, to start without the loss of precious time would require unusual exertion. We immediately despatched an Indian messenger to the owner of the small hacienda across the river while one of our peons carried a second note to a priest of great influence among the forest Indians, Padre Mendoza, then at his other home in the distant mountains.

The answer of Señor Morales was his appearance in person to offer the hospitality of his home and to assist us in securing canoe and oarsmen. To our note the Padre, from his hill-top, sent a polite answer and the offer of his large canoe if we would but guarantee its return. His temporary illness prevented a visit to which we had looked forward with great interest.

The morning after our arrival I started out on foot in company with our *arricro* in search of the Machigangas, who fish and hunt along the river bank during the dry season and retire to their hill camps when the heavy rains begin. We soon left the well-beaten trail and, following a faint woodland path, came to the river bank about a half day's journey below Rosalina. There we found a canoe hidden in an overhanging arch of vines, and crossing the river met an Indian family who gave us further directions. Their vague signs were but dimly understood and we soon found ourselves in the midst of a *carrizo* (reed) swamp filled with tall bamboo and cane and crossed by a network of interlacing streams. We followed a faint path only to find ourselves climbing the adjacent mountain slopes away from our destination. Once again in the swamp we had literally to cut our way through the thick cane, wade the numberless brooks, and follow wild animal trails until, late in the day, famished and thirsty, we came upon a little clearing on a sand-bar, the hut of La Sama, who knew the Machigangas and their villages.

After our long day's work we had fish and yuca, and water to which had been added a little raw cane sugar. Late at night La Sama returned from a trip to the Indian villages down river. He brought with him a half-dozen Machiganga Indians, boys and men, and around the camp fire that night gave us a dramatic account of his former trip down river. At one point he leaped to his feet, and with an imaginary pole shifted the canoe in a swift rapid, turned it aside from imminent wreck, and shouting at the top of his voice over the roar of the water finally succeeded in evading what he had made seem certain death in a whirlpool. We kept a fire going all night long for we slept upon the ground without a covering, and, strange as it may appear, the cold seemed intense, though the minimum thermometer registered 59° F. The next morning the whole party of ten sunned themselves for nearly an hour until the flies and heat once more drove them to shelter.

Returning to camp next day by a different route was an experience of great interest, because of the light it threw on hidden trails known only to the Indian and his friends. Slave raiders in former years devastated the native villages and forced the Indian to conceal his special trails of refuge. At one point we traversed a cliff seventy-five feet above the river, walking on a narrow ledge no wider than a man's foot. At another point the dim trail apparently disappeared, but when we had climbed hand over hand up the face of the cliff, by hanging vines and tree roots, we came upon it again. Crossing the river in the canoe we had used the day before, we shortened the return by wading the swift Chirumbia waist-deep, and by crawling along a cliff face for nearly an eighth of a mile. At the steepest point the river had so undercut the face that there was no trail at all, and we swung fully fifteen feet from one ledge to another, on a hanging vine high above the river.

After two days' delay we left Rosalina late in the afternoon of August 7. My party included several Machiganga Indians, La

Sama, and Dr. W. G. Erving, surgeon of the expedition. Mr. P. B. Lanius, Moscoso (the *arriero*), and two peons were to take the pack train as far as possible toward the rubber station at Pongo de Mainique where preparations were to be made for our arrival. At the first rapid we learned the method of our Indian boatmen. It was to run the heavy boat head on into shallow water at one side of a rapid and in this way "brake" it down stream. Heavily loaded with six men, 200 pounds of baggage, a dog, and supplies of yuca and sugar cane our twenty-five foot dugout canoe was as rigid as a steamer, and we dropped safely down rapid after rapid until long after dark, and by the light of a glorious tropical moon we beached our craft in front of La Sama's hut at the edge of the cane swamp.

Here for five days we endured a most exasperating delay. La Sama had promised Indian boatmen and now said none had yet been secured. Each day Indians were about to arrive, but by nightfall the promise was broken only to be repeated the following morning. To save our food supply—we had taken but six days' provisions—we ate yuca soup and fish and some parched corn, adding to this only a little from our limited stores. At last we could wait no longer, even if the map had to be sacrificed to the work of navigating the canoe. Our determination to leave stirred La Sama to final action. He secured an assistant named Wilson and embarked with us, planning to get Indians farther down river or make the journey himself.

On August 12, at 4.30 P. M., we entered upon the second stage of the journey. As we shot down the first long rapid and rounded a wooded bend the view down river opened up and gave us our first clear notion of the region we had set out to explore. From mountain summits in the clouds long trailing spurs descend to the river bank. In general the slopes are smooth-contoured and forest-clad from summit to base; only in a few places do high cliffs diversify the scenery. The river vista everywhere includes a rapid and small patches of *playa* or flood plain on the inside of the river curves. Although a true canyon hems in the river at two celebrated passes farther down, the upper part of the river flows in a somewhat open valley of moderate relief, with here and there a sentinel-like peak next the river.

A light shower fell at sunset, a typical late-afternoon downpour so characteristic of the tropics. We landed at a small encampment of Machigangas, built a fire against the scarred trunk of a big palm, and made up our beds in the open, covering them with our rubber ponchos. Our Indian neighbors gave us yuca and corn, but their neighborliness went no further, for when our boatmen attempted to sleep under their roofs they drove them out and fastened as securely as possible the shaky door of their hut.

All our efforts to obtain Indians, both here and elsewhere, proved fruitless. One excuse after another was overcome; they plainly coveted the trinkets, knives, machetes, muskets, and ammunition that we offered them; and they appeared to be friendly enough. Only after repeated assurances of our friendship could we learn the real reason for their refusal. Some of them were escaped rubber pickers that had been captured by white raiders several years before, and for them a return to the rubber country meant enslavement, heavy floggings, and separation from their numerous wives. The hardships they had endured, their final escape, the cruelty of the rubber men, and the difficult passage of the rapids below were a set of circumstances that nothing in our list of gifts could overcome. My first request a week before had so sharpened their memory that one of them related the story of his wrongs, a recital intensely dramatic to the whole circle of his listeners, including myself. Though I did not understand the details of his story, his tones and gesticulations were so effective that they held me as well as his kinsmen of the woods spellbound for over an hour.

It is appalling to what extent this great region has been depopulated by the slave raiders and those arch enemies of the savage, smallpox and malaria. At Rosalina, over sixty Indians died of malaria in one year; and only twenty years ago seventy of them, the entire population of the Pongo, were swept away by smallpox. For a week we passed former camps near small abandoned clearings, once the home of little groups of Machigangas.

Even the summer shelter huts on the sand-bars, where the Indians formerly gathered from their hill homes to fish, are now almost entirely abandoned. Though our men carefully reconnoitered each one for fear of ambush, the precaution was needless. Below the Coribeni the Urubamba is a great silent valley. It is fitted by Nature to support numerous villages, but its vast solitudes are unbroken except at night, when a few families that live in the hills slip down to the river to gather yuca and cane.

By noon of the second day's journey we reached the head of the great rapid at the mouth of the Sirialo. We had already run the long Coribeni rapid, visited the Indian huts at the junction of the big Coribeni tributary, exchanged our canoe for a larger and steadier one, and were now to run one of the ugliest rapids of the upper river. The rapid is formed by the gravel masses that the Sirialo brings down from the distant Cordillera Vilcapampa. They trail along for at least a half-mile, split the river into two main currents and nearly choke the mouth of the tributary. For almost a mile above this great barrier the main river is ponded and almost as quiet as a lake.

We let our craft down this rapid by ropes, and in the last difficult passage were so roughly handled by our almost unmanageable canoe as to suffer from several bad accidents. All of the party were injured in one way or another, while I suffered a fracture sprain of the left foot that made painful work of the rest of the river trip.

At two points below Rosalina the Urubamba is shut in by steep mountain slopes and vertical cliffs. Canoe navigation below the Sirialo and Coribeni rapids is no more hazardous than on the rapids of our northern rivers, except at the two "pongos" or narrow passages. The first occurs at the sharpest point of the abrupt curve shown on the map; the second is the celebrated Pongo de Mainique. In these narrow passages in time of high water there is no landing for long stretches. The bow paddler stands well forward and tries for depth and current; the stern paddler keeps the canoe steady in its course. When paddlers are in agreement even a heavy canoe can be directed into the most favorable channels. Our canoemen were always in disagreement, however, and as often as not we shot down rapids at a speed of twenty miles an hour, broadside on, with an occasional bump on projecting rocks or boulders whose warning ordinary boatmen would not let go unheeded.

The scenery at the great bend is unusually beautiful. The tropical forest crowds the river bank, great cliffs rise sheer from the water's edge, their faces overhung with a trailing drapery of vines, and in the longer river vistas one may sometimes see the distant heights of the Cordillera Vilcapampa. We shot the long succession of rapids in the first canyon without mishap, and at night pitched our tent on the edge of the river near the mouth of the Manugali.

From the sharp peak opposite our camp we saw for the first time the phenomenon of cloud-banners. A light breeze was blowing from the western mountains and its vapor was condensed into clouds that floated down the wind and dissolved, while they were constantly forming afresh at the summit. In the night a thunderstorm arose and swept with a roar through the vast forest above us. The solid canopy of the tropical forest fairly resounded with the impact of the heavy raindrops. The next morning all the brooks from the farther side of the river were in flood and the river discolored. When we broke camp the last mist wraiths of the storm were still trailing through the tree-tops and wrapped about the peak opposite our camp, only parting now and then to give us delightful glimpses of a forest-clad summit riding high above the clouds.

The alternation of deeps and shallows at this point in the river and the well-developed canyon meanders are among the most celebrated of their kind in the world. Though shut in by high cliffs and bordered by mountains the river exhibits a succession of curves so regular that one might almost imagine the country a plain from the pattern of the meanders. The succession of smooth curves for a long distance across existing mountains points to a time when a lowland plain with moderate slopes drained by strongly meandering rivers was developed here. Uplift afforded a chance for renewed down-cutting on the part of all the streams, and the incision of the meanders. The present meanders are, of course, not the identical ones that were formed on the lowland plain; they are rather their descendants. Though they still retain their strongly curved quality, and in places have almost cut through the narrow spurs between meander loops, they are not smooth like the meanders of the Mississippi. Here and there are sharp irregular turns that mar the symmetry of the larger curves. The alternating bands of hard and soft rock have had a large part in making the course more irregular. The meanders have responded to the rock structure. Though regular in their broader features they are irregular and deformed in detail.

Deeps and shallows are known in every vigorous river, but it is seldom that they are so prominently developed as in these great canyons. At one point in the upper canyon the river has been broadened into a lake two or three times the average width of the channel and with a scarcely perceptible current; above and below the "laguna," as the boatmen call it, are big rapids with beds so shallow that rocks project in many places. In the Pongo de Mainique the river is at one place only fifty feet wide, yet so deep that there is little current. It is on the banks of the quiet stretches that the red forest deer grazes under leafy arcades. Here, too, are the boa-constrictor trails several feet wide and bare like a roadway. At night the great serpents come trailing down to the river's edge, where the red deer and the wildcat, or so-called "tiger," are their easy prey.

It is in such quiet stretches that one also finds the vast colonies of water skippers. They dance continuously in the sun with an incessant motion from right to left and back again. Occasionally one dances about in circles, then suddenly darts through the entire mass, though without striking his equally erratic neighbors. An up-and-down motion still further complicates the effect. It is positively bewildering to look intently at the whirling multitude and try to follow their complicated motions. Every slight breath of wind brings a shock to the organization of the dance. For though they dance only in the sun, their favorite places are the sunny spots in the shade near the bank, as beneath an overhanging tree. When the wind shakes the foliage the mottled pattern of shade and sunlight is confused, the dance slows down, and the dancers become bewildered. In a storm they seek shelter in the jungle. The hot, quiet, sunlit days bring out literally millions of these tiny creatures.

One of the longest deeps in the whole Urubamba lies just above the Pongo at Mulanquiato. We drifted down with a gentle current just after sunset. Shrill whistles, like those of a steam launch, sounded from either bank, the strange piercing notes of the lowland cicada, *cicada tibicen*. Long decorated canoes, better than any we had yet seen, were drawn up in the quiet coves. Soon we came upon the first settlement. The owner, Señor Pereira, has gathered about him a group of Machigangas, and by marrying into the tribe has attained a position of great influence among the Indians. Upon our arrival a gun was fired to announce to his people that strangers had come, upon which the Machigangas strolled along in twos and threes from their huts, helped us ashore with the baggage, and prepared the evening meal. Here we sat down with five Italians, who had ventured into the rubber fields with golden ideas as to profits. After having lost the larger part of their merchandise, chiefly cinchona, in the rapids the year before, they had established themselves here with the idea of picking rubber. Without capital, they followed the ways of the itinerant rubber picker and had gathered "caucho," the poorer of the two kinds of rubber. No capital is required; the picker simply cuts down the likeliest trees, gathers the coagulated sap, and floats it down-stream to market. After a year of this life they had grown restless and were venturing on other schemes for the great down-river rubber country.

A few weeks later, on returning through the forest, we met their carriers with a few small bundles, the only part of their cargo they had saved from the river. Without a canoe or the means to buy one they had built rafts, which were quickly torn to pieces in the rapids. We, too, should have said *"pobres Italianos"* if their venture had not been plainly foolish. The rubber terri-

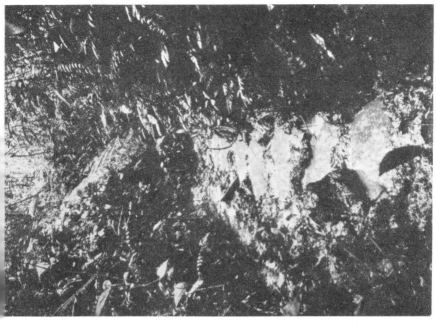

Fig. 14—The mule trail in the rain forest between
Rosalina and Pongo de Mainique. Each pool is from one and
a half to two feet deep. Even in the dry season these holes
are full of water, for the sunlight penetrates the foliage at
a few places only.

Fig. 13—Composition of tropical vegetation in the rain
forest above Pongo de Mainique, elevation 2,500 feet (760 m.).
Scores of species occur within the limits of a single photograph.

FIG. 15.

FIG. 16.

FIG. 15—Topography and vegetation from the Tocate pass, 7,100 feet (2,164 m.), between Rosalina and Pongo de Mainique. See Fig. 53a. This is in the zone of maximum rainfall. The cumulo-nimbus clouds are typical and change to nimbus in the early afternoon.

FIG. 16—The Expedition's thirty-foot canoe at the mouth of the Timpia below Pongo de Mainique.

tory is difficult enough for men with capital; for men without capital it is impossible. Such men either become affiliated
with organized companies or get out of the region when they
can. A few, made desperate by risks and losses, cheat and steal
their way to rubber. Two years before our trip an Italian had
murdered two Frenchmen just below the Pongo and stolen their
rubber cargo, whereupon he was shot by Machigangas under the
leadership of Domingo, the chief who was with us on a journey
from Pongo de Mainique to the mouth of the Timpia. Afterward they brought his skull to the top of a pass along the forest
trail and s、t it up on a cliff at the very edge of Machiganga-land
as a warning to others of his kind.

At Mulanquiato we secured five Machigangas and a boy interpreter, and on August 17 made the last and most difficult portion
of our journey. We found these Indians much more skilful than
our earlier boatmen. Well-trained, alert, powerful, and with excellent team-play, they swept the canoe into this or that thread
of the current, and took one after another of the rapids with the
greatest confidence. No sooner had we passed the Sintulini rapids,
fully a mile long, than we reached the mouth of the Pomareni.
This swift tributary comes in almost at right angles to the main
river and gives rise to a confusing mass of standing waves and
conflicting currents rendered still more difficult by the whirlpool
just below the junction. So swift is the circling current of the
maëlstrom that the water is hollowed out like a great bowl, a really
formidable point and one of our most dangerous passages; a little
too far to the right and we should be thrown over against the cliff-
face; a little too far to the left and we should be caught in the
whirlpool. Once in the swift current the canoe became as helpless as a chip. It was turned this way and that, each turn heading it apparently straight for destruction. But the Indians had
judged their position well, and though we seemed each moment in
a worse predicament, we at last skimmed the edge of the whirlpool and brought our canoe to shore just beyond its rim.

A little farther on we came to the narrow gateway of the
Pongo, where the entire volume of the river flows between cliffs

at one point no more than fifty feet apart. Here are concentrated the worst rapids of the lower Urubamba. For nearly fifteen miles the river is an unbroken succession of rapids, and once within its walls the Pongo offers small chance of escape. At some points we were fortunate enough to secure a foothold along the edge of the river and to let our canoe down by ropes. At others we were obliged to take chances with the current, though the great depth of water in most of the Pongo rapids makes them really less formidable in some respects than the shallow rapids up stream. The chief danger here lies in the rotary motion of the water at the sharpest bends. The effect at some places is extraordinary. A floating object is carried across stream like a feather and driven at express-train speed against a solid cliff. In trying to avoid one of these cross-currents our canoe became turned midstream, we were thrown this way and that, and at last shot through three standing waves that half filled the canoe.

Below the worst rapids the Pongo exhibits a swift succession of natural wonders. Fern-clad cliffs border it, a bush resembling the juniper reaches its dainty finger-like stems far out over the river, and the banks are heavily clad with mosses. The great woods, silent, impenetrable, mantle the high slopes and stretch up to the limits of vision. Cascades tumble from the cliff summits or go rippling down the long inclines of the slate beds set almost on edge. Finally appear the white pinnacles of limestone that hem in the narrow lower entrance or outlet of the Pongo. Beyond this passage one suddenly comes out upon the edge of a rolling forest-clad region, the rubber territory, the country of the great woods. Here the Andean realm ends and Amazonia begins.

From the summits of the white cliffs 4,000 feet above the river we were in a few days to have one of the most extensive views in South America. The break between the Andean Cordillera and the hill-dotted plains of the lower Urubamba valley is almost as sharp as a shoreline. The rolling plains are covered with leagues upon leagues of dense, shadowy, fever-haunted jungle. The great river winds through in a series of splendid meanders, and with so broad a channel as to make it visible almost to the horizon. Down river from our lookout one can reach ocean steamers at Iquitos with less than two weeks of travel. It is three weeks to the Pacific *via* Cuzco and more than a month if one takes the route across the high bleak lava-covered country which we were soon to cross on our way to the coast at Camaná.

CHAPTER III

THE RUBBER FORESTS

The white limestone cliffs at Pongo de Mainique are a boundary between two great geographic provinces (Fig. 17). Down valley are the vast river plains, drained by broad meandering rivers;

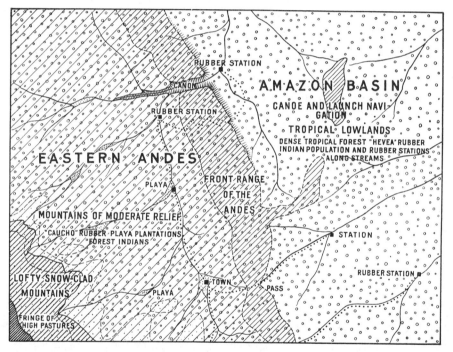

Fig. 17—Regional diagram of the Eastern Andes (here the Cordillera Vilcapampa) and the adjacent tropical plains. For an explanation of the method of construction and the symbolism of the diagram see p. 51.

up valley are the rugged spurs of the eastern Andes and their encanyoned streams (Fig. 18). There are outliers of the Andes still farther toward the northeast where hangs the inevitable haze of the tropical horizon, but the country beyond them differs in no important respect from that immediately below the Pongo.

The foot-path to the summit of the cliffs is too narrow and

steep for even the most agile mules. It is simply impassable for animals without hands. In places the packs are lowered by ropes over steep ledges and men must scramble down from one projecting root or swinging vine to another. In the breathless jungle it is a wearing task to pack in all supplies for the station below the Pongo and to carry out the season's rubber. Recently however the ancient track has been replaced by a road that was cut with great labor, and by much blasting, across the mountain barrier, and at last mule transport has taken the place of the Indian.

In the dry season it is a fair and delightful country—that on the border of the mountains. In the wet season the traveler is either actually marooned or he must slosh through rivers of mud and water that deluge the trails and break the hearts of his beasts (Fig. 14). Here and there a

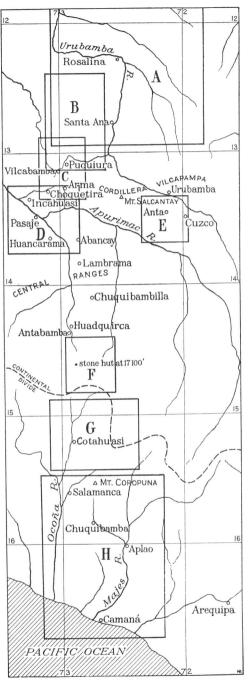

FIG. 18—Index map for the nine regional diagrams in the pages following. A represents Fig. 17; B, 42; C, 36; D, 32; E, 34; F, 25; G, 26; and H, 65.

large shallow-rooted tree has come crashing down across the trail and with its four feet of circumference and ten feet of plank buttress it is as difficult to move as a house. A new trail must be cut around it. A little farther on, where the valley wall steepens and one may look down a thousand feet of slope to the bed of a mountain torrent, a patch of trail has become soaked with water and the mules pick their way, trembling, across it. Two days from Yavero one of our mules went over the trail, and though she was finally recovered she died of her injuries the following night. After a month's work in the forest a mule must run free for two months to recover. The packers count on losing one beast out of five for every journey into the forest. It is not solely a matter of work, though this is terrific; it is quite largely a matter of forage. In spite of its profusion of life (Fig. 13) and its really vast wealth of species, the tropical forest is all but barren of grass. Sugar cane is a fair substitute, but there are only a few cultivated spots. The more tender leaves of the trees, the young shoots of cane in the *carrizo* swamps, and the grass-like foliage of the low bamboo are the chief substitutes for pasture. But they lead to various disorders, besides requiring considerable labor on the part of the dejected peons who must gather them after a day's heavy work with the packs.

Overcoming these enormous difficulties is expensive and some one must pay the bill. As is usual in a pioneer region, the native laborer pays a large part of it in unrequited toil; the rest is paid by the rubber consumer. For this is one of the cases where a direct road connects the civilized consumer and the barbarous producer. What a story it could tell if a ball of smoke-cured rubber on a New York dock were endowed with speech—of the wet jungle path, of enslaved peons, of vile abuses by immoral agents, of all the toil and sickness that make the tropical lowland a reproach!

In the United States the specter of slavery haunted the national conscience almost from the beginning of national life, and the ghost was laid only at the cost of one of the bloodiest wars in history. In other countries, as in sugar-producing Brazil, the freeing of the slaves meant not a war but the verge of financial

FIG. 19.

FIG. 20.

FIG. 19—Moss-draped trees in the rain forest near Abra Tocate between Rosalina and Pongo de Mainique.

FIG. 20—Yavero, a rubber station on the Yavero (Paucartambo) River, a tributary of the Urubamba. Elevation 1,600 feet (490 m.).

Fig. 21—Clearing in the tropical forest between Rosalina and Pabellon. This represents the border region where the forest-dwelling Machiganga Indians and the mountain Indians meet. The clearings are occupied by Machigangas whose chief crops are yuca and corn; in the extreme upper left-hand corner are grassy slopes occupied by Quechua herdsmen and farmers who grow potatoes and corn.

ruin besides a fundamental change in the social order and problems as complex and wearisome as any that war can bring. Everywhere abolition was secured at frightful cost.

The spirit that upheld the new founders of the western republics in driving out slavery was admirable, but as much cannot be said of their work of reconstruction. We like to pass over those dark days in our own history. In South America there has lingered from the old slave-holding days down to the present, a labor system more insidious than slavery, yet no less revolting in its details, and infinitely more difficult to stamp out. It is called peonage; it should be called slavery. In Bolivia, Peru, and Brazil it flourishes now as it ever did in the fruitful soil of the interior provinces where law and order are bywords and where the scarcity of workmen will long impel men to enslave labor when they cannot employ it. Peonage *is* slavery, though as in all slave systems there are many forms under which the system is worked out. We commonly think that the typical slave is one who is made to work hard, given but little food, and at the slightest provocation is tied to a post and brutally whipped. This is indeed the fate of many slaves or ''peons'' so-called, in the Amazon forests; but it is no more the rule than it was in the South before the war, for a peon is a valuable piece of property and if a slave raider travel five hundred miles through forest and jungle-swamp to capture an Indian you may depend upon it that he will not beat him to death merely for the fun of it.

That unjust and frightfully cruel floggings are inflicted at times and in some places is of course a result of the lack of official restraint that drunken owners far from the arm of the law sometimes enjoy. When a man obtains a rubber concession from the government he buys a kingdom. Many of the rubber territories are so remote from the cities that officials can with great difficulty be secured to stay at the customs ports. High salaries must be paid, heavy taxes collected, and grafting of the most flagrant kind winked at. Often the concessionaire himself is chief magistrate of his kingdom by law. Under such a system, remote from all civilizing influences, the rubber producer himself oftentimes a law-

less border character or a downright criminal, no system of government would be adequate, least of all one like peonage that permits or ignores flagrant wrongs because it is so expensive to en-
force justice.

The peonage system continues by reason of that extraordinary
difficulty in the development of the tropical lowland of South
America—the lack of a labor supply. The population of Amazonia
now numbers less than one person to the square mile. The people
are distributed in small groups of a dozen to twenty each in scattered villages along the river banks or in concealed clearings
reached by trails known only to the Indians. Nearly all of them
still live in the same primitive state in which they lived at the
time of the Discovery. In the Urubamba region a single cotton
shirt is worn by the married men and women, while the girls
and boys in many cases go entirely naked except for a loincloth
or a necklace of nuts or monkeys' teeth (Fig. 23). A cane hut
with a thatch to keep out the heavy rains is their shelter and their
food is the yuca, sugar cane, Indian corn, bananas of many kinds,
and fish. A patch of yuca once planted will need but the most
trifling attention for years. The small spider monkey is their
greatest delicacy and to procure it they will often abandon every
other project and return at their own sweet and belated will.

In the midst of this natural life of the forest-dwelling Indian
appears the rubber man, who, to gather rubber, must have rubber
"pickers." If he lives on the edge of the great Andean Cordillera, laborers may be secured from some of the lower valleys, but
they must be paid well for even a temporary stay in the hot and
unhealthful lowlands. Farther out in the great forest country the
plateau Indians will not go and only the scattered tribes remain
from which to recruit laborers. For the nature-life of the Indian
what has the rubber gatherer to offer? Money? The Indian uses
it for ornament only. When I once tried with money to pay an
Indian for a week's services he refused it. In exchange for his
severe labor he wanted nothing more than a fish-hook and a ring,
the two costing not more than a penny apiece! When his love for
ornament has once been gratified the Indian ceases to work. His

FIG. 22—Trading with Machiganga Indians in a reed swamp at Santa Anato, Urubamba Valley, below Rosalina. Just outside the picture on the right is a platform on which corn is stored for protection against rodents and mildew. On the left is the corner of a grass-thatched cane hut.

FIG. 23—Ornaments and fabrics of the Machiganga Indians at Yavero. The nuts are made up into strings, pendants, and heavy necklaces. To the left of the center is one that contains feathers and four drumsticks of a bird about the size of a small wild turkey —probably the so-called turkey inhabiting the eastern mountain valleys and the adjacent border of the plains, and hunted as an important source of food. The cord in the upper right-hand corner is used most commonly for heel supports in climbing trees. The open-work sack is convenient for carrying game, fish, and fruit; the finely woven sacks are used for carrying red ochre for ornamenting or daub-

food and shelter and clothing are of the most primitive kind, but they are the best in the world for him because they are the only kind he has known. So where money and finery fail the lash comes in. The rubber man says that the Indian is lazy and must be made to work; that there is a great deal of work to be done and the Indian is the only laborer who can be found; that if rubber and chocolate are produced the Indian must be made to produce them; and that if he will not produce them for pay he must be enslaved.

It is a law of the rubber country that when an Indian falls into debt to a white man he must work for the latter until the debt is discharged. If he runs away before the debt is canceled or if he refuses to work or does too little work he may be flogged. Under special conditions such laws are wise. In the hands of the rubber men they are the basis of slavery. For, once the rubber interests begin to suffer, the promoters look around for a chance to capture free Indians. An expedition is fitted out that spends weeks exploring this river or that in getting on the track of unattached Indians. When a settlement is found the men are enslaved and taken long distances from home finally to reach a rubber property. There they are given a corner of a hut to sleep in, a few cheap clothes, a rubber-picking outfit, and a name. In return for these articles the unwilling Indian is charged any fanciful price that comes into the mind of his "owner," and he must thereupon work at a per diem wage also fixed by the owner. Since his obligations increase with time, the Indian may die over two thousand dollars in debt!

Peonage has left frightful scars upon the country. In some places the Indians are fugitives, cultivating little farms in secreted places but visiting them only at night or after carefully reconnoitering the spot. They change their camps frequently and make their way from place to place by secret trails, now spending a night or two under the shelter of a few palm leaves on a sandbar, again concealing themselves in almost impenetrable jungle. If the hunter sometimes discovers a beaten track he follows it only to find it ending on a cliff face or on the edge of a lagoon where

concealment is perfect. There are tribes that shoot the white man
at sight and regard him as their bitterest enemy. Experience has
led them to believe that only a dead white is a good white, revers-
ing our saying about the North American Indian; and that even
when he comes among them on peaceful errands he is likely to
leave behind him a trail of syphilis and other venereal diseases
scarcely less deadly than his bullets.

However, the peonage system is not hideous everywhere and in
all its aspects. There are white owners who realize that in the
long run the friendship of the Indians is an asset far greater than
unwilling service and deadly hatred. Some of them have indeed
intermarried with the Indians and live among them in a state but
little above savagery. In the Mamoré country are a few owners
of original princely concessions who have grown enormously
wealthy and yet who continue to live a primitive life among their
scores of illegitimate descendants. The Indians look upon them
as benefactors, as indeed many of them are, defending the Indians
from ill treatment by other whites, giving them clothing and ornaments, and exacting from them only a moderate amount of labor.
In some cases indeed the whites have gained more than simple
gratitude for their humane treatment of the Indians, some of
whom serve their masters with real devotion.

When the "rubber barons" wish to discourage investigation
of their system they invite the traveler to leave and he is given
a canoe and oarsmen with which to make his way out of the district. Refusal to accept an offer of canoes and men is a declara-
tion of war. An agent of one of the London companies accepted
such a challenge and was promptly told that he would not leave
the territory alive. The threat would have held true in the case
of a less skilful man. Though Indians slept in the canoes to prevent their seizure, he slipped past the guards in the night, swam
to the opposite shore, and there secured a canoe within which he
made a difficult journey down river to the nearest post where food
and an outfit could be secured.

A few companies operating on or near the border of the Cordillera have adopted a normal labor system, dependent chiefly upon

people from the plateau and upon the thoroughly willing assistance of well-paid forest Indians. The Compañia Gomera de
Mainique at Puerto Mainique just below the Pongo is one of these
and its development of the region without violation of native
rights is in the highest degree praiseworthy. In fact the whole
conduct of this company is interesting to a geographer, as it
reflects at every point the physical nature of the country.

The government is eager to secure foreign capital, but in eastern Peru can offer practically nothing more than virgin wealth,
that is, land and the natural resources of the land. There are no
roads, virtually no trails, no telegraph lines, and in most cases no
labor. Since the old Spanish grants ran at right angles to the
river so as to give the owners a cross-section of varied resources,
the up-river plantations do not extend down into the rubber country. Hence the more heavily forested lower valleys and plains
are the property of the state. A man can buy a piece of land
down there, but from any tract within ordinary means only a
primitive living can be obtained. The pioneers therefore are the
rubber men who produce a precious substance that can stand the
enormous tax on production and transportation. They do not
want the land—only the exclusive right to tap the rubber trees
upon it. Thus there has arisen the concession plan whereby a
large tract is obtained under conditions of money payment or of
improvements that will attract settlers or of a tax on the export.

The "caucho" or poorer rubber of the Urubamba Valley begins at 3,000 feet (915 m.) and the "hevea" or better class is a
lower-valley and plains product. The rubber trees thereabouts
produce 60 grams (2 ozs.) of dry rubber each week for eight
months. After yielding rubber for this length of time a tree is
allowed to rest four or five years. "Caucho" is produced from
trees that are cut down and ringed with machetes, but it is from
fifty to sixty cents cheaper owing to the impurities that get into
it. The wood, not the nut, of the *Palma carmona* is used for smok-
ing or "curing" the rubber. The government had long been
urged to build a road into the region in place of the miserable
track—absolutely impassable in the wet season—that heretofore

constituted the sole means of exit. About ten years ago Señor Robledo at last built a government trail from Rosalina to Yavero about 100 miles long. While it is a wretched trail it is better than the old one, for it is more direct and it is better drained. In the wet season parts of it are turned into rivers and lakes, but it is probably the best that could be done with the small grant of twenty thousand dollars.

With at least an improvement in the trail it became possible for a rubber company to induce *cargadores* or packers to transport merchandise and rubber and to have a fair chance of success. Whereupon a rubber company was organized which obtained a concession of 28,000 hectares (69,188 acres) of land on condition that the company finish a road one and one-half meters wide to the Pongo, connecting with the road which the government had extended to Yavero. The land given in payment was not continuous but was selected in lots by the company in such a way as to secure the best rubber trees over an area several times the size of the concession. The road was finished by William Tell after four years' work at a cost of about seventy-five thousand dollars. The last part of it was blasted out of slate and limestone and in 1912 the first pack train entered Puerto Mainique.

The first rubber was taken out in November, 1910, and productive possibilities proved by the collection of 9,000 kilos (19,841 pounds) in eight months.

If a main road were the chief problem of the rubber company the business would soon be on a paying basis, but for every mile of road there must be cut several miles of narrow trail (Fig. 14), as the rubber trees grow scattered about—a clump of a half dozen here and five hundred feet farther on another clump and only scattered individuals between. Furthermore, about twenty-five years ago rubber men from the Ucayali came up here in launches and canoes and cut down large numbers of trees within reach of the water courses and by ringing the trunks every few feet with machetes "bled" them rapidly and thus covered a large territory in a short time, and made huge sums of money when the price of rubber was high. Only a few of the small trees that were left are now mature. These, the mature trees that were overlooked, and the virgin stands farther from the rivers are the present sources of rubber.

In addition to the trails small cabins must be built to shelter the hired laborers from the plateau, many of whom bring along their women folk to cook for them. The combined expense to a company of these necessary improvements before production can begin is exceedingly heavy. There is only one alternative for the prospective exploiter: to become a vagrant rubber gatherer. With tents, guns, machetes, cloth, baubles for trading, tinned food for emergencies, and with pockets full of English gold parties have started out to seek fortunes in the rubber forests. If the friendship of a party of Indians can be secured by adequate gifts large amounts of rubber can be gathered in a short time, for the Indians know where the rubber trees grow. On the other hand, many fortunes have been lost in the rubber country. Some of the tribes have been badly treated by other adventurers and attack the newcomers from ambush or gather rubber for a while only to overturn the canoe in a rapid and let the river relieve them of selfish friends.

The Compañia Gomera de Mainique started out by securing the good-will of the forest Indians, the Machigangas. They come and go in friendly visits to the port at Yavero. If one of them is sick he can secure free medicine from the agent. If he wishes goods on credit he has only to ask for them, for the agent knows that the Indian's sense of fairness will bring him back to work for the company. Without previous notice a group of Indians appears:

"We owe," they announce.

"Good," says the agent, "build me a house."

They select the trees. Before they cut them down they address them solemnly. The trees must not hold their destruction against the Indians and they must not try to resist the sharp machetes. Then the Indians set to work. They fell a tree, bind it with light ropes woven from the wild cotton, and haul it to its place. That is all for the day. They play in the sun, do a little hunting, or look over the agent's house, touching everything, talking little, exclaiming much. They dip their wet fingers in the sugar bowl and taste, turn salt out upon their hands, hold colored solutions from the medicine chest up to the light, and pull out and push in the corks of the bottles. At the end of a month or two the house is done. Then they gather their women and babies together and say:

"Now we go," without asking if the work corresponds with the cost of the articles they had bought. Their judgment is good however. Their work is almost always more valuable than the articles. Then they shake hands all around.

"We will come again," they say, and in a moment have disappeared in the jungle that overhangs the trail.

With such labor the Compañia Gomera de Mainique can do something, but it is not much. The regular seasonal tasks of roadbuilding and rubber-picking must be done by imported labor. This is secured chiefly at Abancay, where live groups of plateau Indians that have become accustomed to the warm climate of the Abancay basin. They are employed for eight or ten months at an average rate of fifty cents gold per day, and receive in addition only the simplest articles of food.

At the end of the season the gang leaders are paid a *gratificación,* or bonus, the size of which depends upon the amount of rubber collected, and this in turn depends upon the size of the gang and the degree of willingness to work. In the books of the company I saw a record of *gratificaciónes* running as high as $600 in gold for a season's work.

Some of the laborers become sick and are cared for by the agent until they recover or can be sent back to their homes. Most of them have fever before they return.

The rubber costs the company two *soles* ($1.00) produced at Yavero. The two weeks' transportation to Cuzco costs three and a half soles ($1.75) per twenty-five pounds. The exported rubber, known to the trade as Mollendo rubber, in contrast to the finer "Pará" rubber from the lower Amazon, is shipped to Hamburg. The cost for transportation from port to port is $24.00 per English ton (1,016 kilos). There is a Peruvian tax of 8 per cent of the net value in Europe, and a territorial tax of two soles ($1.00) per hundred pounds. All supplies except the few vegetables grown on the spot cost tremendously. Even dynamite, hoes, clothing, rice—to mention only a few necessities—must pay the heavy cost of transportation after imposts, railroad and ocean freight, storage and agents' percentages are added. The effect of a disturbed market is extreme. When, in 1911, the price of rubber fell to $1.50 a kilo at Hamburg the company ceased exporting. When it dropped still lower in 1912 production also stopped, and it is still doubtful, in view of the growing competition of the East-Indian plantations with their cheap labor, whether operations will ever be resumed. Within three years no less than a dozen large companies in eastern Peru and Bolivia have ceased operations. In one concession on the Madre de Dios the withdrawal of the agents and laborers from the posts turned at last into flight, as the forest Indians, on learning the company's policy, rapidly ascended the river in force, committing numerous depredations. The great war has also added to the difficulties of production.

Facts like these are vital in the consideration of the future of the Amazon basin and especially its habitability. It was the dream of Humboldt that great cities should arise in the midst of the tropical forests of the Amazon and that the whole lowland plain of that river basin should become the home of happy millions. Humboldt's vision may have been correct, though a hundred years have brought us but little nearer its realization. Now, as in the past four centuries, man finds his hands too feeble to control the great elemental forces which have shaped history. The most he can hope for in the next hundred years at least is the ability to dodge Nature a little more successfully, and here and there by studies in tropical hygiene and medicine, by the substitution of water-power for human energy, to carry a few of the outposts and prepare the way for a final assault in the war against the hard conditions of climate and relief. We hear of the Madeira-Mamoré railroad, 200 miles long, in the heart of a tropical forest and of the commercial revolution it will bring. Do we realize that the forest which overhangs the rails is as big as the whole plain between the Rockies and the Appalachians, and that the proposed line would extend only as far as from St. Louis to Kansas City, or from Galveston to New Orleans?

Even if twenty whites were eager to go where now there is but one reluctant pioneer, we should still have but a halting development on account of the scarcity of labor. When, three hundred years ago, the Isthmus of Panama stood in his way, Gomara wrote to his king: "There are mountains, but there are also hands," as if men could be conjured up from the tropical jungle. From that day to this the scarcity of labor has been the chief difficulty in the lowland regions of tropical South America. Even when medicine shall have been advanced to the point where residence in the tropics can be made safe, the Amazon basin will lack an adequate supply of workmen. Where Humboldt saw thriving cities, the population is still less than one to the square mile in an area as large as fifteen of our Mississippi Valley states. We hear much about a rich soil and little about intolerable insects; the climate favors a good growth of vegetation, but a man can starve in a tropical forest as easily as in a desert; certain tributaries of the Negro are bordered by rich rubber forests, yet not a single Indian hut may be found along their banks. Will men of the white race dig up the rank vegetation, sleep in grass hammocks, live in the hot and humid air, or will they stay in the cooler regions of the north and south? Will they rear children in the temperate zones, or bury them in the tropics?

What Gorgas did for Panama was done for intelligent people. Can it be duplicated in the case of ignorant and stupid laborers? Shall the white man with wits fight it out with Nature in a tropical forest, or fight it out with his equals under better skies?

The tropics must be won by strong hands of the lowlier classes who are ignorant or careless of hygiene, and not by the khaki-clad robust young men like those who work at Panama. Tropical medicine can do something for these folk, but it cannot do much. And we cannot surround every laborer's cottage with expensive screens, oiled ditches, and well-kept lawns. There is a practical optimism and a sentimental optimism. The one is based on facts;

the other on assumptions. It is pleasant to think that the tropical forest may be conquered. It is nonsense to say that we are now conquering it in any comprehensive and permanent way. That sort of conquest is still a dream, as when Humboldt wrote over a hundred years ago.

CHAPTER IV

THE FOREST INDIANS

THE people of a tropical forest live under conditions not unlike those of the desert. The Sahara contains 2,000,000 persons within its borders, a density of one-half to the square mile. This is almost precisely the density of population of a tract of equivalent size in the lowland forests of South America. Like the oases groups in the desert of aridity are the scattered groups along the river margins of the forest. The desert trails run from spring to spring or along a valley floor where there is seepage or an intermittent stream; the rivers are the highways of the forest, the flowing roads, and away from them one is lost in as true a sense as one may be lost in the desert.

A man may easily starve in the tropical forest. Before starting on even a short journey of two or three days a forest Indian stocks his canoe with sugar cane and yuca and a little parched corn. He knows the settlements as well as his desert brother knows the springs. The Pahute Indian of Utah lives in the irrigated valleys and makes annual excursions across the desert to the distant mountains to gather the seeds of the nut pine. The Machiganga lives in the hills above the Urubamba and annually comes down through the forest to the river to fish during the dry season.

The Machigangas are one of the important tribes of the Amazon basin. Though they are dispersed to some extent upon the plains their chief groups are scattered through the heads of a large number of valleys near the eastern border of the Andes. Chief among the valleys they occupy are the Pilcopata, Tono, Piñi-piñi, Yavero, Yuyato, Shirineiri, Ticumpinea, Timpia, and Camisea (Fig. 203). In their distribution, in their relations with each other, in their manner of life, and to some extent in their personal traits, they display characteristics strikingly like those

36

seen in desert peoples. Though the forest that surrounds them suggests plenty and the rivers the possibility of free movement with easy intercourse, the struggle of life, as in the desert, is against useless things. Travel in the desert is a conflict with heat and aridity; but travel in the tropic forest is a struggle against space, heat, and a superabundant and all but useless vegetation.

The Machigangas are one of the subtribes of the Campas Indians, one of the most numerous groups in the Amazon Valley. It is estimated that there are in all about 14,000 to 16,000 of them. Each subtribe numbers from one to four thousand, and the territory they occupy extends from the limits of the last plantations— for example, Rosalina in the Urubamba Valley—downstream beyond the edge of the plains. Among them three subtribes are still hostile to the whites: the Cashibos, the Chonta Campas, and the Campas Bravos.

In certain cases the Cashibos are said to be anthropophagous, in the belief that they will assume the strength and intellect of those they eat. This group is also continuously at war with its neighbors, goes naked, uses stone hatchets, as in ages past, because of its isolation and unfriendliness, and defends the entrances to the tribal huts with dart and traps. The Cashibos are diminishing in numbers and are now scattered through the valley of the Gran Pajonal, the left bank of the Pachitea, and the Pampa del Sacramento.[1]

The friendliest tribes live in the higher valley heads, where they have constant communication with the whites. The use of the bow and arrow has not, however, been discontinued among them, in spite of the wide introduction of the old-fashioned muzzle-loading shotgun, which they prize much more highly than the latest rifle or breech-loading shotgun because of its simplicity and cheap-

---

[1] The Cashibos of the Pachitea are the tribe for whom the Piros besought Herndon to produce " some great and infectious disease " which could be carried up the river and let loose amongst them (Herndon, Exploration of the Valley of the Amazon, Washington, 1854, Vol. 1, p. 196). This would-be artfulness suggests itself as something of a match against the cunning of the Cashibos whom rumor reports to imitate the sounds of the forest animals with such skill as to betray into their hands the hunters of other tribes (see von Tschudi, Travels in Peru During the Years 1838-1842, translated from the German by Thomasina Ross, New York, 1849, p. 404).

ness. Accidents are frequent among them owing to the careless use of fire-arms. On our last day's journey on the Urubamba above the mouth of the Timpia one of our Indian boys dropped his canoe pole on the hammer of a loaded shotgun, and not only shot his own fingers to pieces, but gravely wounded his father (Fig. 2). In spite of his suffering the old chief directed our work at the canoe and even was able to tell us the location of the most favorable channel. Though the night that followed was as black as ink, with even the stars obscured by a rising storm, his directions never failed. We poled our way up five long rapids without special difficulties, now working into the lee of a rock whose location he knew within a few yards, now paddling furiously across the channel to catch the upstream current of an eddy.

The principal groups of Machigangas live in the middle Urubamba and its tributaries, the Yavero, Yuyato, Shirineiri, Ticumpinea, Timpia, Pachitea, and others. There is a marked difference in the use of the land and the mode of life among the different groups of this subtribe. Those who live in the lower plains and river "playas," as the patches of flood plain are called, have a single permanent dwelling and alternately fish and hunt. Those that live on hill farms have temporary reed huts on the nearest sandbars and spend the best months of the dry season—April to October—in fishing and drying fish to be carried to their mountain homes (Fig. 21). Some families even duplicate *chacras* or farms at the river bank and grow yuca and sugar cane. In latter years smallpox, malaria, and the rubber hunters have destroyed many of the river villages and driven the Indians to permanent residence in the hills or, where raids occur, along secret trails to hidden camps.

Their system of agriculture is strikingly adapted to some important features of tropical soil. The thin hillside soils of the region are but poorly stocked with humus, even in their virgin condition. Fallen trees and foliage decay so quickly that the layer of forest mold is exceedingly thin and the little that is incorporated in the soil is confined to a shallow surface layer. To meet these special conditions the Indian makes new clearings by girdling and burning the trees. When the soil becomes worn out and the crops diminish, the old clearing is abandoned and allowed to revert to natural growth and a new farm is planted to corn and yuca. The population is so scattered and thin that the land assignment system current among the plateau Indians is not practised among the Machigangas. Several families commonly live together and may be separated from their nearest neighbors by many miles of forested mountains. The land is free for all, and, though some heavy labor is necessary to clear it, once a small patch is cleared it is easy to extend the tract by limited annual cuttings. Local tracts of naturally unforested land are rarely planted, chiefly because the absence of shade has allowed the sun to burn out the limited humus supply and to prevent more from accumulating. The best soil of the mountain slopes is found where there is the heaviest growth of timber, the deepest shade, the most humus, and good natural drainage. It is the same on the playas along the river; the recent additions to the flood plain are easy to cultivate, but they lack humus and a fine matrix which retains moisture and prevents drought or at least physiologic dryness. Here, too, the timbered areas or the cane swamps are always selected for planting.

The traditions of the Machigangas go back to the time of the Inca conquest, when the forest Indians, the "Antis," were subjugated and compelled to pay tribute.[2] When the Inca family itself fled from Cuzco after the Spanish Conquest and sought refuge in the wilderness it was to the Machiganga country that they came by way of the Vilcabamba and Pampaconas Valleys. Afterward came the Spaniards and though they did not exercise governmental au-

[2] The early chronicles contain several references to Antisuyu and the Antis. Garcilaso de la Vega's description of the Inca conquests in Antisuyu are well known (Royal Commentaries of the Yncas, Book 4, Chapters 16 and 17, Hakluyt Soc. Publs., 1st Ser., No. 41, 1869 and Book 7, Chapters 13 and 14, No. 45, 1871). Salcamayhua who also chronicles these conquests relates a legend concerning the tribute payers of the eastern valleys. On one occasion, he says, three hundred Antis came laden with gold from Opatari. Their arrival at Cuzco was coincident with a killing frost that ruined all the crops of the basin whence the three hundred fortunates were ordered with their gold to the top of the high hill of Pachatucsa (Pachatusun) and there buried with it (An Account of the Antiquities of Peru, Hakluyt Soc. Publs., 1st Ser., No. 48, 1873).

thority over the forest Indians they had close relations with them. Land grants were made to white pioneers for special services or through sale and with the land often went the right to exploit the people on it. Some of the concessions were owned by people who for generations knew nothing save by hearsay of the Indians who dwelt in the great forests of the valleys. In later years they have been exploring their lands and establishing so-called relations whereby the savage "buys" a dollar's worth of powder or knives for whatever number of dollars' worth of rubber the owner may care to extract from him.

The forest Indian is still master of his lands throughout most of the Machiganga country. He is cruelly enslaved at the rubber posts, held by the loose bonds of a desultory trade at others, and in a few places, as at Pongo de Mainique, gives service for both love and profit, but in many places it is impossible to establish control or influence. The lowland Indian never falls into the abject condition of his Quechua brother on the plateau. He is self-reliant, proud, and independent. He neither cringes before a white nor looks up to him as a superior being. I was greatly impressed by the bearing of the first of the forest tribes I met in August, 1911, at Santo Anato. I had built a brisk fire and was enjoying its comfort when La Sama returned with some Indians whom he had secured to clear his playa. The tallest of the lot, wearing a colored band of deer skin around his thick hair and a gaudy bunch of yellow feathers down his back, came up, looked me squarely in the eye, and asked

"Tatiry payta?" (What is your name?)

When I replied he quietly sat down by the fire, helping himself to the roasted corn I had prepared in the hot ashes. A few days later when we came to the head of a rapid I was busy sketching-in my topographic map and did not hear his twice repeated request to leave the boat while the party reconnoitered the rapid. Watching his opportunity he came alongside from the rear—he was steersman—and, turning just as he was leaving the boat, gave me a whack in the forehead with his open palm. La Sama saw the motion and protested. The surly answer was:

"I twice asked him to get out and he didn't move. What does he think we run the canoe to the bank for?"

To him the making of a map was inexplicable; I was merely a stupid white person who didn't know enough to get out of a canoe when told!

The plateau Indian has been kicked about so long that all his independence has been destroyed. His goods have been stolen, his services demanded without recompense, in many places he has no right to land, and his few real rights are abused beyond belief. The difference between him and the forest Indian is due quite largely to differences of environment. The plateau Indian is agricultural, the forest Indian nomadic and in a hunting stage of development; the unforested plateau offers no means for concealment of person or property, the forest offers hidden and difficult paths, easy means for concealment, for ambush, and for wide dispersal of an afflicted tribe. The brutal white of the plateau follows altogether different methods when he finds himself in the Indian country, far from military assistance, surrounded by fearless savages. He may cheat but he does not steal, and his brutality is always carefully suited to both time and place.

The Machigangas are now confined to the forest, but the limits of their territory were once farther upstream, where they were in frequent conflict with the plateau Indians. As late as 1835, according to General Miller,[3] they occupied the land as far upstream as the "Encuentro" (junction) of the Urubamba and the Yanatili (Fig. 53). Miller likewise notes that the Chuntaguirus, "a superior race of Indians" who lived "toward the Marañon," came up the river "200 leagues" to barter with the people thereabouts.

"They bring parrots and other birds, monkeys, cotton robes white and painted, wax balsams, feet of the gran bestia, feather ornaments for the head, and tiger and other skins, which they exchange for hatchets, knives, scissors, needles, buttons, and any sort of glittering bauble."

---

[3] Notice of a Journey to the Northward and also to the Northeastward of Cuzco. Royal Geog. Soc. Journ., Vol. 6, 1836, pp. 174-186.

On their yearly excursions they traveled in a band numbering from 200 to 300, since at the mouth of the Paucartambo (Yavero) they were generally set upon by the Pucapacures. The journey upstream required three months; with the current they returned home in fifteen days.

Their place of meeting at the mouth of the Yanatili was a response to a long strip of grassland that extends down the deep and dry Urubamba Valley, as shown in Figs. 53-B and 55. The wet forests, in which the Machigangas live, cover the hills back of the valley plantations; the belt of dry grassland terminates far within the general limits of the red man's domain and only 2,000 feet above the sea. It is in this strip of low grassland that on the one hand the highland and valley dwellers, and on the other the Indians of the hot forested valleys and the adjacent lowland found a convenient place for barter. The same physiographic features are repeated in adjacent valleys of large size that drain the eastern aspect of the Peruvian Andes, and in each case they have given rise to the periodic excursions of the trader.

These annual journeys are no longer made. The planters have crept down valley. The two best playas below Rosalina are now being cleared. Only a little space remains between the lowest valley plantations and the highest rubber stations. Furthermore, the Indians have been enslaved by the rubber men from the Ucayali. The Machigangas, many of whom are runaway peons, will no longer take cargoes down valley for fear of recapture. They have the cautious spirit of fugitives except in their remote valleys. There they are secure and now and then reassert their old spirit when a lawless trader tries to browbeat them into an unprofitable trade. Also, they are yielding to the alluring call of the planter. At Santo Anato they are clearing a playa in exchange for ammunition, machetes, brandy, and baubles. They no longer make annual excursions to get these things. They have only to call at the nearest plantation. There is always a wolf before the door of the planter—the lack of labor. Yet, as on every frontier, he turns wolf himself when the lambs come, and without shame takes a week's work for a penny mirror, or, worse still, supplies them with firewater, for that will surely bring them back to him. Since this is expensive they return to their tribal haunts with nothing except a debauched spirit and an appetite from which they cannot run away as they did from their task masters in the rubber forest. Hence the vicious circle: more brandy, more labor; more labor, more cleared land; more cleared land, more brandy; more brandy, less Indian. But by that time the planter has a large sugar estate. Then he can begin to buy the more expensive plateau labor, and in turn debauch it.

Nature as well as man works against the scattered tribes of Machigangas and their forest kinsmen. Their country is exceedingly broken by ramifying mountain spurs and valleys overhung with cliffs or bordered by bold, wet, fern-clad slopes. It is useless to try to cut your way by a direct route from one point to another. The country is mantled with heavy forest. You must follow the valleys, the ancient trails of the people. The larger valleys offer smooth sand-bars along the border of which canoes may be towed upstream, and there are little cultivated places for camps. But only a few of the tribes live along them, for they are also more accessible to the rubbermen. The smaller valleys, difficult of access, are more secure and there the tribal remnants live today. While the broken country thus offers a refuge to fugitive bands it is the broken country and its forest cover that combine to break up the population into small groups and keep them in an isolated and quarrelsome state. Chronic quarreling is not only the product of mere lack of contact. It is due to many causes, among which is a union of the habit of migration and divergent tribal speech. Every tribe has its own peculiar words in addition to those common to the group of tribes to which it belongs. Moreover each group of a tribe has its distinctive words. I have seen and used carefully prepared vocabularies—no two of which are alike throughout. They serve for communication with only a limited number of families. These peculiarities increase as experiences vary and new situations call for additions to or changes in their vocabularies, and when migrating tribes meet their speech may be so unlike as to make communication difficult.

Thus arise suspicion, misunderstanding, plunder, and chronic war. Had they been a united people their defense of their rough country might have been successful. The tribes have been divided and now and again, to get firearms and ammunition with which to raid a neighbor, a tribe has joined its fortunes to those of vagrant rubber pickers only to find in time that its women were debased, its members decimated by strange and deadly diseases, and its old morality undermined by an insatiable desire for strong drink.[4] The Indian loses whether with the white or against him.

The forest Indian is held by his environment no less strongly than the plateau Indian. We hear much about the restriction of the plateau dweller to the cool zone in which the llama may live. As a matter of fact he lives far below the cool zone, where he no longer depends upon the llama but rather upon the mule for transport. The limits of his range correspond to the limits of the grasslands in the dry valley pockets already described (p. 42), or on the drier mountain slopes below the zone of heaviest rainfall (Fig. 54). It is this distribution that brought him into such intimate contact with the forest Indian. The old and dilapidated coca terraces of the Quechuas above the Yanatili almost overlook the forest patches where the Machigangas for centuries built their rude huts. A good deal has been written about the attempts of the Incas to extend their rule into this forest zone and about the failure of these attempts on account of the tropical climate. But the forest Indian was held by bonds equally secure. The cold climate of the plateau repelled him as it does today. His haunts are the hot valleys where he need wear only a wild-cotton shirt or where he may go naked altogether. That he raided the lands of the plateau Indian is certain, but he could never displace him. Only along the common borders of their domains, where the climates of two zones merged into each other, could the forest Indian and the plateau Indian seriously dispute each other's

---

[4] Walle states (Le Pérou Economique, Paris, 1907, p. 297) that the Conibos, a tribe of the Ucayali, make annual *correrias* or raids during the months of July, August, and September, that is during the season of low water. Over seven hundred canoes are said to participate and the captives secured are sold to rubber exploiters, who, indeed, frequently aid in the organization of the raids.

claims to the land. Here was endless conflict but only feeble trade and only the most minute exchanges of cultural elements.

Even had they been as brothers they would have had little incentive to borrow cultural elements from each other. The forest dweller requires bow and arrow; the plateau dweller requires a hoe. There are fish in the warm river shallows of the forested zone; llamas, vicuña, vizcachas, etc., are a partial source of food supply on the plateau. Coca and potatoes are the chief products of the grassy mountain slopes; yuca, corn, bananas, are the chief vegetable foods grown on the tiny cultivated patches in the forest. The plateau dweller builds a thick-walled hut; the valley dweller a cane shack. So unlike are the two environments that it would be strange if there had been a mixture of racial types and cultures. The slight exchanges that were made seem little more than accidental. Even today the Machigangas who live on the highest slopes own a few pigs obtained from Quechuas, but they never eat their flesh; they keep them for pets merely. I saw not a single woolen article among the Indians along the Urubamba whereas Quechuas with woolen clothing were going back and forth regularly. Their baubles were of foreign make; likewise their few hoes, likewise their guns.

They clear the forest about a wild-cotton tree and spin and weave the cotton fiber into sacks, cords for climbing trees when they wish to chase a monkey, ropes for hauling their canoes, shirts for the married men and women, colored head-bands, and fish nets. The slender strong bamboo is gathered for arrows. The chunta palm, like bone for hardness, supplies them with bows and arrow heads. The brilliant red and yellow feathers of forest birds, also monkey bones and teeth, are their natural ornaments. Their life is absolutely distinct from that of their Quechua neighbors. Little wonder that for centuries forest and plateau Indians have been enemies and that their cultures are so distinct, for their environment everywhere calls for unlike modes of existence and distinct cultural development.

CHAPTER V

THE COUNTRY OF THE SHEPHERDS

THE lofty mountain zones of Peru, the high bordering valleys, and the belts of rolling plateau between are occupied by tribes of shepherds. In that cold, inhospitable region at the top of the country are the highest permanent habitations in the world—17,100 feet (5,210 m.)—the loftiest pastures, the greatest degree of adaptation to combined altitude and frost. It is here only a step from Greenland to Arcady. Nevertheless it is Greenland that has the people. Why do they shun Arcady? To the traveler from the highlands the fertile valleys between 5,000 and 8,000 feet (1,500 to 2,500 m.) seem like the abode of friendly spirits to whose charm the highland dweller must yield. Every pack-train from valley to highland carries luxury in the form of fruit, coca, cacao, and sugar. One would think that every importation of valley products would be followed by a wave of migration from highland to valley. On the contrary the highland people have clung to their lofty pastures for unnumbered centuries. Until the Conquest the last outposts of the Incas toward the east were the grassy ridges that terminate a few thousand feet below the timber line.

In this natural grouping of the people where does choice or blind prejudice or instinct leave off? Where does necessity begin? There are answers to most of these questions to be found in the broad field of geographic comparison. But before we begin comparisons we must study the individual facts upon which they rest. These facts are of almost every conceivable variety. They range in importance from a humble shepherd's stone corral on a mountain slope to a thickly settled mountain basin. Their interpretation is to be sought now in the soil of rich playa lands, now in the fixed climatic zones and rugged relief of deeply dissected, lofty highlands in the tropics. Some of the controlling factors are historical, others economic; still other factors have exerted their influence through obscure psychologic channels almost impossible to trace. The *why* of man's distribution over the earth is one of the most complicated problems in natural science, and the solution of it is the chief problem of the modern geographer.

At first sight the mountain people of the Peruvian Andes seem to be uniform in character and in mode of life. The traveler's first impression is that the same stone-walled, straw-thatched type of hut is to be found everywhere, the same semi-nomadic life, the same degrees of poverty and filth. Yet after a little study the diversity of their lives is seen to be, if not a dominating fact, at least one of surprising importance. Side by side with this diversity there runs a corresponding diversity of relations to their physical environment. Nowhere else on the earth are greater physical contrasts compressed within such small spaces. If, therefore, we accept the fundamental theory of geography that there is a general, necessary, varied, and complex relation between man and the earth, that theory ought here to find a really vast number of illustrations. A glance at the accompanying figures discloses the wide range of relief in the Peruvian Andes. The corresponding range in climate and in life therefore furnishes an ample field for the application of the laws of human distribution.

In analyzing the facts of distribution we shall do well to begin with the causes and effects of migration. Primitive man is in no small degree a wanderer. His small resources often require him to explore large tracts. As population increases the food quest becomes more intense, and thus there come about repeated emigrations which increase the food supply, extend its variety, and draw the pioneers at last into contact with neighboring groups. The farther back we go in the history of the race the clearer it becomes that migrations lie at the root of much of human development. The raid for plunder, women, food, beasts, is a persistent feature of the life of those primitive men who live on the border of unlike regions.

The shepherd of the highland and the forest hunter of the plains perforce range over vast tracts, and each brings back to the home group news that confirms the tribal choice of habitation or sets it in motion toward a more desirable place. Superstitions may lead to flight akin to migration. Epidemics may be interpreted as the work of a malignant spirit from which men must flee. War may drive a defeated group into the fastnesses of a mountain forest where pursuit by stream or trail weakens the pursuer and confines his action, thereby limiting his power. Floods may come and destroy the cultivated spots. Want or mere desire in a hundred forms may lead to movement.

Even among forest tribes long stationary the facile canoe and the light household necessities may easily enable trivial causes to develop the spirit of restlessness. Pressure of population is a powerful but not a general cause of movement. It may affect the settled groups of the desert oases, or the dense population of fertile plains that is rooted in the soil. On the other hand mere whims may start a nomadic group toward a new goal. Often the goal is elusive and the tribe turns back to the old haunts or perishes in the shock of unexpected conflict.

In the case of both primitive societies and those of a higher order the causes and the results of migration are often contradictory. These will depend on the state of civilization and the extremes of circumstance. When the desert blooms the farmer of the Piura Valley in northwestern Peru turns shepherd and drives his flocks of sheep and goats out into the short-lived pastures of the great pampa on the west. In dry years he sends them eastward into the mountains. The forest Indian of the lower Urubamba is a fisherman while the river is low and lives in a reed hut beside his cultivated patch of cane and yuca. When the floods come he is driven to the higher ground in the hills where he has another cultivated patch of land and a rude shelter. To be sure, these are seasonal migrations, yet through them the country becomes better known to each new generation of men. And each generation supplies its pioneers, who drift into the remoter places where population is scarce or altogether wanting.

Dry years and extremely dry years may have opposite effects. When moderate dryness prevails the results may be endurable.

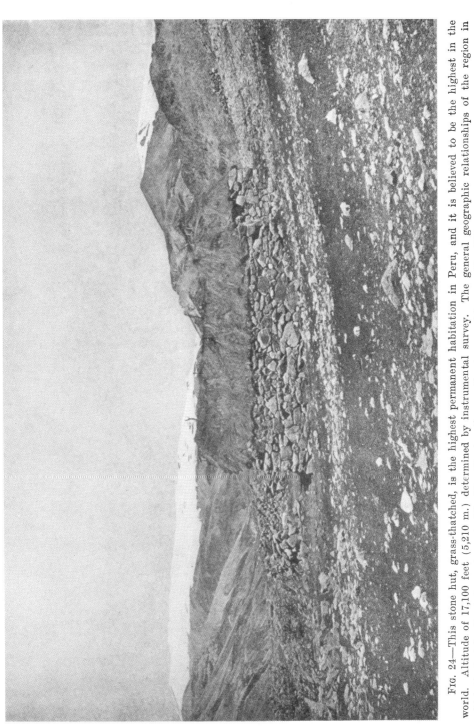

Fig. 24—This stone hut, grass-thatched, is the highest permanent habitation in Peru, and it is believed to be the highest in the world. Altitude of 17,100 feet (5,210 m.) determined by instrumental survey. The general geographic relationships of the region in which the hut is situated are shown in Fig. 25. For location see the topographic map, Fig. 204.

The oases become crowded with men and beasts just when they can ill afford to support them. The alfalfa meadows become overstocked, and cattle become lean and almost worthless. But there is at least bare subsistence. By contrast, if extreme and prolonged drought prevails, some of the people are driven forth to more favored spots. At Vallenar in central Chile some of the workmen in extreme years go up to the nitrate pampa; in wet years they return. When the agents of the nitrate companies hear of hard times in a desert valley they offer employment to the stricken people. It not infrequently happens that when there are droughts in desert Chile there are abundant rains in Argentina on the other side of the Cordillera. There has therefore been for many generations an irregular and slight, though definite, shifting of population from one side of the mountains to the other as periods of drought and periods of rain alternated in the two regions. Some think there is satisfactory evidence to prove that a number of the great Mongolian emigrations took place in wet years when pasture was abundant and when the pastoral nomad found it easy to travel. On the other hand it has been urged that the cause of many emigrations was prolonged periods of drought when the choice lay between starvation and flight. It is evident from the foregoing that both views may be correct in spite of the fact that identical effects are attributed to opposite causes.

It is still an open question whether security or insecurity is more favorable for the broad distribution of the Peruvian Indians of the mountain zone which forms the subject of this chapter. Certainly both tend to make the remoter places better known. Tradition has it that, in the days of intertribal conflict before the Conquest, fugitives fled into the high mountain pastures and lived in hidden places and in caves. Life was insecure and relief was sought in flight. On the other hand peace has brought security to life. The trails are now safe. A shepherd may drive his flock anywhere. He no longer has any one to fear in his search for new pastures. It would perhaps be safe to conclude that there is equally broad distribution of men in the mountain pastures in time of peace and in time of war. There is, however, a difference in

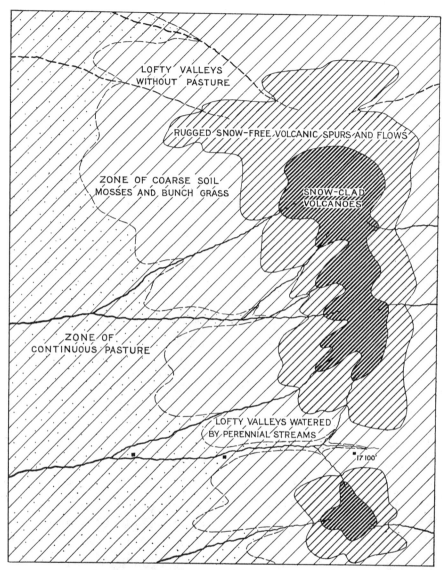

FIG. 25—Regional diagram for the Maritime Cordillera to show the physical relations in the district where the highest habitations in the world are located. For location, see Fig. 20. It should be remembered that the orientation of these diagrams is generalized. By reference to Fig. 20 it will be seen that some portions of the crest of the Maritime Cordillera run east and west and others north and south. The same is true of the Cordillera Vilcapampa, Fig. 36.

the kind of distribution. In time of peace the individual is safe anywhere; in time of unrest he is safe only when isolated and virtually concealed. By contrast, the group living near the trails is scattered by plundering bands and war parties. The remote and isolated group may successfully oppose the smaller band and the individuals that might reach the remoter regions. The fugitive group would have nothing to fear from large bands, for the limited food supply would inevitably cause these to disintegrate upon leaving the main routes of travel. Probably the fullest exploration of the mountain pastures has resulted from the alternation of peace and war. The opposite conditions which these establish foster both kinds of distribution; hence both the remote group life encouraged by war and the individual's lack of restraint in

---

Note on regional diagrams.—For the sake of clearness I have classified the accompanying facts of human distribution in the country of the shepherds and represented them graphically in "regional" diagrams, Figs. 17, 25, 26, 32, 34, 36, 42, 65. These diagrams are constructed on the principle of dominant control. Each brings out the factors of greatest importance in the distribution of the people in a given region. Furthermore, the facts are compressed within the limits of a small rectangle. This compression, though great, respects all essential relations. For example, every location on these diagrams has a concrete illustration but the accidental relations of the field have been omitted; the essential relations are preserved. Each diagram is, therefore, a kind of generalized type map. It bears somewhat the same relation to the facts of human geography that a block diagram does to physiography. The darkest shading represents steep snow-covered country; the next lower grade represents rough but snow-free country; the lightest shading represents moderate relief; unshaded parts represent plain or plateau. Small circles represent forest or woodland; small open-spaced dots, grassland. Fine alluvium is represented by small closely spaced dots; coarse alluvium by large closely spaced dots.

To take an illustration. In Figure 32 we have the Apurimac region near Pasaje (see location map, Fig. 20). At the lower edge of the rectangle is a snow-capped outlier of the Cordillera Vilcapampa. The belt of rugged country represents the lofty, steep, exposed, and largely inaccessible ridges at the mid-elevations of the mountains below the glaciated slopes at the heads of tributary valleys. The villages in the belt of pasture might well be Incahuasi and Corralpata. The floors of the large canyons on either hand are bordered by extensive alluvial fans. The river courses are sketched in a diagrammatic way only, but a map would not be different in its general disposition. Each location is justified by a real place with the same essential features and relations. In making the change there has been no alteration of the general relation of the alluvial lands to each other or to the highland. By suppressing unnecessary details there is produced a diagram whose essentials have simple and clear relations. When such a regional diagram is amplified by photographs of real conditions it becomes a sort of generalized picture of a large group of geographic facts. One could very well extend the method to the whole of South America. It would be a real service to geography to draw up a set of, say, twelve to fifteen regional diagrams, still further generalized, for the whole of the continent. As a broad classification they would serve both the specialist and the general student. As the basis for a regional map of South America they would be invaluable if worked out in sufficient detail and constructed on the indispensable basis of field studies

time of peace are probably in large part responsible for the present widespread occupation of the Peruvian mountains.

The loftiest habitation in the world (Fig. 24) is in Peru. Between Antabamba and Cotahuasi occur the highest passes in the Maritime Cordillera. We crossed at 17,400 feet (5,300 m.), and three hundred feet lower is the last outpost of the Indian shepherds. The snowline, very steeply canted away from the sun, is between 17,200 and 17,600 feet (5,240 to 5,360 m.). At frequent intervals during the three months of winter, snowfalls during the night and terrific hailstorms in the late afternoon drive both shepherds and flocks to the shelter of leeward slopes or steep canyon walls. At our six camps, between 16,000 and 17,200 feet (4,876 and 5,240 m.), in September, 1911, the minimum temperature ranged from 4° to 20° F. The thatched stone hut that we passed at 17,100 feet and that enjoys the distinction of being the highest in the world was in other respects the same as the thousands of others in the same region. It sheltered a family of five. As we passed, three rosy-cheeked children almost as fat as the sheep about them were sitting on the ground in a corner of the corral playing with balls of wool. Hundreds of alpacas and sheep grazed on the hill slopes and valley floor, and their tracks showed plainly that they were frequently driven up to the snowline in those valleys where a trickle of water supported a band of pasture. Less than a hundred feet below them were other huts and flocks.

Here we have the limits of altitude and the limits of resources. The intervalley spaces do not support grass. Some of them are quite bare, others are covered with mosses. It is too high for even the tola bush—that pioneer of Alpine vegetation in the Andes. The distance[1] to Cotahuasi is 75 miles (120 km.), to Antabamba 50 miles (80 km.). Thence wool must be shipped by pack-train to the railroad in the one case 250 miles (400 km.) to Arequipa, in the other case 200 miles (320 km.) to Cuzco. Even the potatoes and barley, which must be imported, come from valleys several days' journey away. The question naturally arises why these people live on the rim of the world. Did they seek out these neglected

---

[1] Distances are not taken from the map but from the trail.

pastures, or were they driven to them? Do they live here by
choice or of necessity? The answer to these questions introduces
two other geographic factors of prime importance, the one physical, the other economic.

The main tracts of lofty pasture above Antabamba cover mountain slopes and valley floor alike, but the moist valley floors supply
the best grazing. Moreover, the main valleys have been intensively glaciated. Hence, though their sides are steep walls, their
floors are broad and flat. Marshy tracts, periodically flooded, are
scattered throughout, and here and there are overdeepened portions where lakes have gathered. There is a thick carpet of grass,
also numerous huts and corrals, and many flocks. At the upper
edge of the main zone of pasture the grasses become thin and with
increasing altitude give out altogether except along the moist valley floors or on shoulders where there is seepage.

If the streams head in dry mountain slopes without snow the
grassy bands of the valley floor terminate at moderate elevations.
If the streams have their sources in snowfields or glaciers there is
a more uniform run-off, and a ribbon of pasture may extend to the
snowline. To the latter class belong the pastures that support
these remote people.

In the case of the Maritime Andes the great elevation of the
snowline is also a factor. If, in Figure 25, we think of the snowline as at the upper level of the main zone of pasture then we
should have the conditions shown in Figure 36, where the limit of
general, not local, occupation is the snowline, as in the Cordillera
Vilcapampa and between Chuquibambilla and Antabamba.

A third factor is the character of the soil. Large amounts of
volcanic ash and lapilli were thrown out in the late stages of volcanic eruption in which the present cones of the Maritime Andes
were formed. The coarse texture of these deposits allows the
ready escape of rainwater. The combination of extreme aridity
and great elevation results in a double restraint upon vegetation.
Outside of the moist valley floors, with their film of ground
moraine on whose surface plants find a more congenial soil, there
is an extremely small amount of pasture. Here are the natural

grazing grounds of the fleet vicuña. They occur in hundreds, and so remote and little disturbed are they that near the main pass one may count them by the score. As we rode by, many of them only stared at us without taking the trouble to get beyond rifle shot. It is not difficult to believe that the Indians easily shoot great numbers in remote valleys that have not been hunted for years.

The extreme conditions of life existing on these lofty plateaus are well shown by the readiness with which even the hardy shepherds avail themselves of shelter. Wherever deep valleys bring a milder climate within reach of the pastures the latter are unpopulated for miles on either side. The sixty-mile stretch between Chuquibamba and Salamanca is without even a single hut, though there are pastures superior to the ones occupied by those loftiest huts of all. Likewise there are no permanent homes between Salamanca and Cotahuasi, though the shepherds migrate across the belt in the milder season of rain. Eastward and northward toward the crest of the Maritime Cordillera there are no huts within a day's journey of the Cotahuasi canyon. Then there is a group of a dozen just under the crest of the secondary range that parallels the main chain of volcanoes. Thence northward there are a number of scattered huts between 15,500 and 16,500 feet (4,700 and 5,000 m.), until we reach the highest habitations of all at 17,100 feet (5,210 m.).

The unpopulated belts of lava plateau bordering the entrenched valleys are, however, as distinctly "sustenance" spaces, to use Penck's term, as the irrigated and fertile alluvial fans in the bottom of the valley. This is well shown when the rains come and flocks of llamas and sheep are driven forth from the valleys to the best pastures. It is equally well shown by the distribution of the shepherds' homes. These are not down on the warm canyon floor, separated by a half-day's journey from the grazing. They are in the intrenched tributary valleys of Figure 26 or just within the rim of the canyon. It is not shelter from the cold but from the wind that chiefly determines their location. They are also kept near the rim of the canyon by the pressure of the farming population from below. Every hundred feet of descent from the arid plateau (Fig. 29) increases the water supply. Springs increase in number and size; likewise belts of seepage make their appearance. The gradients in many places diminish, and flattish spurs and shoulders interrupt the generally steep descents of the canyon

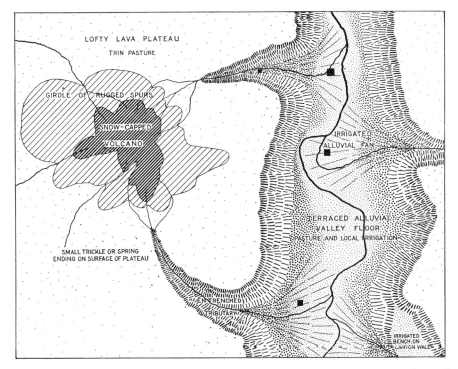

FIG. 26—Regional diagram to show the physical relations in the lava plateau of the Maritime Cordillera west of the continental divide. For location, see Fig. 20. Trails lead up the intrenched tributaries. If the irrigated bench (lower right corner) is large, a town will be located on it. Shepherds' huts are scattered about the edge of the girdle of spurs. There is also a string of huts in the deep sheltered head of each tributary. See also Fig. 29 for conditions on the valley or canyon floor.

wall. Every change of this sort has a real value to the farmer and means an enhanced price beyond the ability of the poor shepherd to pay. If you ask a wealthy *hacendado* on the valley floor (Fig. 29), who it is that live in the huts above him, he will invariably say "los Indios," with a shrug meant to convey the idea of poverty and worthlessness. Sometimes it is "los Indios pobres," or merely "los pobres." Thus there is a vertical stratification of society corresponding to the superimposed strata of climate and land.

At Salamanca (Fig. 62) I saw this admirably displayed under circumstances of unusual interest. The floor and slopes of the valley are more completely terraced than in any other valley I know of. In the photograph, Fig. 30, which shows at least 2,500 feet of descent near the town, one cannot find a single patch of surface that is not under cultivation. The valley is simply filled with people to the limit of its capacity. Practically all are Indians, but with many grades of wealth and importance. When we rode out of the valley before daybreak, one September morning in 1911, there was a dead calm, and each step upward carried us into a colder stratum of air. At sunrise we had reached a point about 2,000 feet above the town, or 14,500 feet (4,420 m.) above sea level. We stood on the frost line. On the opposite wall of the valley the line was as clearly marked out as if it had been an irrigating canal. The light was so fully reflected from the millions of frost crystals above it that both the mountainside and the valley slopes were sparkling like a ruffled lake at sunrise. Below the frost line the slopes were dark or covered with yellow barley and wheat stubble or green alfalfa.

It happened that the frost line was near the line of division between corn and potato cultivation and also near the line separating the steep rough upper lands from the cultivable lower lands. Not a habitation was in sight above us, except a few scattered miserable huts near broken terraces, gullied by wet-weather streams and grown up to weeds and brush. Below us were well-cultivated fields, and the stock was kept in bounds by stone fences and corrals; above, the half-wild burros and mules roamed about everywhere, and only the sheep and llamas were in rude enclosures. Thus in a half hour we passed the frontier between the agricultural folk below the frost line and the shepherd folk above it.

In a few spots the line followed an irregular course, as where flatter lands were developed at unusual elevations or where air drainage altered the normal temperature. And at one place the

FIG. 27.

FIG. 28.

FIG. 27—Terraced valley slopes at Huaynacotas, Cotahuasi Valley, Peru. Elevation 11,500 feet (3,500 m.).

FIG. 28—The highly cultivated and thoroughly terraced floor of the Ollantaytambo Valley at Ollantaytambo. This is a tributary of the Urubamba; elevation, 11,000 feet.

FIG. 29—Cotahuasi on the floor of the Cotahuasi canyon. The even skyline of the background is on a rather even-topped lava plateau. The terrace on the left of the town is formed on limestone, which is overlain by lava flows. A thick deposit of terraced alluvium may be seen on the valley floor, and it is on one of the lower terraces that the city of Cotahuasi stands. The higher terraces are in many cases too dry for cultivation. The canyon is nearly 7,000 feet (2,130 m.) deep and has been cut through one hundred principal lava flows.

frost actually stood on the young corn, which led us to speculate on the possibility of securing from Salamanca a variety of maize that is more nearly resistant to light frosts than any now grown in the United States. In the endless and largely unconscious experimentation of these folk perched on the valley walls a result may have been achieved ahead of that yet reached by our professional experimenters. Certain it is that nowhere else in the world has the potato been grown under such severe climatic conditions as in its native land of Peru and Bolivia. The hardiest varieties lack many qualities that we prize. They are small and bitter. But at least they will grow where all except very few cultivated plants fail, and they are edible. Could they not be imported into Canada to push still farther northward the limits of cultivation? Potatoes are now grown at Forts Good Hope and McPherson in the lower Mackenzie basin. Would not the hardiest Peruvian varieties grow at least as far north as the continental timber line? I believe they could be grown still farther north. They will endure repeated frosts. They need scarcely any cultivation. Prepared in the Peruvian manner, as *chuño,* they could be kept all winter. Being light, the meal derived from them could be easily packed by hunters and prospectors. An Indian will carry in a pouch enough to last him a week. Why not use it north of the continental limit of other cultivated plants since it is the pioneer above the frost line on the Peruvian mountains?

The relation between farmer and shepherd or herdsman grows more complex where deeper valleys interrupt the highlands and mountains. The accompanying sketch, Fig. 32, represents typical relations, though based chiefly on the Apurimac canyon and its surroundings near Pasaje. First there is the snow-clad region at the top of the country. Below it are grassy slopes, the homes of mountain shepherds, or rugged mountain country unsuited for grazing. Still lower there is woodland, in patches chiefly, but with a few large continuous tracts. The shady sides of the ravines and the mountains have the most moisture, hence bear the densest growths. Finally, the high country terminates in a second belt of pasture below the woodland.

Whenever streams descend from the snow or woodland country there is water for the stock above and for irrigation on the
alluvial fan below. But the spur ends dropping off abruptly sev-

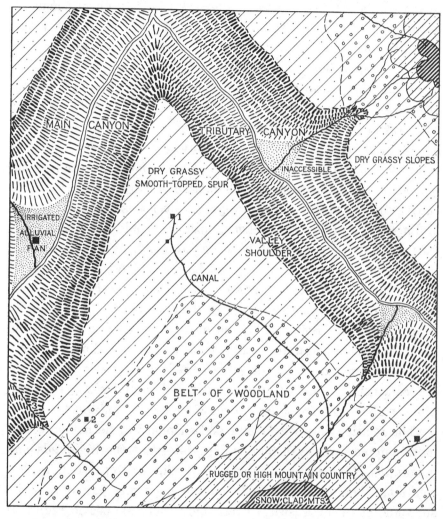

FIG. 32—Regional diagram representing the deep canyoned country west of the
Eastern Cordillera in the region of the Apurimac. For photograph see Fig. 94. For
further description see note on regional diagrams, p. 51. Numbers 1, 2, and 3 correspond in position to the same numbers in Fig. 33.

eral thousand feet have a limited area and no running streams,
and the ground water is hundreds of feet down. There is grass
for stock, but there is no water. In some places the stock is driven

Fig. 31—Alpine pastures in the mountain valley between Chuquibambilla and Lambrama. Huge stone corrals are built on either slope, sheltered from the night winds that blow down-valley.

Fig. 30—Terraced hill slopes near Salamanca. There is no part of the photograph which is not covered with terraces save a few places where bushy growths are visible or where torrents descend through artificial canals.

back and forth every few days. In a few places water is brought
to the stock by canal from the woodland streams above, as at
Corralpata.[2] In the same way a canal brings water to Pasaje
hacienda from a woodland strip many miles to the west. The
little canal in the figure is almost a toy construction a few inches

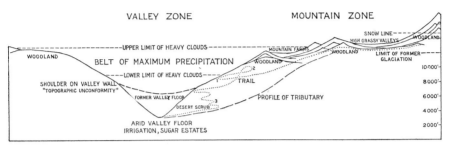

VALLEY ZONE   MOUNTAIN ZONE

SNOW LINE
HIGH GRASSY VALLEYS   WOODLAND
UPPER LIMIT OF HEAVY CLOUDS   MOUNTAIN FARMS
WOODLAND   WOODLAND   LIMIT OF FORMER
BELT OF MAXIMUM PRECIPITATION   WOODLAND   GLACIATION
LOWER LIMIT OF HEAVY CLOUDS   10,000'
SHOULDER ON VALLEY WALL   TRAIL
"TOPOGRAPHIC UNCONFORMITY"   8,000'
FORMER VALLEY FLOOR
DESERT SCRUB   PROFILE OF TRIBUTARY   6,000'
4,000'
ARID VALLEY FLOOR   2,000'
IRRIGATION, SUGAR ESTATES

FIG. 33—Valley climates of the canyoned region shown in Fig. 32.

wide and deep and conveying only a trickle of water. Yet on it
depends the settlement at the spur end, and if it were cut the people would have to repair it immediately or establish new homes.

The canal and the pasture are possible because the slopes are
moderate. They were formed in an earlier cycle of erosion when
the land was lower. They are hung midway between the rough
mountain slopes above and the steep canyon walls below (Fig. 32).
Their smooth descents and gentle profiles are in very pleasing
contrast to the rugged scenery about them. The trails follow them
easily. Where the slopes are flattest, farmers have settled and
produce good crops of corn, vegetables, and barley. Some farmers have even developed three- and four-story farms. On an alluvial fan in the main valley they raise sugar cane and tropical
and subtropical fruits; on the flat upper slopes they produce corn;
in the moister soil near the edge of the woodland are fields of
mountain potatoes; and the upper pastures maintain flocks of

---

[2] Compare with Raimondi's description of Quiches on the left bank of the Marañon
at an elevation of 9,885 feet (3,013 m.): " the few small springs scarcely suffice for
the little patches of alfalfa and other sowings have to depend on the precarious
rains. . . .   Every drop of water is carefully guarded and from each spring a series
of well-like basins descending in staircase fashion make the most of the scant supply."
(El Departamento de Ancachs, Lima, 1873.)

sheep. In one district this change takes place in a distance that may be covered in five hours. Generally it is at least a full and hard day's journey from one end of the series to the other.

Wherever these features are closely associated they tend to be controlled by the planter in some deep valley thereabouts. Where they are widely scattered the people are independent, small groups living in places nearly inaccessible. Legally they are all under the control of the owners of princely tracts that take in the whole country, but the remote groups are left almost wholly to themselves. In most cases they are supposed to sell their few commercial products to the *hacendado* who nominally owns their land, but the administration of this arrangement is left largely to chance. The shepherds and small farmers near the plantation are more dependent upon the planter for supplies, and also their wants are more varied and numerous. Hence they pay for their better location in free labor and in produce sold at a discount.

So deep are some of the main canyons, like the Apurimac and the Cotahuasi, that their floors are arid or semi-arid. The fortunes of Pasaje are tied to a narrow canal from the moist woodland and a tiny brook from a hollow in the valley wall. Where the water has thus been brought down to the arable soil of the fans there are rich plantations and farms. Elsewhere, however, the floor is quite dry and uncultivated. In small spots here and there is a little seepage, or a few springs, or a mere thread of water that will not support a plantation, wherefore there have come into existence the valley herdsmen and shepherds. Their intimate knowledge of the moist places is their capital, quite as much as are the cattle and sheep they own. In a sense their lands are the neglected crumbs from the rich man's table. So we find the shepherd from the hills invading the valleys just as the valley farmer has invaded the country of the shepherd.

The basin type of topography calls into existence a set of relations quite distinct from either of those we have just described. Figure 34 represents the main facts. The rich and comparatively flat floor of the basin supports most of the people. The alluvial fans tributary thereto are composed of fine material on their outer

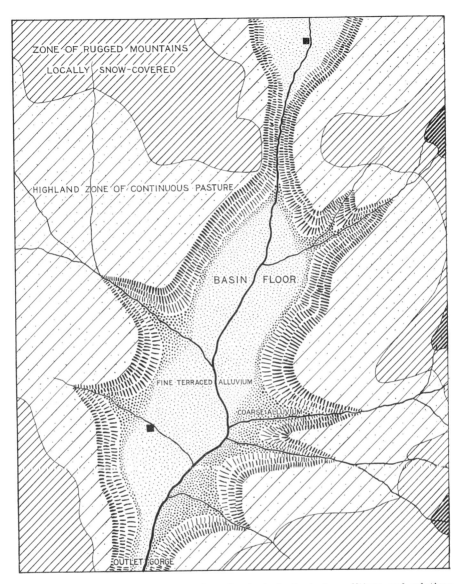

FIG. 34—Regional diagram to show the typical physical conditions and relations in an intermont basin in the Peruvian Andes. The Cuzco basin (see Fig. 37) is an actual illustration; it should, however, be emphasized that the diagram is not a "map" of that basin, for whilst conditions there have been utilized as a basis, the generalization has been extended to illustrate many basins.

margin and of coarse stony waste at their heads. Hence the valley farms also extend over the edges of the fans, while only pasture or dense chaparral occupies the upper portions. Finally

there is the steep margin of the basin where the broad and moderate slopes of the highland break down to the floor of the basin.

If a given basin lies at an elevation exceeding 14,000 feet
(4,270 m.), there will be no cultivation, only pasture. If at 10,000
or 11,000 feet (3,000 or 3,350 m.), there will be grain fields below

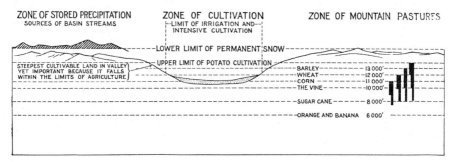

ZONE OF STORED PRECIPITATION   ZONE OF CULTIVATION   ZONE OF MOUNTAIN PASTURES
SOURCES OF BASIN STREAMS |—LIMIT OF IRRIGATION AND—|
                                                    | INTENSIVE CULTIVATION |

- - - - - - - - - LOWER LIMIT OF PERMANENT SNOW - - - - - - - - - - -
- - - - - UPPER LIMIT OF POTATO CULTIVATION - - - - - - - - - - -
STEEPEST CULTIVABLE LAND IN VALLEY
YET IMPORTANT BECAUSE IT FALLS
WITHIN THE LIMITS OF AGRICULTURE
- BARLEY - - - - - - - 13 000' - - -
- WHEAT - - - - - - - 12 000' -
- CORN - - - - - - - 11 000'
- THE VINE - - - - - -10 000'-
- SUGAR CANE - - - - - 8 000'-
- ORANGE AND BANANA   6 000'

FIG. 35—Climatic cross-section showing the location of various zones of cultivation
and pasture in a typical intermont basin in the Peruvian Andes. The thickness of
the dark symbols on the right is proportional to the amount of each staple that is
produced at the corresponding elevation. See also the regional diagram Fig. 34.

and potato fields above (Figs. 34 and 35). If still lower, fruit will
come in and finally sugar cane and many other subtropical products, as at Abancay. Much will also depend upon the amount of
available water and the extent of the pasture land. Thus the
densely populated Cuzco basin has a vast mountain territory
tributary to it and is itself within the limits of barley and wheat
cultivation. Furthermore there are a number of smaller basins, like
the Anta basin on the north, which are dependent upon its better
markets and transportation facilities. A dominance of this kind
is self-stimulating and at last is out of all proportion to the
original differences of nature. Cuzco has also profited as the gateway to the great northeastern valley region of the Urubamba and
its big tributaries. All of the varied products of the subtropical
valleys find their immediate market at Cuzco.

The effect of this natural conspiracy of conditions has been to
place the historic city of Cuzco in a position of extraordinary importance. Hundreds of years before the Spanish Conquest it was
a center of far-reaching influence, the home of the powerful Inca
kings. From it the strong arm of authority and conquest was ex-

tended; to it came tribute of grain, wool, and gold. To one accustomed to look at such great consequences as having at least some ultimate connection with the earth, the situation of Cuzco would be expected to have some unique features. With the glorious past of that city in mind, no one can climb to the surrounding heights and look down upon the fertile mountain-rimmed plain as at an ordinary sight (Fig. 37). The secret of those great conquests lies not only in mind but in matter. If the rise of the Incas to power was not related to the topography and climate of the Cuzco basin, at least it is certain that without so broad and noble a stage the scenes would have been enacted on a far different scale.

The first Inca king and the Spanish after the Incas found here no mobile nomadic tribes melting away at the first touch, no savages hiding in forest fastnesses, but a well-rooted agricultural race in whose center a large city had grown up. Without a city and a fertile tributary plain no strong system of government could be maintained or could even arise. It is a great advantage in ruling to have subjects that cannot move. The agricultural Indians of the Andean valleys and basins, in contrast to the mobile shepherd, are as fixed as the soil from which they draw their life.

The full occupation of the pasture lands about the Cuzco basin is in direct relation to the advantages we have already enumerated. Every part of the region feels the pressure of population. Nowhere else in the Peruvian Andes are the limits between cultivation and grazing more definitely drawn than here. Moreover, there is today a marked difference between the types that inhabit highland and basin. The basin Indian is either a debauched city dweller or, as generally, a relatively alert farmer. The shepherds are exceedingly ignorant and live for the most part in a manner almost as primitive as at the time of the Conquest. They are shy and suspicious. Many of them prefer a life of isolation and rarely go down to the town. They live on the fringe of culture. The new elements of their life have come to them solely by accident and by what might be called a process of ethnic seepage. The slight advances that have been made do not happen by design, they merely happen. Put the highland shepherd in the basin and he would starve in competition with the basin type. Undoubtedly he would live in the basin if he could. He has not been driven out of the basin; he is kept out.

And thus it is around the border of the Abancay basin and others like it. Only, the Abancay basin is lower and more varied as to resources. The Indian is here in competition with the capitalistic white planter. He lives on the land by sufferance alone. Farther up the slopes are the farms of the Indians and above them are the pastures of the ignorant shepherds. Whereas the Indian farmer who raises potatoes clings chiefly to the edge of the Cuzco basin where lie the most undesirable agricultural lands, the Indian farmers of Abancay live on broad rolling slopes like those near the pass northward toward Huancarama. They are unusually prosperous, with fields so well cultivated and fenced, so clean and productive, that they remind one somewhat of the beautiful rolling prairies of Iowa.

It remains to consider the special topographic features of the mountain environments we are discussing, in the Vilcapampa region on the eastern border of the Andes (Fig. 36). The Cordillera Vilcapampa is snow-crested, containing a number of fine white peaks like Salcantay, Soray, and Soiroccocha (Fig. 140). There are many small glaciers and a few that are several miles long. There was here in glacial times a much larger system of glaciers, which lived long enough to work great changes in the topography. The floors of the glaciated valleys were smoothed and broadened and their gradients flattened (Figs. 137 and 190). The side walls were steepened and precipitous cirques were formed at the valley heads. Also, there were built across the valleys a number of stony morainic ridges. With all these changes there was, however, but little effect upon the main masses of the big intervalley spurs. They remain as before—bold, wind-swept, broken, and nearly inaccessible.

The work of the glaciers aids the mountain people. The stony moraines afford them handy sizable building material for their stone huts and their numerous corrals. The thick tufts of grass

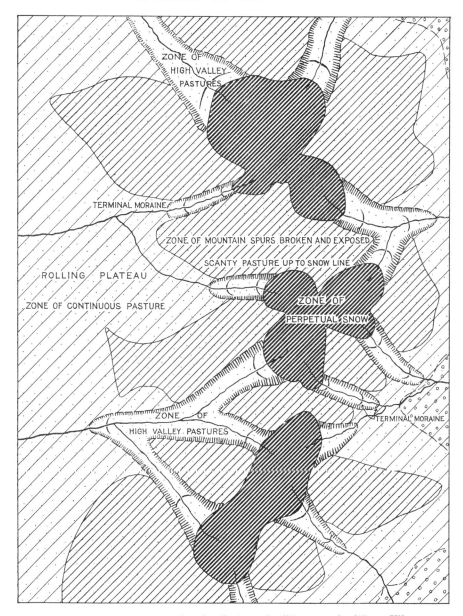

Fig. 36—Regional diagram for the Eastern Cordillera or Cordillera Vilcapampa. Note the crowded zones on the right (east and north) in contrast to the open succession on the left. In sheltered places woodland extends even higher than shown. At several points patches of it grow right under the snowline. Other patches grow on the floors of the glaciated valley troughs.

in the marshy spots in the overdeepened parts of the valleys furnish them with grass for their thatched roofs. And, most im-

portant of all, the flat valley floors have the best pasture in the
whole mountain region. There is plenty of water. There is seclusion, and, if a fence be built from one valley wall to another as can
be done with little labor, an entire section of the valley may be
inclosed. A village like Choquetira, located on a bench on the valley side, commands an extensive view up and down the valley—an
important feature in a grazing village where the corrals cannot
always be built near the houses of the owners. Long, finger-like
belts of highland-shepherd population have thus been extended
into the mountain valleys. Sheep and llamas drift right up to
the snowline.

There is, however, a marked difference between the people on
opposite sides of the Cordillera Vilcapampa. On the west the mountains are bordered by a broad highland devoted to grazing. On
the east there is a narrower grazing belt leading abruptly down
to tropical valleys. The eastern or leeward side is also the
warmer and wetter side of the Cordillera. The snowline is several hundred feet lower on the east. The result is that patches of
scrub and even a little woodland occur almost at the snowline in
favored places. Mist and storms are more frequent. The grass
is longer and fresher. Vegetation in general is more abundant.
The people make less of wool than of cattle, horses, and mules.
Vilcabamba pueblo is famous for its horses, wiry, long-haired little beasts, as hardy as Shetland ponies. We found cattle grazing
only five hundred feet below the limit of perpetual snow. There
are cultivated spots only a little farther down, and only a thousand feet below the snow are abandoned terraces. At the same
elevation are twisted quenigo trees, at least two hundred years
old, as shown by their rings of growth. Thus the limits of agriculture are higher on the east; likewise the limits of cattle grazing
that naturally goes with agriculture. Sheep would thrive, but
llamas do better in drier country, and the shepherd must needs
mix his flocks, for the wool which is his chief product requires
transportation and only the cheap and acclimated llama is at the
shepherd's disposal. From these facts it will be seen that the
anthropo-geographic contrasts between the eastern and western

Fig. 37.

Fig. 38.

FIG. 37—Cuzco and a portion of the famous Cuzco basin with bordering grassy highlands.

FIG. 38—Terraced valley slopes and floor, Urubamba Valley between Urubamba and Ollantaytambo.

Fig. 39.

Fig. 40.

Fig. 39—Huichihua, near Chuquibambilla, a typical mountain village, in the valleys of the Central Ranges, Peruvian Andes.

Fig. 40—Potato field above Vilcabamba at 12,000 feet (3,660 m.). The natural sod is broken by a steel-shod stick and the seed potato dropped into a mere puncture. It receives no attention thereafter until harvest time.

sides of the Cordillera Vilcapampa are as definite as the climatic and vegetal contrasts. This is especially well shown in the differences between dry Arma, deep-sunk in a glaciated valley west of the crest of the mountains, and wet Puquiura, a half-day's journey east of the crest. There is no group on the east at all comparable to the shepherds of Choquetira, either in the matter of thoroughgoing dependence upon grazing or in that of dependence upon glacial topography.

Topography is not always so intimately related to the life of the people as here. In our own country the distribution of available water is a far greater factor. The Peruvian Andes therefore occupy a distinctive place in geography, since, more nearly than in most mountains, their physical conditions have typical human relations that enable one clearly to distinguish the limits of control of each feature of climate or relief.

CHAPTER VI

THE BORDER VALLEYS OF THE EASTERN ANDES

ON the northeastern border of the Peruvian Andes long mountain spurs trail down from the regions of snow to the forested plains of the Amazon. Here are the greatest contrasts in the

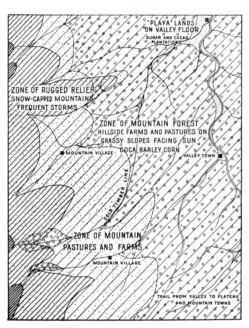

FIG. 41—Regional diagram of the eastern aspect of the Cordillera Vilcapampa. See also Fig. 17 of which this is an enlarged section.

physical and human geography of the Andean Cordillera. So striking is the fact that every serious student of Peru finds himself compelled to cross and recross this natural frontier. The thread of an investigation runs irregularly now into one border zone, now into another. Out of the forest came the fierce marauders who in the early period drove back the Inca pioneers. Down into the forest to escape from the Spaniards fled the last Inca and his fugitive court. Here the Jesuit fathers sowed their missions along the forest margin, and watched over them for two hundred years. From the mountain border one rubber project after another has been launched into the vast swampy lowlands threaded by great rivers. As an ethnic boundary the eastern mountain border of Peru and Bolivia has no equal elsewhere in South America. From the earliest antiquity the tribes of the grass-covered mountains and the hordes of the forested plains have had strongly divergent customs and speech, that bred enduring hatred and led to frequent and bloody strife.

68

Fig. 42—Rug weaver at Cotahuasi. The industry is limited to a small group of related families, living in the Cotahuasi Canyon near Cotahuasi. The rugs are made of alpaca wool. Pure black, pure white, and various shades of mixed gray wool are employed. The result is that the rugs have "fast" colors that always retain their original contrasts. They are made only to order at the homes of the purchasers. The money payment is small, but to it is added board and lodging, besides tobacco, liqueurs, and wine. Before drinking they dip their finger-tips in the wine and sprinkle the earth "that it may be fruitful," the air "that it may be warm," the rug "that it may turn out well," and finally themselves, making the sign of the cross. Then they set to work.

Fig. 43—The floor of the Urubamba Valley from Tarai. The work of the glaciers was not confined to the lofty situations. Mountain débris was delivered to all the streams, many of which aggraded their floors to a depth of several hundred feet, thus increasing the extent of arable soil at elevations where a less rigorous climate permits the production of crops and encourages intensive cultivation,

On the steepest spurs of the Pampaconas Valley the traveler may go from snow to pasture in a half day and from pasture to forest in the same time. Another day he is in the hot zone of the larger valley floors, the home of the Machigangas. The steep descents bring out the superimposed zones with diagrammatic simplicity. The timber line is as sharply marked as the edge of a cultivated field. At a point just beyond the huts of Pampaconas one may stand on a grassy spur that leads directly up—a day's journey—to the white summits of the Cordillera Vilcapampa. Yet so near him is the edge of the forest that he is tempted to try to throw a stone into it. In an hour a bitter wind from the mountains may drive him to shelter or a cold fog come rolling up from the moist region below. It is hard to believe that oppressive heat is felt in the valley just beneath him.

In the larger valleys the geographic contrasts are less sharp and the transition from mountains to plain, though less spectacu-lar, is much more complex and scientifically interesting. The for-est types interfinger along the shady and the sunny slopes. The climate is so varied that the forest takes on a diversified character that makes it far more useful to man. The forest Indians and the valley planters are in closer association. There are many islands and peninsulas of plateau population on the valley floor. Here the zones of climate and the belts of fertile soil have larger areas and the land therefore has greater economic value. Much as the valley people need easier and cheaper communication with the rest of Peru it is no exaggeration to say that the valley prod-ucts are needed far more by the coast and plateau peoples to make the republic self-supporting. Coca, wood, sugar, fruit, are in such demand that their laborious and costly transportation from the valleys to the plateau is now carried on with at least some profit to the valley people. Improved transportation would promote travel and friendship and supply a basis for greater political unity.

A change in these conditions is imminent. Years ago the Peruvian government decreed the construction of a railway from Cuzco to Santa Ana and preliminary surveys were made but without any immediate practical effect. By June, 1914, 12.4 miles (20 km.) had been opened to traffic. The total length of the proposed line is 112 miles (180 km.), the gauge is to be only 2.46 feet (75 cm.),[1] and the proposed cost several millions of dollars. The financial problem may be solved either by a diversion of local revenues, derived from taxes on coca and alcohol, or by borrowed foreign capital guaranteed by local revenues.

A shrubby vegetation is scattered along the valley from the village of Urubamba, 12,000 feet (3,658 m.) above sea level, to the Canyon of Torontoy. It is local and of little value. Trees appear at Ollantaytambo, 11,000 feet (3,353 m.), and here too are more extensive wheat and maize fields besides throngs of cacti and great patches of wild geraniums. On our valley journey we camped in pleasant fields flanked by steep hills whose summits each morning were tipped with snow. Enormous alluvial fans have partly filled up the valleys and furnished broad tracts of fertile soil. The patient farmers have cleared away the stones on the flatter portions and built retaining walls for the smooth fields required for irrigation. In places the lower valley slopes are terraced in the most regular manner (Fig. 38). Some of the fans are too steep and stony for cultivation, exposing bare tracts which wash down and cover the fields. Here and there are stone walls built especially to retain the rush of mud and stones that the rains bring down. Many of them were overthrown or completely buried. Unless the stream channels on the fans are carefully watched and effective works kept up, the labor of years may be destroyed in a single slide from the head of a steep fan.

Each group of fans has a population proportioned to its size and fertility. If there are broad expanses a town like Urubamba or a great hacienda like Huadquiña is sure to be found. One group of huge stony fans below Urubamba (Fig. 180) has only a thin population, for the soil is coarse and infertile and the rivers deeply intrenched. In some places the tiny fans perched high upon the flanks of the mountains where little tributaries burst out

---

[1] Daily Cons. and Trade Report, June 10, 1914, No. 135, and Commerce Reports, March 20, 1916, No. 66.

of steep ravines are cultivated by distant owners who also till parts of the larger fans on the main valley floors. Between the fans of the valley bottoms and the smooth slopes of the high plateaus are the unoccupied lands—the steep canyon walls. Only in the most highly favored places where a small bench or a patch of alluvium occurs may one find even an isolated dwelling. The stair-like trails, in some places cut in solid rock, zigzag up the rocky slopes. An ascent of a thousand feet requires about an hour's travel with fresh beasts. The valley people are therefore walled in. If they travel it is surely not for pleasure. Even business trips are reduced to the smallest number. The prosperity and happiness of the valley people are as well known among the plateau people as is their remarkable bread. Their climate has a combination of winter rain and winter cold with light frosts that is as favorable for good wheat as the continuous winter cold and snow cover of our northern Middle West. The colder grainfields of the plateau are sowed to barley chiefly, though there is also produced some wheat. Urubamba wheat and bread are exported in relatively large quantities, and the market demands greater quantities than the valley can supply. Oregon and Washington flour are imported at Cuzco, two days' muleback journey from the wheat fields of Urubamba.

Such are the conditions in the upper Urubamba Valley The lower valley, beginning at Huadquiña, is 8,000 feet (2,440 m.) above sea level and extends down to the two-thousand-foot contour at Rosalina and to one thousand feet (305 m.) at Pongo de Mainique. The upper and lower sections are only a score of miles (30 km.) apart between Huadquiña and Torontoy, but there is a difference in elevation of three thousand feet (915 m.) at just the level where the maximum contrasts are produced. The cold timber line is at 10,500 feet (3,200 m.).[2] Winter frosts are common

---

[2] Reference to the figures in this chapter will show great variation in the level of the timber line depending upon insolation as controlled by slope exposure and upon moisture directly as controlled largely by exposure to winds. In some places these controls counteract each other; in other places they promote each other's effects. The topographic and climatic cross-sections and regional diagrams elsewhere in this book also emphasize the patchiness of much of the woodland and scrub, some noteworthy examples occurring in the chapter on the Eastern Andes. Two of

at the one place; they are absent altogether at the other. Torontoy
produces corn; Huadquiña produces sugar cane.

These contrasts are still further emphasized by the sharp topographic break between the two unlike portions of the valley. A
few miles below Torontoy the Urubamba plunges into a mile-deep
granite canyon. The walls are so close together that it is impossible from the canyon floor to get into one photograph the highest
and steepest walls. At one place there is over a mile of descent
in a horizontal distance of 2,000 feet. Huge granite slabs fall off
along joint planes inclined but 15° from the vertical. The effect
is stupendous. The canyon floor is littered with coarse waste and
the gradient of the river greatly steepened. There is no cultivation. The trees cling with difficulty to patches of rock waste or
to the less-inclined slopes. There is a thin crevice vegetation that
outlines the joint pattern where seepage supplies the venturesome
roots with moisture. Man has no foothold here, save at the top
of the country, as at Machu Picchu, a typical fortress location
safeguarded by the virtually inaccessible canyon wall and connected with the main ridge slopes only by an easily guarded
narrow spur. Toward the lower end of the canyon a little
finer alluvium appears and settlement begins. Finally, after
a tumble of three thousand feet over countless rapids the river
emerges at Colpani, where an enormous mass of alluvium has
been dumped. The well-intrenched river has already cut a
large part of it away. A little farther on is Huadquiña in
the Salcantay Valley, where a tributary of the Urubamba has
built up a sheet of alluvial land, bright green with cane. From
the distant peaks of Salcantay and its neighbors well-fed streams
descend to fill the irrigation channels. Thus the snow and rock-
waste of the distant mountains are turned into corn and sugar on
the valley lowlands.

---

the most remarkable cases are the patch of woodland at 14,500 feet (4,420 m.) just
under the hanging glacier of Soiroccocha and the other the quenigo scrub on the
lava plateau above Chuquibamba at 13,000 feet (3,960 m.). The strong compression
of climatic zones in the Urubamba Valley below Santa Ana brings into sharp contrast
the grassy ridge slopes facing the sun and the forested slopes that have a high proportion of shade. Fig. 54 represents the general distribution but the details are far
more complicated. See also Figs. 53A and 53B. (See Coropuna Quadrangle.)

FIG. 44.

FIG. 45.

FIG. 44—The snow-capped Cordillera Vilcapampa north of Yucay and the upper canyon of the Urubamba from the wheat fields near Chinchero. In the foreground is one of the well-graded mature slopes of Fig. 123. The crests of the mountains lie along the axis of a granite intrusion. The extent of the snowfields is extraordinary in view of the low latitude, 13° S.

FIG. 45—Rounded slopes due to glacial action at Pampaconas in the Pampaconas Valley near Vilcabamba. A heavy tropical forest extends up the Pampaconas Valley to the hill slopes in the background. Its upper limit of growth is about 10,000 feet (3,050 m.). The camera is pointed slightly downhill.

FIG. 46—Hacienda Huadquiña, in the Salcantay Valley a short distance above its junction with the Urubamba, elevation 8,000 feet (2,440 m.). The cultivated fields are all planted to sugar cane. The mountain slopes are devoted to grazing.

The Cordillera Vilcapampa is a climatic as well as a topographic barrier. The southwestern aspect is dry; the northeastern aspect forested. The gap of the canyon, it should be noticed, comes at a critical level, for it falls just above the upper border of the zone of maximum precipitation. The result is that though mists are driven through the canyon by prolonged up-valley winds, they scatter on reaching the plateau or gather high up on the flanks of the valley or around the snowy peaks overlooking the trail between Ollantaytambo and Urubamba. The canyon walls are drenched with rains and even some of the lofty spurs are clothed with dense forest or scrub.

Farther down the valley winds about irregularly, now pushed to one side by a huge alluvial fan, now turned by some resistant spur of rock. Between the front range of the Andes and the Cordillera Vilcapampa there is a broad stretch of mountain country in the lee of the front range which rises to 7,000 feet (2,134 m.) at Abra Tocate (Fig. 15), and falls off to low hills about Rosalina. It is all very rough in that there are nowhere any flats except for the narrow playa strips along the streams. The dense forest adds to the difficulty of movement. In general appearance it is very much like the rugged Cascade country of Oregon except that the Peruvian forest is much more patchy and its trees are in many places loaded with dense dripping moss which gives the landscape a somber touch quite absent from most of the forests of the temperate zone.

The fertility of the eastern valleys of Peru—the result of a union of favorable climate and alluvial soil—has drawn the planter into this remote section of the country, but how can he dispose of his products? Even today with a railway to Cuzco from the coast it is almost impossible for him to get his sugar and cacao to the outside world.[3] How did he manage before even this railway was built? How could the eastern valley planter live before there were any railways at all in Peru? In part he has solved the problem as the moonshiner of Kentucky tried to solve it, and

---

[3] Commenting on the excellence of the cacao of the montaña of the Urubamba von Tschudi remarked (op. cit., p. 37) that the long land transport prevented its use in Lima where the product on the market is that imported from Guayaquil.

from cane juice makes aguardiente (brandy). The latter is a much more valuable product than sugar, hence (1) it will bear a higher rate of transportation, or (2) it will at the same rate of transportation yield a greater net profit. In a remote valley where sugar could not be exported on account of high freight rates brandy could still be profitably exported.

The same may be said for coca and cacao. They are condensed and valuable products. Both require more labor than sugar but are lighter in bulk and thus have to bear, in proportion to their value, a smaller share of the cost of transportation. At the end of three years coca produces over a ton of leaves per acre per year, and it can be made to produce as much as two tons to the acre. The leaves are picked four times a year. They are worth from eight to twelve cents gold a pound at the plantation or sixteen cents a pound at Cuzco. An orchard of well-cultivated and irrigated cacao trees will do even better. Once they begin to bear the trees require relatively little care except in keeping out weeds and brush and maintaining the water ditches. However, the pods must be gathered at just the right time, the seeds must be raked and dried with expert care, and after that comes the arduous labor of the grinding. This is done by hand on an inclined plane with a heavy round stone whose corners fit the hand. The chocolate must then be worked into cakes and dried, or it must be sacked in heavy cowhide and sewed so as to be practically air tight. When eight or ten years old the trees are mature and each may then bear a thousand pounds of seed.

If labor were cheap and abundant the whole trend of tropical agriculture in the eastern valleys would be toward intensive cultivation and the production of expensive exports. But labor is actually scarce. Every planter must have agents who can send men down from the plateau towns. And the planter himself must use his labor to the best advantage. Aguardiente requires less labor than cacao and coca. The cane costs about as much in labor the first year as the coca bush or the cacao tree, but after that much less. The manufacture of brandy from the cane juice requires little labor though much expensive machinery. For chocolate, a

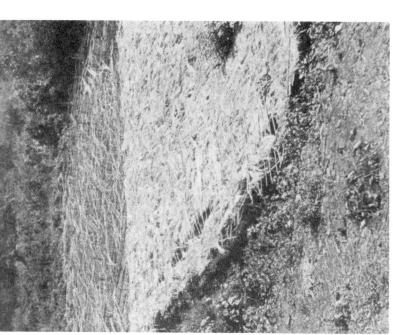

Fig. 47—The Urubamba Valley below Paltaybamba. Harder rocks intruded into the schists that in general compose the valley walls here form steep scarps. It has been suggested (Davis) that such a constricted portion of a valley be called a "shut-in." The old trail climbed to the top of the valley and over the back of a huge spur. The new road is virtually a tunnel blasted along the face of a cliff.

Fig. 48—Coca seed beds near Quillabamba. Urubamba Valley. The young plants are grown under shade and after attaining a height of a foot or more are gradually accustomed to sunlight and finally transplanted to the fields that are to become coca orchards.

FIG. 50—A tiny rubber plant is growing under the tripod made of yuca stems tied with banana leaves. Growing yuca is shown by the naked stalks to the left and right of this canopy, and banana plants fill the background. A plantation scene at Echarati.

FIG. 49—Fig tree formerly attached to a host but now left standing on its stilt-like aërial roots owing to the decay of the host.

storehouse, a grinding stone, and a rake are all that are required. So the planter must work out his own salvation individually. He must take account of the return upon investments in machinery, of the number of hands he can command from among the "faena" or free Indians, of the cost and number of imported hands from the valley and plateau towns, and, finally, of the transportation rates dependent upon the number of mules in the neighborhood, and distance from the market. If in addition the labor is skilfully employed so as to have the tasks which the various products require fall at different periods of the year, then the planter may expect to make money upon his time and get a return upon his initial investment in the land.[4]

The type of tropical agriculture which we have outlined is profitable for the few planters who make up the white population of the valleys, but it has a deplorable effect upon the Indian population. Though the planters, one and all, complain bitterly of the drunken habits of their laborers, they themselves put into the hands of the Indians the means of debauchery. Practically the whole production of the eastern valleys is consumed in Peru. What the valleys do not take is sent to the plateau, where it is the chief cause of vicious conduct. Two-thirds of the prisoners in the city jails are drunkards, and, to be quite plain, they are virtually supplied with brandy by the planter, who could not otherwise make enough money. So although the planter wants more and better labor he is destroying the quality of the little there is, and, if not actually reducing the quantity of it, he is at least very certainly reducing the rate of increase.

The difficulties of the valley planter could be at least partly overcome in several ways. The railway will reduce transportation costs, especially when the playas of the valleys are all cleared and the exports increased. Moreover the eastern valleys

[4] The inadequacy of the labor supply was a serious obstacle in the early days as well as now. In the documents pertaining to the " Obispados y Audiencia del Cuzco " (Vol. 11, p. 349 of the " Juicio de Límites entre el Perú y Bolivia, Prueba Peruana presentada al Gobierno de la República Argentina por Victor M. Maurtua," Barcelona, 1906) we find the report that the natives of the curacy of Ollantaytambo who came down from the hills to Huadquiña to hear mass were detained and compelled to give a day's service on the valley plantations under pain of chastisement.

are capable of producing things of greater utility than brandy and coca leaves. So far as profits are increased by cheaper transportation we may expect the planter to produce more rather than less of brandy and coca, his two most profitable exports, unless other products can be found that are still more profitable. The ratio of profits on sugar and brandy will still be the same unless the government increases the tax on brandy until it becomes no more profitable than sugar. That is what ought to be done for the good of the Indian population. It cannot be done safely without offering in its place the boon of cheaper railway transportation for the sugar crop. Furthermore, with railway improvements should go the blessings that agricultural experiments can bestow. A government farm in a suitable place would establish rice and cotton cultivation. Many of the playas or lower alluvial lands along the rivers can be irrigated. Only a small fraction of the water of the Rio Urubamba is now turned out upon the fields. For a large part of the year the natural rainfall would suffice to keep rice in good condition. Six tons a year are now grown on Hacienda Sahuayaco for local use on account of the heavy rate on rice imported on muleback from Cuzco, whither it comes by sea and by trail from distant coastal valleys. The lowland people also need rice and it could be sent to them down river by an easier route than that over which their supplies now come. It should be exported to the highlands, not imported therefrom. There are so many varieties adapted to so many kinds of soil and climate that large amounts should be produced at fair profits.

The cotton plant, on the other hand, is more particular about climate and especially the duration of dry and wet seasons; in spite of this its requirements are all met in the Santa Ana Valley. The rainfall is moderate and there is an abundance of dry warm soil. The plant could make most of its growth in the wet season, and the four months of cooler dry season with only occasional showers would favor both a bright staple and a good picking season. More labor would be required for cotton and rice and for the increased production of cacao than under the present system. This would not be a real difficulty if the existing labor supply were conserved by the practical abolition, through heavy taxation, of the brandy that is the chief cause of the laborer's vicious habits. This is the first step in securing the best return upon the capital invested in a railway. Economic progress is here bound up with a very practical morality. Colonization in the eastern valleys, of which there have been but a few dismal attempts, will only extend the field of influence, it will not solve the real problem of bringing the people of the rich eastern territory of Peru into full and honorable possession of their natural wealth.

The value of the eastern valleys was known in Inca times, for their stone-faced terraces and coca-drying patios may still be seen at Echarati and on the border of the Chaupimayu Valley at Sahuayaco. Tradition has it that here were the imperial coca lands, that such of the forest Indians as were enslaved were obliged to work upon them, and that the leaves were sent to Cuzco over a paved road now covered with "montaña" or forest. The Indians still relate that at times a mysterious, wavering, white light appears on the terraces and hills where old treasure lies buried. Some of the Indians have gold and silver objects which they say were dug from the floors of hill caves. There appears to have been an early occupation of the best lands by the Spaniards, for the long extensions down them of Quechua population upon which the conquerors could depend no doubt combined with the special products of the valley to draw white colonists thither.[5]

---

[5] The Spanish occupation of the eastern valleys was early and extensive. Immediately after the capture of the young Inca Tupac Amaru and the final subjugation of the province of Vilcapampa colonists started the cultivation of coca and cane. Development of the main Urubamba Valley and tributary valleys proceeded at a good rate: so also did their troubles. Baltasar de Ocampo writing in 1610 (Account of the Province of Vilcapampa, Hakluyt Soc. Publs., Ser. 2, Vol. 22, 1907, pp. 203-247) relates the occurrence of a general uprising of the negroes employed on the sugar plantations of the region. But the peace and prosperity of every place on the eastern frontier was unstable and quite generally the later eighteenth and earlier nineteenth centuries saw a retreat of the border of civilization. The native rebellion of the mid-eighteenth century in the montaña of Chanchamayo caused entire abandonment of a previously flourishing area. When Raimondi wrote in 1885 (La Montaña de Chanchamayo, Lima, 1885) some of the ancient hacienda sites were still occupied by savages. In the Paucartambo valleys, settlement began by the end of the sixteenth century and at the beginning of the nineteenth before their complete desolation by the savages they were highly prosperous. Paucartambo town, itself, once important for its commerce in coca is now in a sadly decadent condition.

General Miller,[6] writing in 1836, mentions the villages of Incharate (Echarati) and Sant' Ana (Santa Ana) but discourages the idea of colonization " . . . since the river . . . has lofty mountains on either side of it, and is not navigable even for boats."

In the "Itinerario de los viajes de Raimondi en el Peru"[7] there is an interesting account of the settlement by the Rueda family of the great estate still held by a Rueda, the wife of Señor Duque. José Rueda, in 1829, was a government deputy representative and took his pay in land, acquiring valuable territory on which there was nothing more than a mission. In 1830 Rueda ceded certain lands in "arriendo" (rent) and on these were founded the haciendas Pucamoco, Sahuayaco, etc.

Señor Gonzales, the present owner of Hacienda Sahuayaco, recently obtained his land—a princely estate, ten miles by forty— for 12,000 soles ($6,000). In a few years he has cleared the best tract, built several miles of canals, hewed out houses and furniture, planted coca, cacao, cane, coffee, rice, pepper, and cotton, and would not sell for $50,000. Moreover, instead of being a superintendent on a neighboring estate and keeping a shop in Cuzco, where his large family was a source of great expense, he has become a wealthy landowner. He has educated a son in the United States. He is importing machinery, such as a rice thresher and a distilling plant. His son is looking forward to the purchase of still more playa land down river. He pays a sol a day to each laborer, securing men from Cotabambas and Abancay, where there are many Indians, a low standard of wages, little unoccupied land, and a hot climate, so that the immigrants do not need to become acclimatized.

The deepest valleys in the Eastern Andes of Peru have a semi-arid climate which brings in its train a variety of unusual geographic relations. At first as one descends the valley the shady and sunny slopes show sharply contrasted vegetation.

---

[6] Notice of a Journey to the Northward and also to the Eastward of Cuzco, and among the Chunchos Indians, in July, 1835. Journ. Royal Geog. Soc., Vol. 6, 1836, pp. 174-186.

[7] Bol. Soc. Geog. de Lima, Vol. 8, 1898, p. 45.

Fig. 51.

Fig. 52.

Fig. 51—Robledo's mountain-side trail in the Urubamba Valley below Rosalina.

Fig. 52—An epiphyte partly supported by a dead host at Rosalina, elevation 2,000 feet. The epiphyte bears a striking resemblance to a horned beast whose arched back, tightly clasped fingers, and small eyes give it a peculiarly malignant and life-like expression.

FIG. 53A.

FIG. 53B.

FIG. 53A—The smooth grassy slopes at the junction of the Yanatili (left) and Urubamba (right) rivers near Pabellon.

FIG. 53B—Distribution of vegetation in the Urubamba Valley near Torontoy. The patches of timber in the background occupy the shady sides of the spurs; the sunny slopes are grass-covered; the valley floor is filled with thickets and patches of woodland but not true forest.

The one is forested, the other grass-covered. Slopes that receive the noon and afternoon sun the greater part of the year are hottest and therefore driest. For places in 11° south latitude the sun is well to the north six months of the year, nearly overhead for about two months, and to the south four months. Northwesterly aspects are therefore driest and warmest, hence also grass-covered. In many places the line between grass and forest is developed so sharply that it seems to be the artificial edge of a cut-over tract. This is true especially if the relief is steep and the hill or ridge-crests sharp.[8]

At Santa Ana this feature is developed in an amazingly clear manner, and it is also combined with the dry timber line and with productivity in a way I have never seen equaled elsewhere. The diagram will explain the relation. It will be seen that the front range of the mountains is high enough to shut off a great deal of rainfall. The lower hills and ridges just within the front range are relatively dry. The deep valleys are much drier. Each broad expansion of a deep valley is therefore a dry pocket. Into it the sun pours even when

[8] Marcoy who traveled in Peru in the middle of the last century was greatly impressed by the sympathetic changes of aspect and topography and vegetation in the eastern valleys. He thus describes a sudden change of scene in the Occobamba valley: ". . . the trees had disappeared, the birds had taken wing, and great sandy spaces, covered with the latest deposits of the river, alternated with stretches of yellow grass and masses of rock half-buried in the ground." (Travels in South America, translated by Elihu Rich, 2 vols. New York, 1875, Vol. 1, p. 326.)

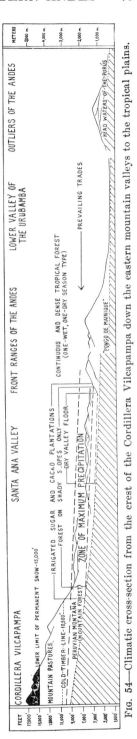

FIG. 54—Climatic cross-section from the crest of the Cordillera Vilcapampa down the eastern mountain valleys to the tropical plains.

all the surrounding hills and mountains are wrapped in cloud. The greater number of hours of sunshine hastens the rate of evaporation and still further increases the dryness. Under the spur of much sunlight and of ample irrigation water from the wetter hill slopes, the dry valley pockets produce huge crops of fruit and cane.

The influence of the local climate upon tree growth is striking. Every few days, even in the relatively dry winter season, clouds gather about the hills and there are local showers. The lower limit of the zone of clouds is sharply marked and at both Santa Ana and Echarati it is strikingly constant in elevation—about five thousand feet above sea level. From the upper mountains the forest descends, with only small patches of glade and prairie. At the lower edge of the zone of cloud it stops abruptly on the warmer and drier slopes that face the afternoon sun and continues on the moister slopes that face the forenoon sun or that slope away from the sun.

But this is not the only response the vegetation makes. The forest changes in character as well as in distribution. The forest in the wet zone is dense and the undergrowth luxuriant. In the selective slope forest below the zone of cloud the undergrowth is commonly thin or wanting and the trees grow in rather even-aged stands and by species. Finally, on the valley floor and the tributary fans, there is a distinct growth of scrub with bands of trees along the water courses. Local tracts of coarse soil, or less rain on account of a deep "hole" in a valley surrounded by steeper and higher mountains, or a change in the valley trend that brings it into less free communication with the prevailing winds, may still further increase the dryness and bring in a true xerophytic or drought-resisting vegetation. Cacti are common all through the Santa Ana Valley and below Sahuayaco there is a patch of tree cacti and similar forms several square miles in extent. Still farther down and about half-way between Sahuayaco and Pabellon are immense tracts of grass-covered mountain slopes (Fig. 53). These extend beyond Rosalina, the last of them terminating near Abra Tocate (Fig. 15). The sudden interruption is due to a turn in the valley giving freer access to the up-valley winds that sweep through the pass at Pongo de Mainique.

Northward from Abra Tocate (Fig. 55) the forest is practically continuous. The break between the two vegetal regions is emphasized by a corral for cattle and mules, the last outpost of the plateau herdsmen. Not three miles away, on the opposite forested slope of the valley, is the first of the Indian clearings where several families of Machigangas spend the wet season when the lower river is in flood (Fig. 21). The grass lands will not yield corn and coca because the soil is too thin, infertile, and dry. The Indian farms are therefore all in the forest and begin almost at its very edge. Here finally terminates a long peninsula of grass-

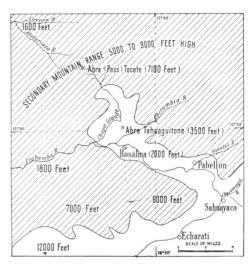

FIG. 55—Map to show the relation of the grasslands of the dry lower portion of the Urubamba Valley (unshaded) to the forested lands at higher elevations (shaded). See Fig. 54 for climatic conditions. Patches and slender tongues of woodland occur below the main timber line and patches of grassland above it.

covered country. Below this point the heat and humidity rapidly increase; the rains are heavier and more frequent; the country becomes almost uninhabitable for stock; transportation rates double. Here is the undisputed realm of the forest with new kinds of trees and products and a distinctive type of forest-dwelling Indian.

At the next low pass is the skull of an Italian who had murdered his companions and stolen a season's picking of rubber, attempting to escape by canoe to the lower Urubamba from the Pongo de Mainique. The Machigangas overtook him in their swiftest dugouts, spent a night with him, and the next morning shot him in the back and returned with their rightful property—

a harvest of rubber. For more than a decade foreigners have been coming down from the plateau to exploit them. They are an independent and free tribe and have simple yet correct ideas of right and wrong. Their chief, a man of great strength of character and one of the most likeable men I have known, told me that he placed the skull in the pass to warn away the whites who came to rob honest Indians.

The Santa Ana Valley between the Canyon of Torontoy and the heavy forest belt below Rosalina is typical of many of the eastern valleys of Peru, both in its physical setting and in its economic and labor systems. Westward are the outliers of the Vilcapampa range; on the east are the smaller ranges that front the tropical lowlands. Steep valleys descend from the higher country to join the main valley and at the mouth of every tributary is an alluvial fan. If the alluvium is coarse and steeply inclined there is only pasture on it or a growth of scrub. If fine and broad it is cleared and tilled. The sugar plantations begin at Huadquiña and end at Rosalina. Those of Santa Ana and Echarati are the most productive. It takes eighteen months for the cane to mature in the cooler weather at Huadquiña (8,000 feet). Less than a year is required at Santa Ana (3,400 feet). Patches of alluvium or playas, as they are locally called, continue as far as Santo Anato, but they are cultivated only as far as Rosalina. The last large plantation is Pabellon; the largest of all is Echarati. All are irrigated. In the wet months, December to March inclusive, there is little or no irrigation. In the four months of the dry season, June to September inclusive, there is frequent irrigation. Since the cane matures in about ten months the harvest seasons fall irregularly with respect to the seasons of rain. Therefore the land is cleared and planted at irregular intervals and labor distributed somewhat through the year. There is however a concentration of labor toward the end of the dry season when most of the cane is cut for grinding.

The combined freight rate and government tax on coca, sugar, and brandy take a large part of all that the planter can get for his crop. It is 120 miles (190 km.) from Santa Ana to Cuzco and it takes five days to make the journey. The freight rate on coca and sugar for mule carriage, the only kind to be had, is two cents per pound. The national tax is one cent per pound (0.45 kg.). The coca sells for twenty cents a pound. The cost of production is unknown, but the paid labor takes probably one-half this amount. The planter's time, capital, and profit must come out of the rest. On brandy there is a national tax of seven cents per liter (0.26 gallon) and a municipal tax of two and a half cents. It costs five cents a liter for transport to Cuzco. The total in taxes and transport is fourteen and a half cents a liter. It sells for twenty cents a liter. Since brandy (aguardiente), cacao (for chocolate), and coca leaves (for cocaine) are the only precious substances which the valleys produce it takes but a moment's inspection to see how onerous these taxes would be to the planter if labor did not, as usual, pay the penalty.

Much of the labor on the plantations is free of cost to the owner and is done by the so-called *faena* or free Indians. These are Quechuas who have built their cabins on the hill lands of the planters, or on the floors of the smaller valleys. The disposition of their fields in relation to the valley plantations is full of geographic interest. Each plantation runs at right angles to the course of the valley. Hacienda Sahuayaco is ten miles (16 km.) in extent down valley and forty miles (64 km.) from end to end across the valley, and it is one of the smaller plantations! It follows that about ten square miles lie on the valley floor and half of this can ultimately be planted. The remaining three hundred and ninety square miles include some mountain country with possible stores of mineral wealth, and a great deal of "fells" country—grassy slopes, graded though steep, excellent for pasture, with here and there patches of arable land. But the hill country can be cultivated only by the small farmer who supplements his supply of food from cultivated plants like potatoes, corn, and vegetables, by keeping cattle, mules, pigs, and poultry, and by raising coca and fruit.

The Indian does not own any of the land he tills. He has the right merely to live on it and to cultivate it. In return he must

work a certain number of days each year on the owner's plantation. In many cases a small money payment is also made to the
planter. The planter prefers labor to money, for hands are
scarce throughout the whole eastern valley region. No Indian
need work on the planter's land without receiving pay directly
therefor. Each also gets a small weekly allotment of aguardiente
while in the planter's employ.

The scene every Saturday night outside the office of the *con-*
tador (treasurer) of a plantation is a novel one. Several hundred
Indians gather in the dark patio in front of the office. Within
the circle of the feeble candlelight that reaches only the margin
of the crowd one may see a pack of heavy, perspiring faces. Many
are pock-marked from smallpox; here and there an eye is missing;
only a few are jovial. A name is shouted through the open door
and an Indian responds. He pulls off his cap and stands stupid
and blinking, while the contador asks:

"Faena" (free)?

"Si, Señor," he answers.

"Un sol" (one "sol" or fifty cents gold). The assistant hands
over the money and the man gives way to the next one on the list.
If he is a laborer in regular and constant employ he receives five
soles (two fifty gold) per week. There are interruptions now and
then. A ragged, half-drunken man has been leaning against the
door post, suspiciously impatient to receive his money. Finally
his name is called.

"Faena?" asks the contador.

"No, Señor, cinco (five) soles."

At that the field *superintendente* glances at his time card and
speaks up in protest.

"You were the man that failed to show up on Friday and Saturday. You were drunk. You should receive nothing."

"No, mi patrón," the man contends, "I had to visit a sick
cousin in the next valley. Oh, he was very sick, Señor," and he
coughs harshly as if he too were on the verge of prostration. The
sick cousin, a faena Indian, has been at work in another cane field
on the same plantation for two days and now calls out that he is

present and has never had a sick day in his life. Those outside laugh uproariously. The contador throws down two soles and the drunkard is pushed back into the sweating crowd, jostled right and left, and jeered by all his neighbors as he slinks away grumbling.

Another Indian seems strangely shy. He scarcely raises his voice above a whisper. He too is a faena Indian. The contador finds fault.

"Why didn't you come last month when I sent for you?"

The Indian fumbles his cap, shuffles his feet, and changes his coca cud from one bulging cheek to the other before he can answer. Then huskily:

"I started, Señor, but my woman overtook me an hour afterward and said that one of the ewes had dropped a lamb and needed care."

"But your woman could have tended it!"

"No, Señor, she is sick."

"How, then, could she have overtaken you?" he is asked.

"She ran only a little way and then shouted to me."

"And what about the rest of the month?" persists the contador.

"The other lambs came, Señor, and I should have lost them all if I had left."

The contador seems at the end of his complaint. The Indian promises to work overtime. His difficulties seem at an end, but the superintendent looks at his old record.

"He always makes the same excuse. Last year he was three weeks late."

So the poor shepherd is fined a sol and admonished that his lands will be given to some one else if he does not respond more promptly to his patron's call for work. He leaves behind him a promise and the rank mixed smell of coca and much unwashed woolen clothing.

It is not alone at the work that they grumble. There is malaria in the lower valleys. Some of them return to their lofty mountain homes prostrated with the unaccustomed heat and alternately shaking with chills and burning with fever. Without aid they may die or become so weakened that tuberculosis carries them off. Only their rugged strength enables the greater number to return in good health.

A plantation may be as large as a principality and draw its laborers from places fifty miles away. Some of the more distant Indians need not come to work in the canefields. Part of their flock is taken in place of work. Or they raise horses and mules and bring in a certain number each year to turn over to the patron. Hacienda Huadquiña (Fig. 46) takes in all the land from the snow-covered summits of the Cordillera Vilcapampa to the canefields of the Urubamba. Within the broad domain are half the climates and occupations characteristic of Peru. It is difficult to see how a thousand Indians can be held to even a mixed allegiance. It seems impossible that word can be got to them. However the native "telegraph" is even more perfect than that among the forest Indians. From one to the other runs the news that they are needed in the canefields. On the trail to and from a mountain village, in their ramblings from one high pasture to another, within the dark walls of their stone and mud huts when they gather for a feast or to exchange drinks of brandy and *chicha*—the word is passed that has come up from the valleys.

For every hundred faena Indians there are five or six regular laborers on the plantations, so with the short term passed by the faena Indians their number is generally half that of the total laborers at work at any one time. They live in huts provided for them by the planter, and in the houses of their friends among the regular laborers. Here there are almost nightly carousals. The regular laborer comes from the city or the valley town. The faena laborer is a small hill farmer or shepherd. They have much to exchange in the way of clothing, food, and news. I have frequently had their conversations interpreted for me. They ask about the flocks and the children, who passed along the trails, what accidents befell the people.

"Last year," droned one to another over their chicha, "last year we lost three lambs in a hailstorm up in the high fields near the snow. It was very cold. My foot cracked open and, though

I have bound it with wet coca leaves every night, it will not cure,'' and he displays his heel, the skin of which is like horn for hardness and covered with a crust of dirt whose layers are a record of the weather and of the pools he has waded for years.

Their wanderings are the main basis of conversation. They know the mountains better than the condors do. We hired a small boy of twelve at Puquiura. He was to build our fires, carry water, and help drive the mules. He crossed the Cordillera Vilcapampa on foot with us. He scrambled down into the Apurimac canyon and up the ten thousand feet of ascent on the other side, twisted the tails of the mules, and shouted more vigorously then the arrieros. He was engaged to go with us to Pasaje, where his father would return with him in a month. But he climbed to Huascatay with us and said he wanted to see Abancay. When an Indian whom we pressed into service dropped the instruments on the trail and fled into the brush the boy packed them like a man. The soldier carried a tripod on his back. The boy, not to be outdone, insisted on carrying the plane table, and to his delight we called him a soldier too. He went with us to Huancarama. When I paid him he smiled at the large silver soles that I put into his hand; and when I doubled the amount for his willingness to work his joy was unbounded. Forthwith he set out, this time on muleback, on the return journey. The last I saw of him he was holding his precious soles in a handkerchief and kicking his beast with his bare heels, as light-hearted as a cavalier. Often I find myself wondering whether he returned safely with his money. I should very much like to see him again, for with him I associate cheerfulness in difficult places and many a pleasant camp-fire.

CHAPTER VII

THE GEOGRAPHIC BASIS OF REVOLUTIONS AND OF HUMAN CHARACTER IN THE PERUVIAN ANDES

HUMAN character as a spontaneous development has always been a great factor in shaping historical events, but it is a striking fact that in the world of our day its influence is exerted chiefly in the lowest and highest types of humanity. The savage with his fetishes, his taboos, and his inherent childlikeness and suspicion needs only whim or a slight religious pretext to change his conduct. Likewise the really educated and the thoughtful act from motives often wholly unrelated to economic conditions or results. But the masses are deeply influenced by whatever affects their material welfare. A purely idealistic impulse may influence a people, but in time its effects are always displayed against an economic background.

There is a way whereby we may test this theory. In most places in the world we have history in the making, and through field studies we can get an intimate view of it. It is peculiarly the province of geography to study the present distribution and character of men in relation to their surroundings and these are the facts of mankind that must forever be the chief data of economic history. It is not vain repetition to say that this means, first of all, the study of the character of men in the fullest sense. It means, in the second place, that a large part of the character must be really understood. Whenever this is done there is found a geographic basis of human character that is capable of the clearest demonstration. It is in the geographic environment that the material motives of humanity have struck their deepest roots.

These conclusions might be illustrated from a hundred places in the field of study covered in this book. Almost every chapter of Part I contains facts of this character. I wish, however, to discuss the subject specifically and for that purpose now turn to the conditions of life in the remoter mountain valleys and to one or two aspects of the revolutions that occur now and then in Peru. The last one terminated only a few months before our arrival and it was a comparatively easy matter to study both causes and effects.

A caution is necessary however. It is a pity that we use the term "revolution" to designate these little disturbances. They affect sometimes a few, again a few hundred men. Rarely do they involve the whole country. A good many of them are on a scale much smaller than our big strikes. Most of them involve a loss of life smaller than that which accompanies a city riot. They are in a sense strikes against the government, marked by local disorders and a little violence.

Early in 1911 the Prefect of the Department of Abancay had crowned his long career by suppressing a revolution. He had been Subprefect at Andahuaylas, and when the rebels got control of the city of Abancay and destroyed some of the bridges on the principal trails, he promptly organized a military expedition, constructed rafts, floated his small force of men across the streams, and besieged the city. The rebel force was driven at last to take shelter in the city jail opposite the Prefectura. There, after the loss of half their number, they finally surrendered. Seventy-five of them were sent to the government penitentiary at Arequipa. Among the killed were sons fro.n nearly half the best families of Abancay. All of the rebels were young men.

It would be difficult to give an adequate idea of the hatred felt by the townspeople toward the government. Every precaution was taken to prevent a renewal of the outbreak. Our coming was telegraphed ahead by government agents who looked with suspicion upon a party of men, well armed and provisioned, coming up from the Pasaje crossing of the Apurimac, three days' journey north. The deep canyon affords shelter not only to game, but also to fugitives, rebels, and bandits. The government generally abandons pursuit on the upper edge of the canyon, for only a prolonged guerilla warfare could completely subdue an armed force

scattered along its rugged walls and narrow floor. The owner of
the hacienda at Pasaje is required to keep a record of all passengers rafted across the Apurimac, but he explains significantly that
some who pass are too hurried to write their names in his book.
Once he reaches the eastern wall of the canyon a fugitive may
command a view of the entire western wall and note the approach
of pursuers. Thence eastward he has the whole Cordillera Vilcapampa in which to hide. Pursuit is out of the question.

When we arrived, the venerable Prefect, a model of old-fashioned courtesy, greeted us with the utmost cordiality. He told us
of our movements since leaving Pasaje, and laughingly explained
that since we had sent him no friendly message and had come
from a rebel retreat, he had taken it for granted that we intended
to storm the town. I assured him that we were ready to join his
troops, if necessary, whereupon, with a delightful frankness, he
explained his method of keeping the situation in hand. Several
troops of cavalry and two battalions of infantry were quartered
at the government barracks. Every evening the old gentleman,
a Colonel in the Peruvian army, mounted a powerful gray horse
and rode, quite unattended, through the principal streets of the
town. Several times I walked on foot behind him, again I pre-
ceded him, stopping in shops on the way to make trivial purchases,
to find out what the people had to say about him and the government as he rode by. One old gentleman interested me particularly.
He had only the day before called at the Prefectura to pay his
respects. Although his manner was correct there was lacking to
a noticeable degree the profusion of sentiment that is apt to be
exhibited on such an occasion. He now sat on a bench in a shop.
Both his own son and the shopkeeper's son had been slain in the
revolution. It was natural that they should be bitter. But the
precise nature of their complaint was what interested me most.
One said that he did not object to having his son lose his life for
his country. But that his country's officials should hire Indians
to shoot his son seemed to him sheer murder. Later, at Lambrama, I talked with a rebel fugitive, and that was also his complaint. The young men drafted into the army are Indians, or

Fig. 57.—Arboreal cacti in the mixed forest of the dry valley floor below Sahuayaco.

Fig. 56.—The type of forest in the moister tracts of the valley floor at Sahuayaco. In the center of the photograph is a tree known as the "sandy matico" used in making canoes for river navigation.

FIG. 58.

FIG. 59.

FIG. 58—Crossing the Apurimac at Pasaje. These are mountain horses, small and wiry, with a protective coat of long hair. They are accustomed to graze in the open without shelter during the entire winter.

FIG. 59—Crossing the Apurimac at Pasaje. The mules are blindfolded and pushed off the steep bank into the water and rafted across.

mixed, never whites. White men, and men with a small amount
of Indian blood, officer the army. When a revolutionary party
organizes it is of course made up wholly of men of white and
mixed blood, never Indians. The Indians have no more grievance
against one white party than another. Both exploit him to the
limit of law and beyond the limit of decency. He fights if he must,
but never by choice.

Thus Indian troops killed the white rebels of Abancay.

"Tell me, Señor," said the fugitive, "if you think that just.
Tell me how many Indians you think a white man worth. Would
a hundred dead Indians matter? But how replace a white man
where there are so few? The government *assassinated* my com-
patriots!"

"But," I replied, "why did you fight the government? All of
you were prosperous. Your fathers may have had a grievance
against the government, but of what had you young men to complain?"

His reply was far from convincing. He was at first serious, but
his long abstract statements about taxes and government waste-
fulness trailed off into vagueness, and he ended in a laughing
mood, talking about adventure, the restless spirit of young men,
and the rich booty of confiscated lands and property had the
rebels won. He admitted that it was a reckless game, but when I
called him a mere soldier of fortune he grew serious once more
and reverted to the iniquitous taxation system of Peru. Further
inquiry made it quite clear that the ill-fated revolution of Abancay
was largely the work of idle young men looking for adventure.
It seemed a pity that their splendid physical energy could not
have been turned into useful channels. The land sorely needs engineers, progressive ranchmen and farmers, upright officials, and
a spirit of respect for law and order. Old men talked of the unstable character of the young men of the time, but almost all of
them had themselves been active participants in more than one
revolution of earlier years.

Every night at dinner the Prefect sent off by government telegraph a long message to the President of the Republic on the

state of the Department, and received similar messages from the central government about neighboring departments. These he read to us, and, curiously enough, to the entire party, made up of army officers and townsmen. I was surprised to find later that the company included one government official whose son had been among the imprisoned rebels at Arequipa. We met the young man a week later at a mountain village, a day after a general amnesty had been declared. His escape had been made from the prison a month before. He forcibly substituted the mess-boy's clothing for his own, and thus passed out unnoticed. After a few days' hiding in the city, he set out alone across the desert of Vitor, thence across the lofty volcanic country of the Maritime Andes, through some of the most deserted, inhospitable land in Peru, and at the end of three weeks had reached Lambrama, near Abancay, the picture of health!

Later I came to have a better notion of the economic basis of the revolution, for obviously the planters and the reckless young men must have had a mutual understanding. Somewhere the rebels had obtained the sinews of war. The planters did not take an open part in the revolution, but they financed it. When the rebels were crushed, the planters, at least outwardly, welcomed the government forces. Inwardly they cursed them for thwarting their scheme. The reasons have an interesting geographic basis. Abancay is the center of a sugar region. Great irrigated estates are spread out along the valley floor and the enormous alluvial fans built into the main valley at the mouths of the tributary streams. There is a heavy tax on sugar and on aguardiente (brandy) manufactured from cane juice. The hacendados had dreamed of lighter taxes. The rebels offered the means of securing relief. But taxes were not the real reason for the unrest, for many other sugar producers pay the tax without serious complaint. Abancay is cut off from the rest of Peru by great mountains. Toward the west, via Antabamba, Cotahuasi, and Chuquibamba, two hundred miles of trail separate its plantations from the Pacific. Twelve days' hard riding is required to reach Lima over the old colonial trade route. It is three days to Cuzco at the end of the three-hundred-mile railway from the port of Mollendo. The trails to the Atlantic rivers are impossible for trading purposes. Deep sunk in a subtropical valley, the irrigable alluvial land of Abancay tempts the production of sugar.

But nature offers no easy route out of the valley. For centuries the product has been exported at almost prohibitive cost, as in the eastern valley of Santa Ana. The coastal valleys enjoy easy access to the sea. Each has its own port at the valley mouth, where ocean steamers call for cargo. Many have short railway lines from port to valley head. The eastern valleys and Abancay have been clamoring for railways, better trails, and wagon roads. From the public fund they get what is left. The realization of their hopes has been delayed too long. It would be both economic and military strategy to give them the desired railway. Revolutions in Peru always start in one of two ways: either by a *coup* at Lima or an unchecked uprising in an interior province. Bolivia has shown the way out of this difficulty. Two of her four large centers—La Paz and Oruro—are connected by rail, and the line to Cochabamba lacks only a few kilometres of construction.[1] To Sucre a line has been long projected. Formerly a revolution at one of the four towns was exceedingly difficult to stamp out. Diaz had the same double motive in encouraging railway building in the remote desert provinces of Northern Mexico, where nine out of ten Mexican revolutions gather headway. Argentina has enjoyed a high degree of political unity since her railway system was extended to Córdoba and Tucumán. The last uprising, that of 1906, took place on her remotest northeastern frontier.

We had ample opportunity to see the hatred of the rebels. At nightfall of September 25th we rode into the courtyard of Hacienda Auquibamba. We had traveled under the worst possible

[1] According to the latest information (August, 1916) of the Bolivia Railway Co., trains are running from Oruro to Buen Retiro, 35 km. from Cochabamba. Thence connection with Cochabamba is made by a tram-line operated by the Electric Light and Power Co. of that city. The Bulletin of the Pan-American Union for July, 1916, also reports the proposed introduction of an automobile service for conveyance of freight and passengers.

circumstances. Our mules had been enfeebled by hot valley work at Santa Ana and the lower Urubamba and the cold mountain climate of the Cordillera Vilcapampa. The climb out of the Apurimac canyon, even without packs, left them completely exhausted. We were obliged to abandon one and actually to pull another along. It had been a hard day in spite of a prolonged noon rest. Everywhere our letters of introduction had won an outpouring of hospitality among a people to whom hospitality is one of the strongest of the unwritten laws of society. Our soldier escort rode ahead of the pack train.

As the clatter of his mules' hoofs echoed through the dark buildings the manager rushed out, struck a light and demanded "Who's there?" To the soldier's cheerful "Buena noche, Señor," he sneeringly replied "Halto! Guardia de la República, aqui hay nada para un soldado del gobierno." Whereupon the soldier turned back to me and said we should not be able to stop here, and coming nearer me he whispered "He is a revolutionary." I dismounted and approached the haughty manager, who was in a really terrible mood. Almost before I could begin to ask him for accommodations he rattled off that there was no pasture for our beasts, no food for us, and that we had better go on to the next hacienda. "Absolutamente nada!" he repeated over and over again, and at first I thought him drunk. Since it was then quite dark, with no moon, but instead heavy black clouds over the southern half of the sky and a brisk valley wind threatening rain, I mildly protested that we needed nothing more than shelter. Our food boxes would supply our wants, and our mules, even without fodder, could reach Abancay the next day. Still he stormed at the government and would have none of us. I reminded him that his fields were filled with sugar cane and that it was the staple forage for beasts during the part of the year when pasture was scarce. The cane was too valuable, he said. It was impossible to supply us. I was on the point of pitching camp beside the trail, for it was impossible to reach the next hacienda with an exhausted outfit.

Just then an older man stepped into the circle of light and amiably inquired the purpose of our journey. When it was explained, he turned to the other and said it was unthinkable that men should be treated so inhospitably in a strange land. Though he himself was a guest he urged that the host should remember the laws of hospitality, whereupon the latter at last grudgingly asked us to join him at his table and to turn our beasts over to his servants. It was an hour or more before he would exhibit any interest in us. When he had learned of our object in visiting Abancay he became some-what more friendly, though his hostility still manifested itself. Nowhere else in South America have I seen exhibited such boorish conduct. Nevertheless the next morning I noticed that our mules had been well fed. He said good-by to us as if he were glad to be rid of any one in any way connected with the hostile govern-ment. Likewise the manager at Hacienda Pasaje held out almost until the last before he would consent to aid us with fresh beasts. Finally, after a day of courting I gave him a camp chair. He was so pleased that he not only gave us beasts, but also a letter of introduction to one of his caretakers on a farm at the top of the cuesta. Here on a cold, stormy night we found food and fuel and the shelter of a friendly roof.

A by-product of the revolution, as of all revolutions in thinly settled frontier regions, was the organization of small bands of outlaws who infested the lonely trails, stole beasts, and left their owners robbed and helpless far from settlements. We were cau-tioned to beware of them, both by Señor Gonzales, the Prefect at Abancay, and by the Subprefect of Antabamba. Since some of the bandits had been jailed, I could not doubt the accuracy of the reports, but I did doubt stories of murder and of raids by large companies of mountain bandits. As a matter of fact we were robbed by the Governor of Antabamba, but in a way that did not enable us to find redress in either law or lead. The story is worth telling because it illustrates two important facts: first, the vile so-called government that exists in some places in the really remote sections of South America, and second, the character of the mountain Indians.

The urgent letter from the Prefect of Abancay to the Subprefect of Antabamba quickly brought the latter from his distant home. When we arrived we found him drinking with the Governor. The Subprefect was most courteous. The Governor was good-natured, but his face exhibited a rare combination of cruelty and vice. We were offered quarters in the municipal building for the day or two that we were obliged to stop in the town. The delay enabled us to study the valley to which particular interest attaches because of its situation in the mountain zone between the lofty pastures of the Alpine country and the irrigated fields of the valley farmers.

Antabamba itself lies on a smooth, high-level shoulder of the youthful Antabamba Valley. The valley floor is narrow and rocky, and affords little cultivable land. On the valley sides are steep descents and narrow benches, chiefly structural in origin, over which there is scattered a growth of scrub, sufficient to screen the deer and the bear, and, more rarely, vagrant bands of vicuña that stray down from their accustomed haunts in the lofty Cordillera. Three thousand feet above the valley floor a broad shoulder begins (Fig. 60) and slopes gently up to the bases of the true mountains that surmount the broad rolling summit platform. Here are the great pasture lands of the Andes and their semi-nomadic shepherds. The highest habitation in the world is located here at 17,100 feet (5,210 m.), near a secondary pass only a few miles from the main axis of the western chain, and but 300 feet (91 m.) below it.

The people of Antabamba are both shepherds and farmers. The elevation is 12,000 feet (3,658 m.), too high and exposed for anything more than potatoes. Here is an Indian population pure-blooded, and in other respects, too, but little altered from its original condition. There is almost no communication with the outside world. A deep canyon fronts the town and a lofty mountain range forms the background.

At nightfall, one after another, the Indians came in from the field and doffed their caps as they passed our door. Finally came the "Teniente Gobernador," or Lieutenant Governor. He had only a slight strain of white blood. His bearing was that of a sneak, and he confirmed this impression by his frank disdain for his full-blooded townsmen. "How ragged and ugly they are! You people must find them very stupid," etc. When he found that we had little interest in his remarks, he asked us if we had ever seen Lima. We replied that we had, whereupon he said, "Do you see the gilded cross above the church yonder? I brought that on muleback all the way from Lima! Think of it! These ignorant people have never seen Lima!" His whole manner as he drew himself up and hit his breast was intended to make us think that he was vastly superior to his neighbors. The sequel shows that our first estimate of him was correct.

We made our arrangements with the Governor and departed. To inspire confidence, and at the Governor's urgent request, we had paid in advance for our four Indians and our fresh beasts— and at double the usual rates, for it was still winter in the Cordillera. They were to stay with us until we reached Cotahuasi, in the next Department beyond the continental divide, where a fresh outfit could be secured. The Lieutenant Governor accompanied us to keep the party together. They appeared to need it. Like our Indian peons at Lambrama the week before, these had been taken from the village jail and represented the scum of the town. As usual they behaved well the first day. On the second night we reached the Alpine country where the vegetation is very scanty and camped at the only spot that offered fuel and water. The elevation was 16,000, and here we had the lowest temperature of the whole journey, + 6° F. (—14.4° C.). Ice covered the brook near camp as soon as the sun went down and all night long the wind blew down from the lofty Cordillera above us, bringing flurries of snow and tormenting our unprotected beasts. It seemed to me doubtful if our Indians would remain. I discussed with the other members of the party the desirability of chaining the peons to the tent pole, but this appeared so extreme a measure that we abandoned the idea after warning the Teniente that he must not let them escape.

At daybreak I was alarmed at the unusual stillness about camp. A glance showed that half our hobbled beasts had drifted back toward Antabamba and no doubt were now miles away. The four Indian peons had left also, and their tracks, half buried by the last snowfall, showed that they had left hours before and that it was useless to try to overtake them. Furthermore we were making a topographic map across the Cordillera, and, in view of the likelihood of snow blockading the 17,600-foot (5,360 m.) pass which we had to cross, the work ought not to be delayed. With all these disturbing conditions to meet, and suffering acutely from mountain sickness, I could scarcely be expected to deal gently with our official. I drew out the sleeping Teniente and set him on his feet. To my inquiry as to the whereabouts of the Indians that he had promised to guard, he blinked uncertainly, and after a stupid ''Quien sabe?'' peered under the cover of a sheepskin near by as if the peons had been transformed into insects and had taken refuge under a blade of grass. I ordered him to get breakfast and after that to take upon his back the instruments that two men had carried up to that time, and accompany the topographer. Thus loaded, the Lieutenant Governor of Antabamba set out on foot a little ahead of the party. Hendriksen, the topographer, directed him to a 17,000-foot peak near camp, one of the highest stations occupied in the traverse. When the topographer reached the summit the instruments were there but the Teniente had fled. Hendriksen rapidly followed the tracks down over the steep snow-covered wall of a deeply recessed cirque, but after a half-hour's search could not get sight of the runaway, whereupon he returned to his station and took his observations, reaching camp in the early afternoon.

In the meantime I had intercepted two Indians who had come from Cotahuasi driving a llama train loaded with corn. They held a long conversation at the top of the pass above camp and at first edged suspiciously away. But the rough ground turned them back into the trail and at last they came timidly along. They pretended not to understand Spanish and protested vigorously that they had to keep on with their llamas. I thought from the belligerent attitude of the older, which grew rapidly more threatening as he saw that I was alone, that I was in for trouble, but when

I drew my revolver he quickly obeyed the order to sit down to breakfast, which consisted of soup, meat, and army biscuits. I also gave them coca and cigarettes, the two most desirable gifts one can make to a plateau Indian, and thereupon I thought I had gained their friendship, for they at last talked with me in broken Spanish. The older one now explained that he must at all hazards reach Matará by nightfall, but he would be glad to leave his son to help us. I agreed, and he set out forthwith. The *arriero* (muleteer) had now returned with the lost mules and with the assistance of the Indian we soon struck camp and loaded our mules. I cautioned the arriero to keep close watch of the Indian, for at one time I had caught on his face an expression of hatred more intense than I had ever seen before. The plateau Indian of South America is usually so stupid and docile that the unexpectedly venomous look of the man after our friendly conversation and my good treatment alarmed me. At the last moment, and when our backs were turned, our Indian, under the screen of the packs, slipped away from us. The arriero called out to know where he had gone. It took us but a few moments to gain the top of a hill that commanded the valley. Fully a half-mile away and almost indistinguishable against the brown of the valley floor was our late assistant, running like a deer. No mule could follow over that broken ground at an elevation of 16,000 feet, and so he escaped.

Fortunately that afternoon we passed a half-grown boy riding back toward Antabamba and he promised to hand the Governor a note in Spanish, penciled on a leaf of my traverse book. I dropped all the polite phrases that are usually employed and wrote as follows:

" Señor Gobernador:

"Your Indians have escaped, likewise the Lieutenant Governor. They have taken two beasts. In the name of the Prefect of Abancay, I ask you immediately to bring a fresh supply of men and animals. We shall encamp near the first pass, three days west of Antabamba, until you come."

We were now without Indians to carry the instruments, which had therefore to be strapped to the mules. Without guides we started westward along the trail. At the next pass the topographer rode to the summit of a bluff and asked which of the two trails I intended to follow. Just then a solitary Indian passed and I shouted back that I would engage the Indian and precede the party, and he could tell from my course at the fork of the trail how to direct his map and where to gain camp at nightfall. But the Indian refused to go with us. All my threatening was useless and I had to force myself to beat him into submission with my quirt. Several repetitions on the way, when he stubbornly refused to go further, kept our guide with us until we reached a camp site. I had offered him a week's pay for two hours' work, and had put coca and cigarettes into his hands. When these failed I had to resort to force. Now that he was about to leave I gave him double the amount I had promised him. He could scarcely believe his eyes. He rushed up to the side of my mule, and reaching around my waist embraced me and thanked me again and again. The plateau Indian is so often waylaid in the mountains and impressed for service, then turned loose without pay or actually robbed, that a *promise* to pay holds no attraction for him. I had up to the last moment resembled this class of white. He was astonished to find that I really meant to pay him well.

Then he set out upon the return, faithfully delivering my note to the topographer about the course of the trail and the position of the camp. He had twelve miles to go to the first mountain hut, so that he could not have traveled less than that distance to reach shelter. The next morning a mantle of snow covered everything, yet when I pushed back the tent flap there stood my scantily clad Indian of the night before, shivering, with sandaled feet in the snow, saying that he had come back to work for me!

This camp was number thirteen out of Abancay, and here our topographer was laid up for three days. Heretofore the elevation had had no effect upon him, but the excessively lofty stations of the past few days and the hard climbing had finally prostrated him. We had decided to carry him out by the fourth day if he felt no better, but happily he recovered sufficiently to continue the work. The delay enabled the Governor to overtake us with a fresh outfit. On the morning of our third day in camp he overtook us with a small escort of soldiers accompanied by the fugitive Teniente. He said that he had come to arrest me on the charge of maltreating an official of Peru. A few packages of cigarettes and a handful of raisins and biscuits so stirred his gratitude that we parted the best of friends. Moreover he provided us with four fresh beasts and four new men, and thus equipped we set out for a rendezvous about ten miles away. But the faithless Governor turned off the trail and sought shelter at the huts of a company of mountain shepherds. That night his men slept on the ground in a bitter wind just outside our camp at 17,200 feet. They complained that they had no food. The Governor had promised to join us with llama meat for the peons. We fed them that night and also the next day. But we had by that time passed the crest of the western Cordillera and were outside the province of Antabamba. The next morning not only our four men but also our four beasts were missing. We were stranded and sick just under the pass. To add to our distress the surgeon, Dr. Erving, was obliged to leave us for the return home, taking the best saddle animal and the strongest pack mule. It was impossible to go on with the map. That morning I rode alone up a side valley until I reached a shepherd's hut, where I could find only a broken-down, shuffling old mule, perfectly useless for our hard work.

Then there happened a piece of good luck that seems almost providential. A young man came down the trail with three pack mules loaded with llama meat. He had come from the Cotahuasi Valley the week before and knew the trail. I persuaded him to let us hire one of his mules. In this way and by leaving the instruments and part of our gear in the care of two Indian youths we managed to get to Cotahuasi for rest and a new outfit.

The young men who took charge of part of our outfit interested me very greatly. I had never seen elsewhere so independent and clear-eyed a pair of mountain Indians. At first they would have nothing to do with us. They refused us permission to store our goods in their hut. To them we were railroad engineers. They said that the railway might come and when it did it would depopulate the country. The railway was a curse. Natives were obliged to work for the company without pay. Their uncle had told them of frightful abuses over at Cuzco and had warned them not to help the railway people in any way. They had moved out here in a remote part of the mountains so that white men could not exploit them.

In the end, however, we got them to understand the nature of our work. Gifts of various sorts won their friendship, and they consented to guard the boxes we had to leave behind. Two weeks later, on his return, the topographer found everything unmolested.

I could not but feel that the spirit of those strong and independent young men was much better for Peru than the cringing, subservient spirit of most of the Indians that are serfs of the whites. The policy of the whites has been to suppress and exploit the natives, to abuse them, and to break their spirit. They say that it keeps down revolution; it keeps the Indian in his place. But certainly in other respects it is bad for the Indian and it is worse for the whites. Their brutality toward the natives is incredible. It is not so much the white himself as the vicious half-breed who is often allied with him as his agent.

I shall never forget the terror of two young girls driving a donkey before them when they came suddenly face to face with our party, and we at the same time hastily scrambled off our beasts to get a photograph of a magnificent view disclosed at the bend of the steep trail. They thought we had dismounted to attack them, and fled screaming in abject fear up the mountain side, abandoning the donkey and the pack of potatoes which must have represented a large part of the season's product. It is a kind of highway robbery condoned because it is only robbing an Indian. He is considered to be lawful prey. His complaint goes unnoticed. In the past a revolution has offered him sporadic chances to wreak vengeance. More often it adds to his troubles by scattering through the mountain valleys the desperate refugees or lawless bands of marauders who kill the flocks of the mountain shepherds and despoil their women.

There are still considerable numbers of Indians who shun the white man and live in the most remote corners of the mountains. I have now and again come upon the most isolated huts, invisible from the valley trails. They were thatched with grass; the walls were of stone; the rafters though light must have required prodigious toil, for all timber stops at 12,000 feet on the mountain borders. The shy fugitive who perches his hut near the lip of a hanging valley far above the trail may look down himself unseen as an eagle from its nest. When the owner leaves on a journey, or to take his flock to new pastures, he buries his pottery or hides it in almost inaccessible caves. He locks the door or bars it, thankful if the spoiler spares rafters and thatch.

At length we reached Cotahuasi, a town sprawled out on a terrace just above the floor of a deep canyon (Fig. 29). Its flower gardens and pastures are watered by a multitude of branching canals lined with low willows. Its bright fields stretch up the lower slopes and alluvial fans of the canyon to the limits of irrigation where the desert begins. The fame of this charming oasis is widespread. The people of Antabamba and Lambrama and even the officials of Abancay spoke of Cotahuasi as practically the end of our journey. Fruits ripen and flowers blossom every month of the year. Where we first reached the canyon floor near Huaynacotas, elevation 11,500 feet (3,500 m.), there seemed to be acres of rose bushes. Only the day before at an elevation of 16,800 feet (5,120 m.) we had broken thick ice out of a mountain spring in order to get water; now we were wading a shallow river, and grateful for the shade along its banks. Thus we came to the town prepared to find the people far above their plateau neighbors in character. Yet, in spite of friendly priests and officials and courteous shopkeepers, there was a spirit strangely out of harmony with the pleasant landscape.

Inquiries showed that even here, where it seemed that only sylvan peace should reign, there had recently been let loose the spirit of barbarism. We shall turn to some of its manifestations and look at the reasons therefor.

In the revolution of 1911 a mob of drunken, riotous citizens gathered to storm the Cotahuasi barracks and the jail. A full-blooded Indian soldier, on duty at the entrance, ordered the rioters to stop and when they paid no heed he shot the leader and scattered the crowd. The captain thereupon ordered the soldier to Arequipa because his life was no longer safe outside the barracks. A few months later he was assigned to Professor Bingham's Coropuna expedition. Professor Bingham reached the Cotahuasi Valley as I was about to leave it for the coast, and the soldier was turned over to me so that he might leave Cotahuasi at the earliest possible moment, for his enemies were plotting to kill him.

He did not sleep at all the last night of his stay and had us called at three in the morning. He told his friends that he was going to leave with us, but that they were to announce his leaving a day later. In addition, the Subprefect was to accompany us until daybreak so that no harm might befall me while under the protection of a soldier who expected to be shot from ambush.

At four o'clock our whispered arrangements were made, we opened the gates noiselessly, and our small cavalcade hurried through the pitch-black streets of the town. The soldier rode ahead, his rifle across his saddle, and directly behind him rode the Subprefect and myself. The pack mules were in the rear. We had almost reached the end of the street when a door opened suddenly and a shower of sparks flew out ahead of us. Instantly the soldier struck spurs into his mule and turned into a side street. The Subprefect drew his horse back savagely and when the next shower of sparks flew out pushed me against the wall and whispered: "Por Dios, quien es?" Then suddenly he shouted: "Sopla no mas, sopla no mas" (stop blowing).

Thereupon a shabby penitent man came to the door holding in his hand a large tailor's flatiron. The base of it was filled with glowing charcoal and he was about to start his day's work. The sparks were made in the process of blowing through the iron to start the smoldering coals. We greeted him with more than ordinary friendliness and passed on.

At daybreak we had reached the steep western wall of the canyon where the real ascent begins, and here the Subprefect turned back with many *felicidades* for the journey and threats for the soldier if he did not look carefully after the pack train. From every angle of the zigzag trail that climbs the "cuesta" the soldier scanned the valley road and the trail below him. He was anxious lest news of his escape reach his enemies who had vowed to take his life. Half the day he rode turned in his saddle so as to see every traveler long before he was within harm's reach. By nightfall we safely reached Salamanca, fifty miles away (Fig. 62).

The alertness of the soldier was unusual and I quite enjoyed his close attention to the beasts and his total abstinence, for an alert and sober soldier on detail is a rare phenomenon in the interior of Peru. But all Salamanca was drunk when we arrived —Governor, alcaldes, citizens. Even the peons drank up in brandy the money that we gave them for forage and let the beasts starve. The only sober person I saw was the white telegraph operator from Lima. He said that he had to stay sober, for the telegraph office—the outward sign of government—was the special object of attack of every drink-crazed gang of rioters. They had tried to break in a few nights before and he had fired his revolver point-blank through the door. The town offered no shelter but the dark filthy hut of the Gobernador and the tiny telegraph office. So I made up my bed beside that of the operator. We shared our meals and chatted until a late hour, he recounting the glories of Lima, to which he hoped to return at the earliest possible moment, and cursing the squalid town of Salamanca. His operator's keys were old, the batteries feeble, and he was in continual anxiety lest a message could not be received. In the night he sprang out of bed shouting frantically:

"Estan llamando" (they are calling), only to stumble over my bed and awaken himself and offer apologies for walking in his sleep.

Meanwhile my soldier, having regained his courage, began drinking. It was with great difficulty that I got started, after a day's delay, on the trail to Chuquibamba. There his thirst quite overcame him. To separate him from temptation it became necessary to lock him up in the village jail. This I did repeatedly on the way to Mollendo, except beyond Quilca, where we slept in the hot marshy valley out of reach of drink, and where the mosquitoes kept us so busy that either eating or drinking was almost out of the question.

The drunken rioters of Cotahuasi and their debauched brothers at Salamanca are chiefly natives of pure or nearly pure Indian blood. They are a part of the great plateau population of the Peruvian Andes. Have they degenerated to their present low state, or do they display merely the normal condition of the plateau people? Why are they so troublesome an element? To this as to so many questions that arise concerning the highland population we find our answer not chiefly in government, or religion, or inherited character, but in geography. I doubt very much if a greater relative difference would be seen if two groups of whites were set down, the one in the cold terrace lands of Salamanca, the other in the warm vineyards of Aplao, in the Majes Valley. The common people of these two towns were originally of the same race, but the lower valley now has a white element including even most of those having the rank of peons. Greater differences in character could scarcely be found between the Aztecs and the Iroquois. In the warm valley there is of coarse drunkenness, but it is far from general; there is stupidity, but the people are as a whole alert; and finally, the climate and soil produce grapes from which famous wines are made, they produce sugar cane, cotton, and alfalfa, so that the whites have come in, diluted the Indian blood, and raised the standard of life and behavior. Undoubtedly their influence would tend to have the same general effect if they mixed in equal numbers with the plateau groups. There is, however, a good reason for their not doing so.

The lofty towns of the plateau have a really wretched climate. White men cannot live comfortably at Antabamba and Salamanca. Further, they are so isolated that the modest comforts and the smallest luxuries of civilization are very expensive. To pay for them requires a profitable industry managed on a large scale and there is no such industry in the higher valleys. The white who goes there must be satisfied to live like an Indian. The result is easy to forecast. Outside of government officers, only the disso-

FIG. 60.

FIG. 61.

FIG. 60—View across the Antabamba canyon just above Huadquirca.

FIG. 61—Huancarama, west of Abancay, on the famous Lima to Buenos Aires road. Note the smooth slopes in the foreground. See Chapter XI.

FIG. 62—Salamanca, on the floor of the deep Arma Valley (a tributary of one of the major coast valleys, the Ocoña), which is really a canyon above this point and which, in spite of its steepness, is thoroughly terraced and intensively cultivated up to the frost line.

lute or unsuccessful whites live in the worst towns, like Salamanca and Antabamba. A larger valley with a slightly milder climate and more accessible situation, like Chuquibamba, will draw a still better grade of white citizen and in the largest of all—Cuzco and the Titicaca basin—we find normal whites in larger numbers, though they nowhere live in such high ratios to the Indian as on the coast and in the lower valleys near the coast. With few exceptions the white population of Peru is distributed in response to favorable combinations of climate, soil, accessibility, and general opportunities to secure a living without extreme sacrifice.

These facts are stated in a simple way, for I wish to emphasize the statement that the Indian population responds to quite other stimuli. Most of the luxuries and comforts of the whites mean nothing to the Indian. The machine-made woolens of the importers will probably never displace his homespun llama-wool clothing. His implements are few in number and simple in form. His tastes in food are satisfied by the few products of his fields and his mountain flocks. Thus he has lived for centuries and is quite content to live today. Only coca and brandy tempt him to engage in commerce, to toil now and then in the hot valleys, and to strive for more than the bare necessities of life. Therefore it matters very little to him if his home town is isolated, or the resources support but a small group of people. He is so accustomed to a solitary existence in his ramblings with his flocks that a village of fifty houses offers social enjoyments of a high order. Where a white perishes for lack of society the Indian finds himself contented. Finally, he is not subject to the white man's exploitation when he lives in remote places. The pastures are extensive and free. The high valley lands are apportioned by the alcalde according to ancient custom. His life is unrestricted by anything but the common law and he need have no care for the morrow, for the seasons here are almost as fixed as the stars.

Thus we have a sort of segregation of whites in the lower places where a modern type of life is maintained and of Indians in the higher places where they enjoy advantages that do not appeal to the whites. Above 8,000 feet the density of the white population bears a close inverse proportion to the altitude, excepting in the case of the largest valleys whose size brings together such numbers as to tempt the commercial and exploiting whites to live in them. Furthermore, we should find that high altitude, limited size, and greater isolation are everywhere closely related to increasing immorality or decreasing character among the whites. So to the low Indian population there is thus added the lowest of the white population. Moreover, because it yields the largest returns, the chief business of these whites is the sale of coca and brandy and the downright active debauchery of the Indian. This is all the easier for them because the isolated Indian, like the average isolated white, has only a low and provincial standard of morality and gets no help from such stimulation as numbers usually excite.

For example, the Anta basin at harvest time is one of the fairest sights in Peru. Sturdy laborers are working diligently. Their faces are bright and happy, their skin clear, their manner eager and animated. They sing at their work or gather about their mild *chicha* and drink to the patron saints of the harvest. The huts are filled with robust children; all the yards are turned into threshing floors; and from the stubbly hillslopes the shepherd blows shrill notes upon his barley reeds and bamboo flute. There is drinking but there is little disorder and there is always a sober remnant that exercises a restraining influence upon the group.

In the most remote places of all one may find mountain groups of a high order of morality unaffected by the white man or actually shunning him. Clear-eyed, thick-limbed, independent, a fine, sturdy type of man this highland shepherd may be. But in the town he succumbs to the temptation of drink. Some writers have tried to make him out a superior to the plains and low valley type. He is not that. The well-regulated groups of the lower elevations are far superior intellectually and morally in spite of the fact that the poorly regulated groups may fall below the highland dweller in morality. The coca-chewing highlander is a clod. Surely, as a whole, the mixed breed of the coastal valleys is a far worthier type, save in a few cases where a Chinese or negroid element or both have led to local inferiority. And surely, also, that is the worst combination which results in adding the viciousness of the inferior or debased white to the stupidity of the highland Indian. It is here that the effects of geography are most apparent. If the white is tempted in large numbers because of exceptional position or resources, as at La Paz, the rule of altitude may have an exception. And other exceptions there are not due to physical causes, for character is practically never a question of geography alone. There is the spiritual factor that may illumine a strong character and through his agency turn a weak community into a powerful one, or hold a weakened group steadfast against the forces of disintegration. Exceptions arise from this and other causes and yet with them all in mind the geographic factor seems predominant in the types illustrated herewith.[2]

---

[2] During his travels Raimondi collected many instances of the isolation and conservatism of the plateau Indian: thus there is the village of Pampacolca near Coropuna, whose inhabitants until recently carried their idols of clay to the slopes of the great white mountain and worshiped them there with the ritual of Inca days (El Perú, Lima, 1874, Vol. 1).

CHAPTER VIII

THE COASTAL DESERT

To the wayfarer from the bleak mountains the warm green valleys of the coastal desert of Peru seem like the climax of scenic beauty. The streams are intrenched from 2,000 to 4,000 feet, and the valley walls in some places drop 500 feet by sheer descents from one level to another. The cultivated fields on the valley floors look like sunken gardens and now and then one may catch the distant glint of sunlight on water. The broad white path that winds through vineyards and cotton-fields, follows the foot of a cliff, or fills the whole breadth of a gorge is the waste-strewn, half-dry channel of the river. In some places almost the whole floor is cultivated from one valley wall to the other. In other places the fields are restricted to narrow bands between the river and the impending cliffs of a narrow canyon. Where tributaries enter from the desert there may be huge banks of mud or broad triangular fans covered with raw, infertile earth. The picture is generally touched with color—a yellow, haze-covered horizon on the bare desert above, brown lava flows suspended on the brink of the valley, gray-brown cliffs, and greens ranging from the dull shade of algarrobo, olive and fig trees, to the bright shade of freshly irrigated alfalfa pastures.

After several months' work on the cold highlands, where we rode almost daily into hailstorms or wearisome gales, we came at length to the border of the valley country. It will always seem to me that the weather and the sky conspired that afternoon to reward us for the months of toil that lay behind. And certainly there could be no happier place to receive the reward than on the brink of the lava plateau above Chuquibamba. There was promise of an extraordinary view in the growing beauty of the sky, and we hurried our tired beasts forward so that the valley below

FIG. 63.

FIG. 64.

FIG. 63—The deep fertile Majes Valley below Cantas. Compare with Fig. 6 showing the Chili Valley at Arequipa.

FIG. 64—The Majes Valley, desert coast, western Peru. The lighter patches on the valley floor are the gravel beds of the river at high water. Much of the alluvial land is still uncleared.

might also be included in the picture. The head of the Majes Valley is a vast hollow bordered by cliffs hundreds of feet high, and we reached the rim of it only a few minutes before sunset.

I remember that we halted beside a great wooden cross and that our guide, dismounting, walked up to the foot of it and kissed and embraced it after the custom of the mountain folk when they reach the head of a steep "cuesta." Also that the trail seemed to drop off like a stairway, which indeed it was.[1] Everything else about me was completely overshadowed by snowy mountains, colored sky, and golden-yellow desert. One could almost forget the dark clouds that gather around the great mass of Coropuna and the bitter winds that creep down from its glaciers at night—it seemed so friendly and noble. Behind it lay bulky masses of rose-tinted clouds. We had admired their gay colors only a few minutes, when the sun dropped behind the crest of the Coast Range and the last of the sunlight played upon the sky. It fell with such marvelously swift changes of color upon the outermost zone of clouds as these were shifted with the wind that the eye had scarcely time to comprehend a tint before it was gone and one more beautiful still had taken its place. The reflected sunlight lay warm and soft upon the white peaks of Coropuna, and a little later the Alpine glow came out delicately clear.

When we turned from this brilliant scene to the deep valley, we found that it had already become so dark that its greens had turned to black, and the valley walls, now in deep shadow, had lost half their splendor. The color had not left the sky before the lights of Chuquibamba began to show, and candles twinkled from the doors of a group of huts close under the cliff. We were not long in starting the descent. Here at last were friendly habitations and happy people. I had worked for six weeks between 12,000 and 17,000 feet, constantly ill from mountain sickness, and it was with no regret that I at last left the plateau and got down

---

[1] Raimondi (op. cit., p. 109) has a characteristic description of the "Camino del Peñon" in the department of La Libertad: ". . . the ground seems to disappear from one's feet; one is standing on an elevated balcony looking down more than 6,000 feet to the valley . . . the road which descends the steep scarp is a masterpiece."

to comfortable altitudes. It seemed good news when the guide
told me that there were mosquitoes in the marshes of Camaná.
Any low, hot land would have seemed like a health resort. I had
been in the high country so long that, like the Bolivian mining
engineer, I wanted to get down not only to sea level, but below it!

If the reader will examine Figs. 65 and 66, and the photographs
that accompany them, he may gain an idea of the more important

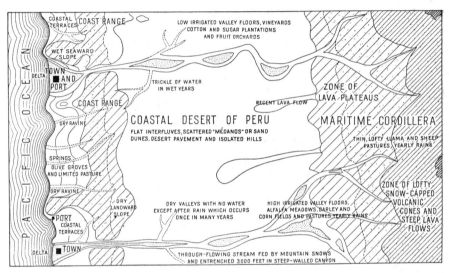

FIG. 65—Regional diagram to show the physical relations in the coastal desert
of Peru. For location, see Fig. 20.

features of the coastal region. We have already described, in
Chapters V and VII, the character of the plateau region and its
people. Therefore, we need say little in this place of the part
of the Maritime Cordillera that is included in the figure. Its
unpopulated rim (see p. 54), the semi-nomadic herdsmen and shepherds from Chuquibamba that scour its pastures in the moist
vales about Coropuna, and the gnarled and stunted trees at 13,000
feet (3,960 m.) which partly supply Chuquibamba with firewood,
are its most important features. A few groups of huts just under
the snowline are inhabited for only a part of the year. The delightful valleys are too near and tempting. Even a plateau
Indian responds to the call of a dry valley, however he may shun
the moist, warm valleys on the eastern border of the Cordillera.

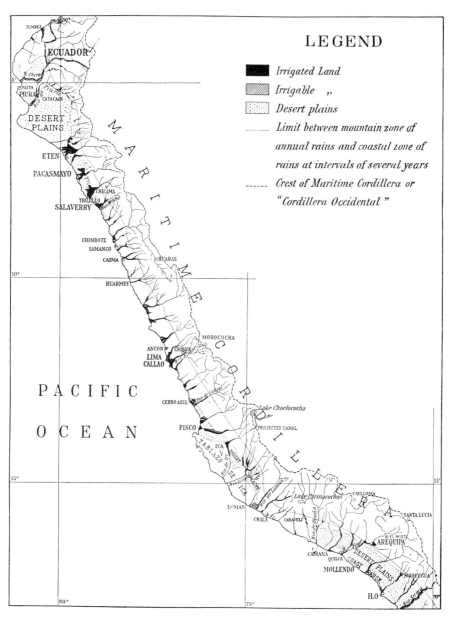

Fig. 66—Irrigated and irrigable land of the coastal belt of Peru. The map exhibits in a striking manner how small a part of the whole Pacific slope is available for cultivation. Pasture grows over all but the steepest and the highest portions of the Cordillera to the right of (above) the dotted line. Another belt of pasture too narrow to show on the map, grows in the fog belt on the seaward slopes of the Coast Range. Scale, 170 miles to the inch.

The greater part of the coastal region is occupied by the desert. Its outer border is the low, dry, gentle, eastward-facing slope of the Coast Range. Its inner border is the foot of the steep descent that marks the edge of the lava plateau. This descent is a fairly well-marked line, here and there broken by a venturesome lava flow that extends far out from the main plateau. Within these definite borders the desert extends continuously northwestward for hundreds of miles along the coast of Peru from far beyond the Chilean frontier almost to the border of Ecuador. It is broken up by deep tranverse valleys and canyons into so-called "pampas," each of which has a separate name; thus west of Arequipa between the Vitor and Majes valleys are the "Pampa de Vitor" and the "Pampa de Sihuas," and south of the Vitor is the "Pampa de Islay."

The pampa surfaces are inclined in general toward the sea. They were built up to their present level chiefly by mountain streams before the present deep valleys were cut, that is to say, when the land was more than a half-mile lower. Some of their material is wind-blown and on the walls of the valleys are alternating belts of wind-blown and water-laid strata from one hundred to four hundred feet thick as if in past ages long dry and long wet periods had succeeded each other. The wind has blown sand and dust from the desert down into the valleys, but its chief work has been to drive the lighter desert waste up partly into the mountains and along their margins, partly so high as to carry it into the realm of the lofty terrestrial winds, whence it falls upon surfaces far distant from the fields of origin. There are left behind the heavier sand which the wind rolls along on the surfaces and builds into crescentic dunes called médanos, and the pebbles that it can sandpaper but cannot remove bodily. Thus there are belts of dunes, belts of irregular sand drifts, and belts of true desert "pavement" (a residual mantle of faceted pebbles and irregular stones).

Yet another feature of the desert pampa are the "dry" valleys that join the through-flowing streams at irregular intervals, as shown in the accompanying regional diagram. If one follow a dry valley to its head he will find there a set of broad and shallow tributaries. Sand drifts may clog them and appear to indicate that water no longer flows through them. They are often referred to by unscientific travelers as evidences of a recent change of climate. I had once the unusual opportunity (in the mountains of Chile) of seeing freshly fallen snow melted rapidly and thus turned suddenly into the streams. In 1911 this happened also at San Pedro de Atacama, northern Chile, right in the desert at 8,000 feet (2,440 m.) elevation, and in both places the dry, sand-choked valleys were cleaned out and definite channels reëstablished. From a large number of facts like these we know that the dry valleys represent the work of the infrequent rains. No desert is absolutely rainless, although until recently it was the fashion to say so. Naturally the wind, which works incessantly, partly offsets the work of the water. Yet the wind can make but little impression upon the general outlines of the dry valleys. They remain under the dominance of the irregular rains. These come sometimes at intervals of three or four years, again at intervals of ten to fifteen years, and some parts of the desert have probably been rainless for a hundred years. Some specific cases are discussed in the chapter on Climate.

The large valleys of the desert zone have been cut by snow-fed streams and then partly filled again so that deep waste lies on their floors and abuts with remarkable sharpness against the bordering cliffs (Fig. 155). Extensive flats are thus available for easy cultivation, and the through-flowing streams furnish abundant water to the irrigating canals. The alluvial floor begins almost at the foot of the steep western slope of the lava plateau, but it is there stony and coarse—hence Chuquibamba, or plain of stones (chuqui=stone; bamba=plain). Farther down and about half-way between Chuquibamba and Aplao (Camaná Quadrangle) it is partly covered with fresh mud and sand flows from the bordering valley walls and the stream is intrenched two hundred feet. A few miles above Aplao the stream emerges from its narrow gorge and thenceforth flows on the surface of the alluvium right to the sea. Narrow places occur between Cantas and Aplao, where there is a projection of old and hard quartzitic rock, and again above Camaná, where the stream cuts straight across the granite axis of the Coast Range. Elsewhere the rock is either a softer sandstone or still unindurated sands and gravels, as at the top of the desert series of strata that are exposed on the valley wall. The changing width of the valley is thus a reflection of the changing hardness of the rock.

There is a wide range of products between Chuquibamba at 10,000 feet (3,050 m.) at the head of the valley and Camaná near the valley mouth. At the higher levels fruit will not grow—only alfalfa, potatoes, and barley. A thousand feet below Chuquibamba fruit trees appear. Then follows a barren stretch where there are mud flows and where the river is intrenched. Below this there is a wonderful change in climate and products. The elevation falls off 4,000 feet and the first cultivated patches below the middle unfavorable section are covered with grape vines. Here at 3,000 feet (900 m.) elevation above the sea begin the famous vineyards of the Majes Valley, which support a wine industry that dates back to the sixteenth century. Some of the huge buried earthenware jars for curing the wine at Hacienda Cantas were made in the reign of Philip II.

The people of Aplao and Camaná are among the most hospitable and energetic in Peru, as if these qualities were but the reflection of the bounty of nature. Nowhere could I see evidences of crowding or of the degeneracy or poverty that is so often associated with desert people. Water is always plentiful; sometimes indeed too plentiful, for floods and changes in the bed of the river are responsible for the loss of a good deal of land. This abundance of water means that both the small and the large landowners receive enough. There are none of the troublesome official regulations, as in the poorer valleys with their inevitable favoritism or downright graft. Yet even here the valley is not fully occupied; at many places more land could be put under cultivation. The Belaunde brothers at Cantas have illustrated this in their new cotton plantation, where clearings and new canals have turned into cultivated fields tracts long covered with brush.

The Majes Valley sorely lacks an adequate port. Its cotton, sugar, and wine must now be shipped to Camaná and thence to Mollendo, either by a small bi-weekly boat, or by pack-train over the coast trail to Quilca, where ocean steamers call. This is so roundabout a way that the planters of the mid-valley section and the farmers of the valley head now export their products over the desert trail from Cantas to Vitor on the Mollendo-Arequipa railroad, whence they can be sent either to the cotton mills or the stores of Arequipa, the chief distributing market of southern Peru, or to the ocean port.

The foreshore at Camaná is low and marshy where the salt water covers the outer edge of the delta. In the hollow between two headlands a broad alluvial plain has been formed, through which the shallow river now discharges. Hence the natural indentation has been filled up and the river shoaled. To these disadvantages must be added a third, the shoaling of the sea bottom, which compels ships to anchor far off shore. Such shoals are so rare on this dry and almost riverless coast as to be a menace to navigation. The steamer *Tucapelle,* like all west-coast boats, was sailing close to the unlighted shore on a very dark night in April, 1911, when the usual fog came on. She struck the reef just off Camaná. Half of her passengers perished in trying to get through the tremendous surf that broke over the bar. The most practicable scheme for the development of the port would seem to be a floating dock and tower anchored out of reach of the surf, and connected by cable with a railway on shore. Harbor works would be extraordinarily expensive. The valley can support only a modest project.

The relations of Fig. 65, representing the Camaná-Vitor region, are typical of southern Peru, with one exception. In a few valleys the streams are so small that but little water is ever found beyond the foot of the mountains, as at Moquegua. In the Chili Valley is Arequipa (8,000 feet), right at the foot of the big cones of the Maritime Cordillera (see Fig. 6). The green valley floor narrows rapidly and cultivation disappears but a few miles below the town. Outside the big valleys cultivation is limited to the best spots along the foot of the Coast Range, where tiny streams or small springs derive water from the zone of clouds and fogs on the seaward slopes of the Coast Range. Here and there are olive groves, a vegetable garden, or a narrow alfalfa meadow, watered

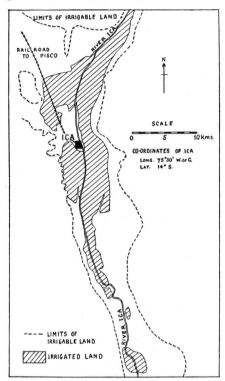

FIG. 67—Irrigated and irrigable land in the Ica Valley of the coastal desert of Peru.

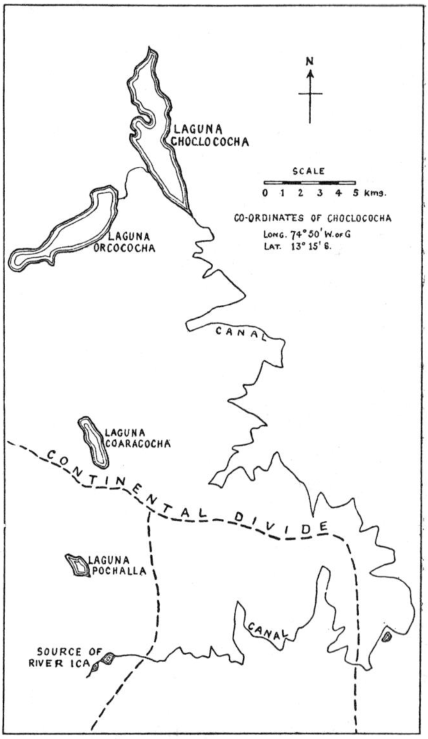

FIG. 68—The projected canal to convey water from the Atlantic slope to the Pacific slope of the Maritime Cordillera.[2]

by uncertain springs that issue below the hollows of the bordering mountains.

In central and northern Peru the coastal region has aspects quite different from those about Camaná. At some places, for example north of Cerro Azul, the main spurs of the Cordillera extend down to the shore. There is neither a low Coast Range nor a broad desert pampa. In such places flat land is found only on the alluvial fans and deltas. Lima and Callao are typical. Fig. 66, compiled from Adams's reports on the water resources of

_____

[2] Figs. 67 and 68 are from Bol. de Minas del Perú, 1906, No. 37, pp. 82 and 84 respectively.

the coastal region of Peru, shows this distinctive feature of the central region. Beyond Salaverry extends the northern region, where nearly all the irrigated land is found some distance back from the shore. The farther north we go the more marked is this

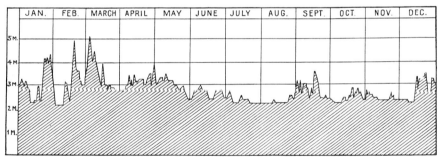

	JAN	FEB	MARCH	APRIL	MAY	JUNE	JULY	AUG	SEPT	OCT.	NOV	DEC

Fɪɢ. 69—A stream of the intermittent type in the coastal desert of Peru. Depth of water in the Puira River at Puira, 1905. (Bol. de Minas del Perú, 1906, No. 45, p. 2.)

feature, because the coastal belt widens. Catacaos is several miles from the sea, and Piura is an interior place. At the extreme north, where the rains begin, as at Tumbez, the cultivated land once more extends to the coast.

These three regions contain all the fertile coastal valleys of Peru. The larger ones are impressive—with cities, railways,

	JAN.	FEB.	MARCH	APRIL	MAY	JUNE	JULY	AUG.	SEPT.	OCT.	NOV.	DEC.

Fɪɢ. 70—A stream of the perennial type in the coastal desert of Peru. Depth of water in the Chira River at Sullana, 1905. Data from May to September are approximate. (Bol. de Minas del Perú, 1906, No. 45, p. 2.)

ports, and land in a high state of cultivation. But they are after all only a few hundred square miles in extent. They contain less than a quarter of the people. The whole Pacific slope from the crest of the Cordillera has about 15,000 square miles (38,850 sq. km.), and of this only three per cent is irrigated valley land, as shown in Fig. 66. Moreover, only a small additional amount may be irrigated, perhaps one half of one per cent. Even this amount may be added not only by a better use of the water but also by the diversion of streams and lakes from the Atlantic to the Pacific. Figs. 67 and 68 represent such a project, in which it is proposed to carry the water of Lake Choclococha through a canal and tunnel under the continental divide and so to the head of the Ica Valley. A little irrigation can be and is carried on by the use of well water, but this will never be an important source because of the great depth to the ground water, and the fact that it, too, depends ultimately upon the limited rains.

The inequality of opportunity in the various valleys of the coastal region depends in large part also upon inequality of river discharge. This is dependent chiefly upon the sources of the streams, whether in snowy peaks of the main Cordillera with fairly constant run-off, or in the western spurs where summer rains bring periodic high water. A third type has high water during the time of greatest snow melting, combined with summer rains, and to this class belongs the Majes Valley with its sources in the snow-cap of Coropuna. The other two types are illustrated by the accompanying diagrams for Puira and Chira, the former intermittent in flow, the latter fairly constant.[3]

---

[3] The Boletín de Minas del Perú, No. 34, 1905, contains a graphic representation of the régime of. the Rio Chili at Arequipa for the years 1901-1905.

CHAPTER IX

CLIMATOLOGY OF THE PERUVIAN ANDES

CLIMATIC BELTS

The noble proportions of the Peruvian Andes and their position in tropical latitudes have given them climatic conditions of great diversity. Moreover, their great breadth and continuously lofty summits have distributed the various climatic types over spaces sufficiently ample to affect large and important groups of people. When we add to this the fact that the topographic types developed on a large scale are distributed at varying elevations, and that upon them depend to a large degree the chief characteristics of the soil, another great factor in human distribution, we are prepared to see that the Peruvian Andes afford some striking illustrations of combined climatic and topographic control over man.

The topographic features in their relations to the people have been discussed in preceding chapters. We shall now examine the corresponding effects of climate. It goes without saying that the topographic and climatic controls cannot and need not be kept rigidly apart. Yet it seems desirable, for all their natural interdependence, to give them separate treatment, since the physical laws upon which their explanations depend are of course entirely distinct. Further, there is an independent group of human responses to detailed climatic features that have little or no connection with either topography or soil.

The chief climatic belts of Peru run roughly from north to south in the direction of the main features of the topography. Between 13° and 18° S., however, the Andes run from northwest to southeast, and in short stretches nearly west-east, with the result that the climatic belts likewise trend westward, a condition well illustrated on the seventy-third meridian. Here are developed important climatic features not found elsewhere in Peru. The trade winds are greatly modified in direction and effects; the northward-trending valleys, so deep as to be secluded from the trades, have floors that are nearly if not quite arid; a restricted coastal region enjoys a heavier rainfall; and the snowline is much more strongly canted from west to east than anywhere else in the long belt of mountains from Patagonia to Venezuela. These exceptional features depend, however, upon precisely the same physical laws as the normal climatic features of the Peruvian Andes. They can, therefore, be more easily understood after attention has been given to the larger aspects of the climatic problem of which they form a part.

The critical relations of trade winds, lofty mountains, and ocean currents that give distinction to Peruvian climate are shown in Figs. 71 to 73. From them and Fig. 74 it is clear that the two sides of the Peruvian mountains are in sharp contrast climatically. The eastern slopes have almost daily rains, even in the dry season, and are clothed with forest. The western leeward slopes are so dry that at 8,000 feet even the most drought-resisting grasses stop—only low shrubs live below this level, and over large areas there is no vegetation whatever. An exception is the Coast Range, not shown on these small maps, but exhibited in the succeeding diagram. These have moderate rains on their seaward (westerly) slopes during some years and grass and shrubby vegetation grow between the arid coastal terraces below them and the parched desert above. The greatest variety of climate is enjoyed by the mountain zone. Its deeper valleys and basins descend to tropical levels; its higher ranges and peaks are snow-covered. Between are the climates of half the world compressed, it may be, between 6,000 and 15,000 feet of elevation and with extremes only a day's journey apart.

In the explanation of these contrasts we have to deal with relatively simple facts and principles; but the reader who is interested chiefly in the human aspects of the region should turn to p. 138 where the effects of the climate on man are set forth. The ascending trades on the eastern slopes pass successively into

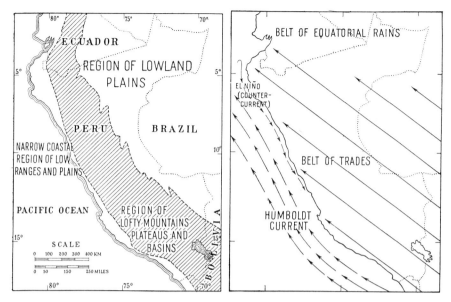

FIG. 71.   FIG. 72.

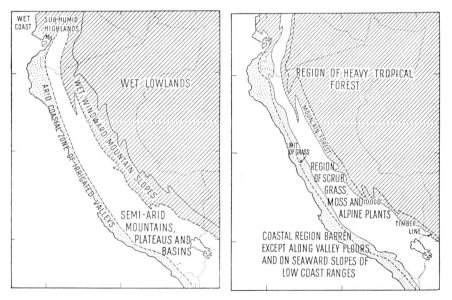

FIG. 73.   FIG. 74.

FIG. 71—The three chief topographic regions of Peru.
FIG. 72—The wind belts of Peru and ocean currents of adjacent waters.
FIG. 73—The climatic belts of Peru.
FIG. 74—Belts of vegetation in Peru.

atmospheric levels of diminishing pressure; hence they expand, deriving the required energy for expansion from the heat of the air itself. The air thereby cooled has a lower capacity for the retention of water vapor, a function of its temperature; the colder the air the less water vapor it can take up. As long as the actual amount of water vapor in the air is less than that which the air can hold, no rain falls. But the cooling process tends constantly to bring the warm, moist, ascending air currents to the limit of their capacity for water vapor by diminishing the temperature. Eventually the air is saturated and if the capacity diminishes still further through diminishing temperature some of the water vapor must be condensed from a gaseous to a liquid form and be dropped as rain.

The air currents that rise thousands of feet per day on the eastern slopes of the Andes pass again and again through this practically continuous process and the eastern aspect of the mountains is kept rain-soaked the whole year round. For the trades here have only the rarest reversals. Generally they blow from the east day after day and repeat a fixed or average type of weather peculiar to that part of the tropics under their steady domination. During the southern summer, when the day-time temperature contrasts between mountains and plains are strongest, the force of the trade wind is greatly increased and likewise the rapidity of the rain-making processes. Hence there is a distinct seasonal difference in the rainfall—what we call, for want of a better name, a "wet" and a "dry" season.

On the western or seaward slopes of the Peruvian Andes the trade winds descend, and the process of rain-making is reversed to one of rain-taking. The descending air currents are compressed as they reach lower levels where there are progressively higher atmospheric pressures. The energy expended in the process is expressed in the air as heat, whence the descending air gains steadily in temperature and capacity for water vapor, and therefore is a drying wind. Thus the leeward, western slopes of the mountains receive little rain and the lowlands on that side are desert.

A series of narrow but pronounced climatic zones coincide with the topographic subdivisions of the western slope of the country between the crest of the Maritime Cordillera and the Pacific Ocean. This belted arrangement is diagrammatically shown in Fig. 75. From the zone of lofty mountains with a well-marked summer rainy season descent is made by lower slopes with successively

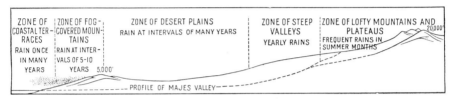

FIG. 75—Topographic and climatic provinces in the coastal region of Peru. The broadest division, into the zones of regular annual rains and of irregular rains, occurs approximately at 8,000 feet but is locally variable. To the traveler it is always clearly defined by the change in architecture, particularly of the house roofs. Those of the coast are flat; those of the sierra are pitched to facilitate run off.

less and less precipitation to the desert strip, where rain is only known at irregular intervals of many years' duration. Beyond lies the seaward slope of the Coast Range, more or less constantly enveloped in fog and receiving actual rain every few years, and below it is the very narrow band of dry coastal terraces.

The basic cause of the general aridity of the region has already been noted; the peculiar circumstances giving origin to the variety in detail can be briefly stated. They depend upon the meteorologic and hydrographic features of the adjacent portion of the South Pacific Ocean and upon the local topography.

The lofty Andes interrupt the broad sweep of the southeast trades passing over the continent from the Atlantic; and the wind circulation of the Peruvian Coast is governed to a great degree by the high pressure area of the South Pacific. The prevailing winds blow from the south and the southeast, roughly paralleling the coast or, as onshore winds, making a small angle with it. When the Pacific high pressure area is best developed (during the southern winter), the southerly direction of the winds is emphasized, a condition clearly shown on the Pilot Charts of the South Pacific Ocean, issued by the U. S. Hydrographic Office.

The hydrographic feature of greatest importance is the Humboldt Current. To its cold waters is largely due the remarkably low temperatures of the coast.[1] In the latitude of Lima its mean surface temperature is about 10° below normal. Lima itself has a mean annual temperature 4.6° F. below the theoretical value for that latitude, (12° S.). An accompanying curve shows the low temperature of Callao during the winter months. From mid-June to mid-September the mean was 61° F., and the annual mean is only 65.6° F. (18° C.). The reduction in temperature is accompanied by a reduction in the vapor capacity of the super-incumbent air, an effect of which much has been made in explanation of

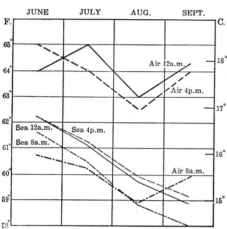

Fig. 76—Temperatures at Callao, June-September, 1912, from observations taken by Captain A. Taylor, of Callao. Air temperatures are shown by heavy lines; sea temperatures by light lines. In view of the scant record for comparative land and water temperatures along the Peruvian coast this record, short as it is, has special interest.

the west-coast desert. That it is a contributing though not exclusive factor is demonstrated in Fig. 77. Curve A represents the hypothetical change of temperature on a mountainous coast with temporary afternoon onshore winds from a *warm* sea. Curve B represents the change of temperature if the sea be cold (actual case of Peru). The more rapid rise of curve B to the right of X-X′, the line of transition, and its higher elevation above its former saturation level, as contrasted with A, indicates greater dryness (lower relative humidity). There has been precipitation in case A, but at a higher temperature, hence

---

[1] Hann (Handbook of Climatology, translated by R. De C. Ward, New York, 1903) indicates a contributory cause in the upwelling of cold water along the coast caused by the steady westerly drift of the equatorial current.

more water vapor remains in the air after precipitation has ceased. Curve *B* ultimately rises nearly to the level of *A*, for with less water vapor in the air of case *B* the temperature rises more rapidly (a general law). Moreover, the higher the temperature the greater the radiation. To summarize, curve *A* rises more slowly than curve *B*, (1) because of the greater amount of water vapor it contains, which must have its temperature raised with that of the air, and thus absorbs energy which would

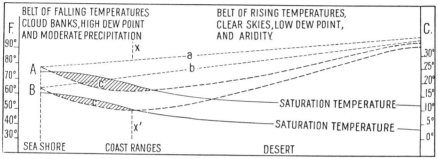

Fig. 77—To show progressive lowering of saturation temperature in a desert under the influence of the mixing process whereby dry and cool air from aloft sinks to lower levels thus displacing the warm surface air of the desert. The evaporated moisture of the surface air is thus distributed through a great volume of upper air and rain becomes increasingly rarer. Applied to deserts in general it shows that the effect of any cosmic agent in producing climatic change from moist to dry or dry to moist will be disproportionately increased. The shaded areas C and C' represent the fog-covered slopes of the Coast Range of Peru as shown in Fig. 92. X—X' represents the crest of the Coast Range.

otherwise go to increase the temperature of the air, and (2) because its loss of heat by radiation is more rapid on account of its higher temperature. We conclude from these principles and deductions that under the given conditions a cold current intensifies, but does not cause the aridity of the west-coast desert.

Curves *a* and *b* represent the rise of temperature in two contrasted cases of warm and cold sea with the coastal mountains eliminated, so as to simplify the principle applied to *A* and *B*. The steeper gradient of *b* also represents the fact that the lower the initial temperature the dryer will the air become in passing over the warm land. For these two curves the transition line *X-X'* coincides with the crest of the Coast Range. It will also be seen that curve *a* is never so far from the saturation level as

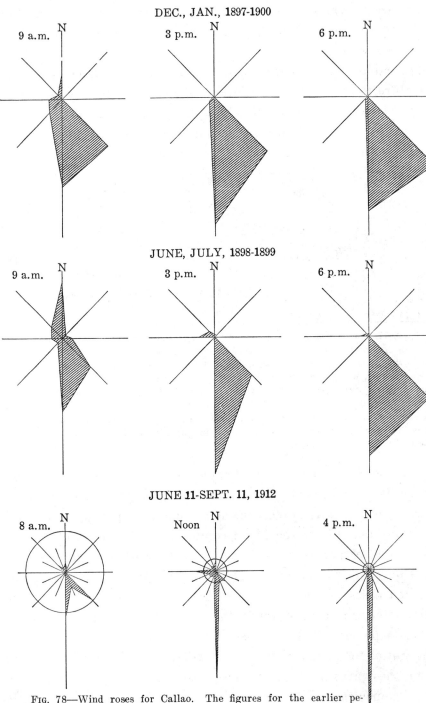

FIG. 78—Wind roses for Callao. The figures for the earlier period (1897-1900) are drawn from data in the Boletín de la Sociedad
Geográfica de Lima, Vols. 7 and 8, 1898-1900: for the latter period
data from observations of Captain A. Taylor, of Callao. The diameter of the circle represents the proportionate number of observations
when calm was registered.

curve *b*. Hence, unusual atmospheric disturbances would result in heavier and more frequent showers.

Turning now to local factors we find on the west coast a regional topography that favors a diurnal periodicity of air movement. The strong slopes of the Cordillera and the Coast Range create up-slope or eastward air gradients by day and opposite

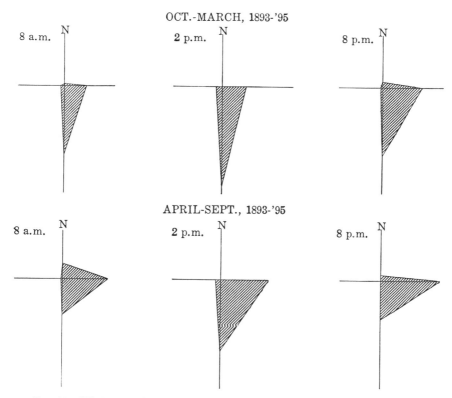

FIG. 79—Wind roses for Mollendo. The figures are drawn from data in Peruvian Meteorology (1892-1895), Annals of the Astronomical Observatory of Harvard College, Vol. 39, Pt. 2, Cambridge, Mass., 1906. Observations for an earlier period, Feb. 1889-March 1890, (Id. Vol. 39, Pt. 1, Cambridge, Mass. 1899) record S. E. wind at 2 p. m. 97 per cent of the observation time.

gradients by night. To this circumstance, in combination with the low temperature of the ocean water and the direction of the prevailing winds, is due the remarkable development of the sea-breeze, without exception the most important meteorological feature of the Peruvian Coast. Several graphic representations are appended to show the dominance of the sea-breeze (see wind roses for Callao, Mollendo, Arica, and Iquique), but interest in the phenomenon is far from being confined to the theoretical. Everywhere along the coast the *virazon*, as the sea-breeze is called in contradistinction to the *terral* or land-breeze, enters deeply into the affairs of human life. According to its strength it aids or hinders shipping; sailing boats may enter port on it or it

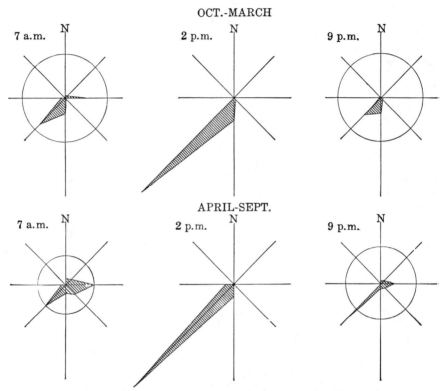

FIG. 80—Wind roses for the summer and winter seasons of the years 1911-1913. The diameter of the circle in each case shows the proportion of calm. Figures are drawn from data in the Anuario Meteorológico de Chile, Publications No. 3, (1911), 6 (1912) and 13 (1913), Santiago, 1912, 1914, 1914.

may be so violent, as, for example, it commonly is at Pisco, that cargo cannot be loaded or unloaded during the afternoon. On the nitrate pampa of northern Chile (20° to 25° S.) it not infrequently breaks with a roar that heralds its coming an hour in advance. In the Majes Valley (12° S.) it blows gustily for a half-hour and about noon (often by eleven o'clock) it settles down to an uncomfortable gale. For an hour or two before the sea-breeze begins the air is hot and stifling, and dust clouds hover about the traveler. The maximum temperature is attained at this time and not around 2.00 P. M. as is normally the case. Yet so boisterous is the noon wind that the laborers time their siesta by it, and not by the high temperatures of earlier

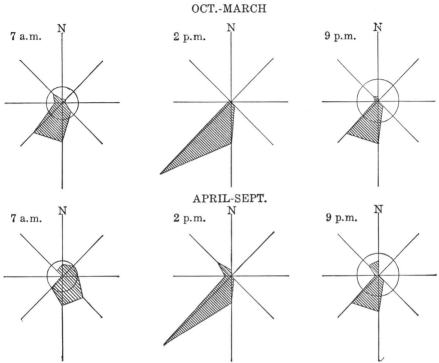

FIG. 81—Wind roses for Iquique for the summer and winter seasons of the years 1911-1913. The diameter of the circle in each case shows the proportion of calm. For source of data see Fig. 80.

hours. In the afternoon it settles down to a steady, comfortable, and dustless wind, and by nightfall the air is once more calm.

Of highest importance are the effects of the sea-breeze on precipitation. The bold heights of the Coast Range force the nearly or quite saturated air of the sea-wind to rise abruptly several thousand feet, and the adiabatic cooling creates fog, cloud, and even rain on the seaward slope of the mountains. The actual form and amount of precipitation both here and in the interior region vary greatly, according to local conditions and to season and also from year to year. The coast changes height and contour from place to place. At Arica the low coastal chain of northern Chile terminates at the Morro de Arica. Thence northward is a stretch of open coast, with almost no rainfall and little fog. But in the stretch of coast between Mollendo and the Majes Valley a coastal range again becomes prominent. Fog enshrouds the hills almost daily and practically every year there is rain somewhere along their western aspect.

During the southern winter the cloud bank of the coast is best developed and precipitation is greatest. At Lima, for instance,

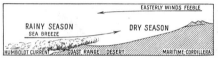

FIG. 82—The wet and dry seasons of the Coast Range and the Cordillera are complementary in time. The "wet" season of the former occurs during the southern winter; the cloud bank on the seaward slopes of the hills is best developed at that time and actual rains may occur.

FIG. 83—During the southern summer the seaward slopes of the Coast Range are comparatively clear of fog. Afternoon cloudiness is characteristic of the desert and increases eastward (compare Fig. 86), the influence of the strong sea winds as well as that of the trades (compare Fig. 93B) being felt on the lower slopes of the Maritime Cordillera.

the clear skies of March and April begin to be clouded in May, and the cloudiness grows until, from late June to September, the sun is invisible for weeks at a time. This is the period of the *garua* (mist) or the "tiempo de lomas," the "season of the hills," when the moisture clothes them with verdure and calls thither the herds of the coast valleys.

During the southern summer on account of the greater relative difference between the temperatures of land and water, the seabreeze attains its maximum strength. It then accomplishes its greatest work in the desert. On the pampa of La Joya, for example, the sand dunes move most rapidly in the summer. According to the Peruvian Meteorological Records of the Harvard Astronomical Observatory the average movement of the dunes from April to September, 1900, was 1.4 inches per day, while during the summer months of the same year it was 2.7 inches. In close agreement are the figures for the wind force, the record for which also shows that 95 per cent of the winds with strength over 10 miles per hour blew from a southerly direction. Yet during this season the coast is generally clearest of fog and cloud. The explanation appears to lie in the exceedingly delicate nature of the adjustments between the various rain-making forces. The relative humidity of the air from the sea is always high, but on the immediate coast is slightly less so in summer than in winter. Thus in Mollendo the relative humidity during the winter of 1895 was 81 per cent; during the summer 78 per cent. Moreover, the temperature of the Coast Range is considerably higher in summer than in winter, and there is a tendency to reëvaporation of any moisture that may be blown against it. The immediate shore, indeed, may still be cloudy as is the case at Callao, which actually has its cloudiest season in the summer, but the hills are comparatively clear. In consequence the sea-air passes over into the desert, where the relative increase in temperature has not been so great (compare Mollendo and La Joya in the curve for mean monthly temperature), with much higher vapor content than in winter. The relative humidity for the winter season at La Joya, 1895, was 42.5 per cent; for the summer season 57 per cent. The influence of the great barrier of the Maritime Cordillera, aided

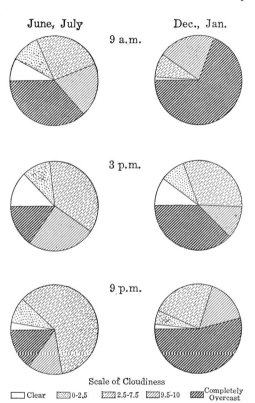

Fig. 84—Cloudiness at Callao. Figures are drawn from data in the Boletín de la Sociedad Geográfica de Lima, Vols. 7 and 8, 1898-1900. They represent the conditions at three observation hours during the summers (Dec., Jan.) of 1897-1898, 1898-1899, 1899-1900 and the winters (June, July) of 1898 and 1899.

doubtless by convectional rising, causes ascent of the comparatively humid air and the formation of cloud. Farther eastward, as the topographic influence is more strongly felt, the cloudiness

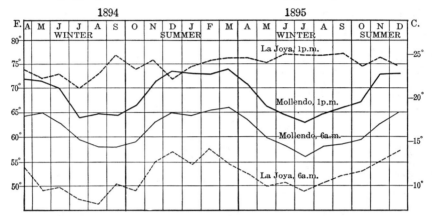

FIG. 85—Temperature curves for Mollendo (solid lines) and La Joya (broken lines) April, 1894, to December, 1895, drawn from data in Peruvian Meteorology, 1892-1895, Annals of the Astronomical Observatory of Harvard College, Vol. 49, Pt. 2, Cambridge, Mass., 1908. The approximation of the two curves of maximum temperature during the winter months contrasts with the well-maintained difference in minimum temperatures throughout the year.

increases until on the border zone, about 8,000 feet in elevation, it may thicken to actual rain. Data have been selected to demonstrate this eastern gradation of meteorological phenomena.

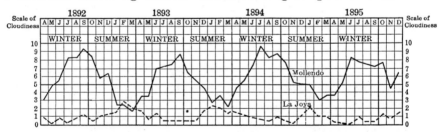

FIG. 86—Mean monthly cloudiness for Mollendo (solid line) and La Joya (broken line) from April, 1892, to December, 1895. Mollendo, 80 feet elevation, has the maximum winter cloudiness characteristic of the seaward slope of the Coast Range (compare Fig. 82) while the desert station of La Joya, 4,140 feet elevation, has typical summer cloudiness (compare Fig. 83). Figures are drawn from data in Peruvian Meteorology, 1892-1895, Annals of the Astronomical Observatory of Harvard College, Vol. 49, Pt. 2, Cambridge, Mass., 1908.

At La Joya, a station on the desert northeast of Mollendo at an elevation of 4,140 feet, cloudiness is always slight, but it increases markedly during the summer. Caraveli, at an altitude of

5,635 feet,[2] and near the eastern border of the pampa, exhibits a tendency toward the climatic characteristics of the adjacent zone. Data for a camp station out on the pampa a few leagues from the town, were collected by Mr. J. P. Little of the staff of the

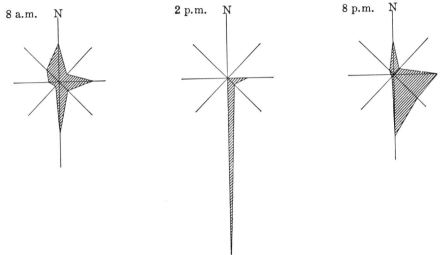

8 a.m.   N   2 p.m.   N   8 p.m.   N

FIG. 87—Wind roses for La Joya for the period April, 1892, to December, 1895. Compare the strong afternoon indraught from the south with the same phenomenon at Mollendo, Fig. 79. Figures drawn from data in Peruvian Meteorology, 1892-1895, Annals of the Astronomical Observatory of Harvard College, Vol. 39, Pt. 2, Cambridge, Mass., 1906.

Peruvian Expedition of 1912-13. They relate to the period January to March, 1913. Wind roses for these months show the characteristic light northwesterly winds of the early morning hours, in sharp contrast with the strong south and southwesterly indraught of the afternoon. The daily march of cloudiness is closely coördinated. Quotations from Mr. Little's field notes follow:

"In the morning there is seldom any noticeable wind. A breeze starts at 10 A. M., generally about 180° (i. e. due south), increases to 2 or 3 velocity at noon, having veered some 25° to the southwest. It reaches a maximum velocity of 3 to 4 at about 4.00 P. M., now coming about 225° (i. e. southwest). By 6 P. M. the wind

---

[2] This is the elevation obtained by the Peruvian Expedition. Raimondi's figure (1,832 m.) is higher.

has died down considerably and the evenings are entirely free from it. The wind action is about the same every day. It is not a cold wind and, except with the fog, not a damp one, for I have not worn a coat in it for three weeks. It has a free unobstructed sweep across fairly level pampas. . . . At an interval of every three or four days a dense fog sweeps up from the southwest, dense enough for one to be easily lost in it. It seldom makes even

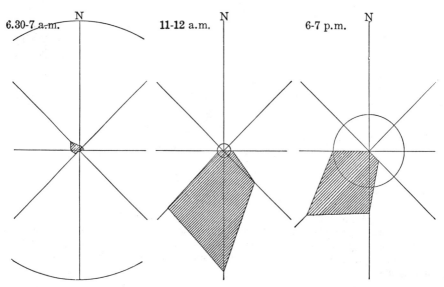

FIG. 88—Wind roses for a station on the eastern border of the Coast Desert near Caraveli during the summer (January to March) of 1913. Compare with Fig. 87. The diameter of the circle in each case represents the proportion of calm. Note the characteristic morning calm.

a sprinkle of rain, but carries heavy moisture and will wet a man on horseback in 10 minutes. It starts about 3 P. M. and clears away by 8.00 P. M. . . . During January, rain fell in camp twice on successive days, starting at 3.00 P. M. and ceasing at 8.00 P. M. It was merely a light, steady rain, more the outcome of a dense fog than a rain-cloud of quick approach. In Caraveli, itself, I am told that it rains off and on all during the month in short, light showers." This record is dated early in February and, in later notes, that month and March are recorded rainless.

Chosica (elevation 6,600 feet), one of the meteorological stations of the Harvard Astronomical Observatory, is still nearer the border. It also lies farther north, approximately in the latitude of Lima, and this in part may help to explain the greater cloudiness and rainfall. The rainfall for the year 1889-1890 was 6.14 inches, of which 3.94 fell in February. During the winter months when the principal wind observations were taken, over 90 per cent showed noon winds from a southerly direction while in the early

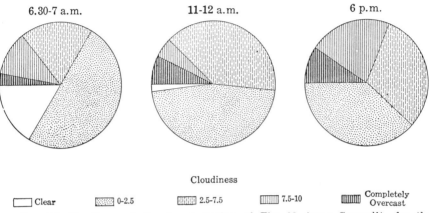

Cloudiness

☐ Clear   ▦ 0-2.5   ▦ 2.5-7.5   ▥ 7.5-10   ▥ Completely Overcast

FIG. 89—Cloudiness at the desert station of Fig. 88 (near Caraveli), for the summer (January to March) of 1913.

morning northerly winds were frequent. It is also noteworthy that the "directions of the upper currents of the atmosphere as recorded by the motion of the clouds was generally between N. and E." Plainly we are in the border region where climatic influences are carried over from the plateau and combine their effects with those from Pacific sources. Arequipa, farther south, and at an altitude of 7,550 feet, resembles Chosica. For the years 1892 to 1895 its mean rainfall was 5.4 inches.

Besides the seasonal variations of precipitation there are longer periodic variations that are of critical importance on the Coast Range. At times of rather regular recurrence, rains that are heavy and general fall there. Every six or eight years is said to be a period of rain, but the rains are also said to occur sometimes at intervals of four years or ten years. The regularity is only approximate. The years of heaviest rain are commonly associated with an unusual frequency of winds from the north, and an abnormal development of the warm current, El Niño, from the

THE ANDES OF SOUTHERN PERU

Gulf of Guayaquil. Such was the case in the phenomenally rainy year of 1891. The connection is obscure, but undoubtedly exists.

The effects of the heavy rains are amazing and appear the more so because of the extreme aridity of the country east of them. During the winter the desert traveler finds the air temperature rising to uncomfortable levels. Vegetation of any sort may be completely lacking. As he approaches the leeward slope of the Coast Range, a cloud mantle full of refreshing promise may be seen just peeping over the crest (Fig. 91). Long, slender cloud filaments project eastward over the margin of the desert. They are traveling rapidly but they never advance far over the hot wastes, for their eastern margins are constantly undergoing evaporation. At times the top of the cloud bank rises

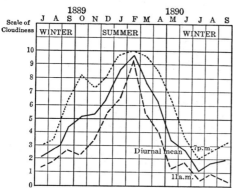

Fig. 90—Cloudiness at Chosica, July, 1889, to September, 1890. Chosica, a station on the Oroya railroad east of Lima, is situated on the border region between the desert zone of the coast and the mountain zone of yearly rains. The minimum cloudiness recorded about 11 a. m. is shown by a broken line; the maximum cloudiness, about 7 p. m., by a dotted line, and the mean for the 24 hours by a heavy solid line. The curves are drawn from data in Peruvian Meteorology, 1889-1890, Annals of the Astronomical Observatory of Harvard College, Vol. 39, Pt. 1, Cambridge, Mass., 1899.

well above the crest of the Coast Range, and it seems to the man from the temperate zone as if a great thunderstorm were rising in the west. But for all their menace of wind and rain the clouds never get beyond the desert outposts. In the summer season the aspect changes, the heavy yellow sky of the desert displaces the murk of the coastal mountains and the bordering sea.

It is an age-old strife renewed every year and limited to a narrow field of action, wonderfully easy to observe. We saw it in its most striking form at the end of the winter season in October, 1911, and for more than a day watched the dark clouds rise ominously only to melt into nothing where the desert holds sway. At night we camped beside a scum-coated pool of alkali water no larger than a wash basin. It lay in a valley that headed in the Coast Range, and carried down into the desert a mere trickle that seeped through the gravels of the valley floor. A little below the pool the valley cuts through a mass of granite and becomes a steep-walled gorge. The bottom is clogged with waste, here boulders, there masses of both coarse and fine alluvium. The water in the valley was quite incapable of accomplishing any work except that associated with solution and seepage, and we saw it in the wet season of an unusually wet year. Clearly there has been a diminution in the water supply. But time prevented us from exploring this particular valley to its head, to see if the reduction were due to a change of climate, or only to capture of the head-waters by the vigorous rain-fed streams that enjoy a favorable position on the wet seaward slopes and that are extending their watershed aggressively toward the east at the expense of their feeble competitors in the dry belt.

An early morning start enabled me to witness the whole series of changes between the clear night and the murky day, and to pass in twelve hours from the dry desert belt through the wet belt, and emerge again into the sunlit terraces at the western foot of the Coast Range. Two hours before daylight a fog descended from the hills and the going seemed to be curiously heavy for the beasts. At daybreak my astonishment was great to find that it was due to the distinctly moist sand. We were still in the desert. There was not a sign of a bush or a blade of grass. Still, the surface layer, from a half inch to an inch thick, was really wet. The fog that overhung the trail lifted just before sunrise, and at the first touch of the sun melted away as swiftly as it had come. With it went the surface moisture and an hour after sunrise the dust was once more rising in clouds around us.

We had no more than broken camp that morning when a merchant with a pack-train passed us, and shouted above the bells of the leading animals that we ought to hurry or we should get caught in the rain at the pass. My guide, who, like many of his kind, had never before been over the route he pretended to know, asked him in heaven's name what drink in distant Camaná whence he had come produced such astonishing effects as to make a man talk about rain in a parched desert. We all fell to laughing and at our banter the stranger stopped his pack-train and earnestly urged us to hurry, for, he said, the rains beyond the pass were exceptionally heavy this year. We rode on in a doubtful state of mind. I had heard about the rains, but I could not believe that they fell in real showers!

About noon the cloud bank darkened and overhung the border of the desert. Still the sky above us was clear. Then happened what I can yet scarcely believe. We rode into the head of a tiny valley that had cut right across the coast chain. A wisp of cloud, an outlier of the main bank, lay directly ahead of us. There were grass and bushes not a half-mile below the bare dry spot on which we stood. We were riding down toward them when of a sudden the wind freshened and the cloud wisp enveloped us, shutting out the view, and ten minutes later the moisture had gathered in little beads on the manes of our beasts and the trail became slippery. In a half-hour it was raining and in an hour we were in the midst of a heavy downpour. We stopped and pastured our famished beasts in luxuriant clover. While they gorged themselves a herd of cattle drifted along, and a startled band of burros that suddenly confronted our beasts scampered out of sight in the heavy mist. Later we passed a herdsman's hut and long before we reached him he shouted to us to alter our course, for just ahead the old trail was wet and treacherous at this time of year. The warning came too late. Several of our beasts lost their footing and half rolled, half slid, down hill. One turned completely over, pack and all, and lay in the soft mud calmly taking advantage of the delay to pluck a few additional mouthfuls of grass. We were glad to reach firmer ground on the other side of the valley.

The herdsmen were a hospitable lot. They had come from Camaná and rarely saw travelers. Their single-roomed hut was mired so deeply that one found it hard to decide whether to take shelter from the rain inside or escape the mud by standing in the rain outside. They made a little so-called cheese, rounded up and counted the cattle on clear days, drove them to the springs from time to time, and talked incessantly of the wretched rains in the hills and the delights of dry Camaná down on the coast. We could not believe that only some hours' traveling separated two localities so wholly unlike.

The heavy showers and luxuriant pastures of the wet years and the light local rains of the dry years endow the Coast Range with many peculiar geographic qualities. The heavy rains provide the desert people at the foot of the mountains such a wealth of pasture for their burdensome stock as many oases dwellers possess only in their dreams. From near and far cattle are driven to the wet hill meadows. Some are even brought in from distant valleys by sea, yet only a very small part of the rich pastures can be used. It is safe to say that they could comfortably support ten times the number of cattle, mules, and burros that actually graze upon them. The grass would be cut for export if the weather were not so continually wet and if there were not so great a mixture of weeds, flowers, and shrubs.

Then come the dry years. The surplus stock is sold, and what remains is always maintained at great expense. In 1907 I saw stock grazing in a small patch of dried vegetation back of Mollendo, although they had to be driven several miles to water. They looked as if they were surviving with the greatest difficulty and their restless search for pasture was like the search of a desperate hunter of game. In 1911 the same tract was quite devoid of grass, and except for the contour-like trails that completely covered the hills no one would even guess that this had formerly been a cattle range. The same year, but five months later, a carpet of grass, bathed in heavy mist, covered the soil; a trickle of water had collected in pools on the valley floor; several happy families from the town had laid out a prosperous-looking garden; there were romping children who showed me where to pick up the trail to the port; on every hand was life and activity because the rains had returned bringing plenty in their train. I asked a native how often he was prosperous.

"Segun el temporal y la Providencia" (according to the

weather and to Providence), he replied, as he pointed significantly
to the pretty green hills crowned with gray mist.

It, therefore, seems fortunate that the Coast Range is so placed
as to intercept and concentrate a part of the moisture that the sea-
winds carry, and doubly fortunate that its location is but a few
miles from the coast, thereby giving temporary relief to the relatively crowded people of the lower irrigated valleys and the towns.
The wet years formerly developed a crop of prospectors. Pack
animals are cheaper when there is good pasture and they are also
easier to maintain. So when the rains came the hopeful pick-and-
shovel amateurs began to emigrate from the towns to search for
ore among the discolored bands of rock intruded into the granite
masses of the coastal hills. However, the most likely spots have
been so thoroughly and so unsuccessfully prospected for many
years that there is no longer any interest in the "mines."

Transportation rates are still most intimately related to the
rains. My guide had two prices—a high price if I proposed to
enter a town at night and thus require him to buy expensive
forage; a low price if I camped in the hills and reached the town
in time for him to return to the hills with his animals. Inquiry
showed that this was the regular custom. I also learned that in
packing goods from one part of the coast to another forage must
be carried in dry years or the beasts required to do without.
In wet years by a very slight detour the packer has his beasts in
good pasture that is free for all. The merchant who dispatches
the goods may find his charges nearly doubled in extremely dry
years. Goods are more expensive and there is a decreased con-
sumption. The effects of the rains are thus transmitted from one
to another, until at last nearly all the members of a community
are bearing a share of the burdens imposed by drought. As always there are a few who prosper in spite of the ill wind. If the
pastures fail, live stock *must* be sold and the dealers ship south
to the nitrate ports or north to the large coast towns of Peru,
where there is always a demand. Their business is most active
when it is dry or rather at the beginning of the dry period. Also
if transport by land routes becomes too expensive the small trad-

ers turn to the sea routes and the carriers have an increased business. But so far as I have been able to learn, dry years favor only a few scattered individuals.

To the traveler on the west coast it is a source of constant surprise that the sky is so often overcast and the ports hidden by fog, while on every hand there are clear evidences of extreme aridity. Likewise it is often inquired why the sunsets there should be often so superlatively beautiful during the winter months when the coast is fog bound. Why a desert when the air is so humid? Why striking sunsets when so many of the days are marked by dull skies? As we have seen in the first part of this chapter, the big desert tracts lie east of the Coast Range, and there, excepting slight summer cloudiness, cloudless skies are the rule. The desert just back of the coast is in many parts of Peru only a narrow fringe of dry marine terraces quite unlike the real desert in type of weather and in resources. The fog bank overhanging it forms over the Humboldt Current which lies off shore; it drifts landward with the onshore wind; it forms over the upwelling cold water between the current and the shore; it gathers on the seaward slopes of the coastal hills as the inflowing air ascends them in its journey eastward. Sometimes it lies on the surface of the land and the water; more frequently it is some distance above them. On many parts of the coast its characteristic position is from 2,000 to 4,000 feet above sea level, descending at night nearly or quite to the surface, ascending by day and sometimes all but disappearing except as rain-clouds on the hills.[3] Upon the local behavior of the fog bank depends in large measure the local climate. A general description of the coastal climate will have many

---

[3] According to Ward's observations the base of the cloud belt averages between 2,000 and 3,000 feet above sea level (Climatic Notes Made During a Voyage Around South America, Journ. of School Geogr., Vol. 2, 1898). On the south Peruvian coast, specifically at Mollendo, Middendorf found the cloud belt beginning about 1,000 feet and extending upwards to elevations of 3,000 to 4,000 feet. At Lima the clouds descend to lower levels (El Clima de Lima, Bol. Soc. Geogr. de Lima, Vol. 15, 1904). In the third edition of his Süd- und Mittelamerika (Leipzig and Vienna, 1914) Sievers says that at Lima in the winter the cloud on the coast does not exceed an elevation of 450 m. (1,500 feet) while on the hills it lies at elevations between 300 and 700 m. (1,000 and 2,300 feet).

exceptions. The physical principles involved are, however, the same everywhere. I take for discussion therefore the case illustrated by Fig. 92, since this also displays with reasonable fidelity the conditions along that part of the Peruvian coast between Camaná and Mollendo which lies in the field of work of the Yale Peruvian Expedition of 1911.

Three typical positions of the fog bank are shown in the figure, and a fourth—that in which the bank extends indefinitely westward—may be supplied by the imagination.

If the cloud bank be limited to C only the early morning hours at the port are cloudy. If it extend to B the sun is obscured until midday. If it reach as far west as A only a few late afternoon hours are sunny. Once in a while there is a sudden splash of rain —a few drops which astonish the traveler who looks out upon a parched landscape. The smaller drops are evaporated before reaching the earth. In spite of the ever-present threat of rain the coast is extremely arid. Though the vegetation appears to be dried and burned up, the air is humid and for months the sky may be overcast most of the time. So nicely are the rain-making conditions balanced that if one of our ordinary low-pressure areas, or so-called cyclonic storms, from the temperate zone were set in motion along the foot of the mountains, the resulting deluge would immediately lay the coast in ruins. The cane-thatched, mud-walled huts and houses would crumble in the heavy rain like a child's sand pile before a rising sea; the alluvial valley land would be coated with infertile gravel; and mighty rivers of sand, now delicately poised on arid slopes, would inundate large tracts of fertile soil.

If the fog and cloud bank extend westward indefinitely, the entire day may be overcast or the sun appear for a few moments only through occasional rifts. Generally, also, it will make an appearance just before sunset, its red disk completely filling the narrow space between the under surface of the clouds and the water. I have repeatedly seen the ship's passengers and even the crew leave the dinner table and collect in wondering groups about the port-holes and doorways the better to see the marvelous play of

FIG. 91.

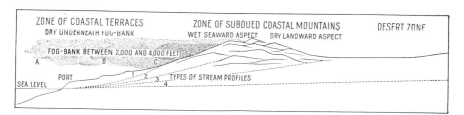

FIG. 92.

FIG. 91—Looking down the canyon of the Majes River to the edge of the cloud bank formed against the Coast Range back of Camaná.

FIG. 92—Topographic and climatic cross-section to show the varying positions of the cloud bank on the coast of Peru, the dry terrace region, and the types of stream profiles in the various belts.

colors between sky and sea. It is impossible not to be profoundly moved by so majestic a scene. A long resplendent path of light upon the water is reflected in the clouds. Each cloud margin is tinged with red and, as the sun sinks, the long parallel bands of light are shortened westward, changing in color as they go, until at last the full glory of the sunset is concentrated in a blazing arc of reds, yellows, and purples, that to most people quite atones for the dull gray day and its humid air.

At times the clouds are broken up by the winds and scattered helter-skelter through the west. A few of them may stray into the path of the sun temporarily to hide it and to reflect its primary colors when the sun reappears. From the main cloud masses there reach out slender wind-blown streamers, each one delicately lighted as the sun's rays filter through its minute water particles. Many streamers are visible for only a short distance, but when the sun catches them their filmy invisible fingers become delicate bands of light, some of which rapidly grow out almost to the dome of the sky. Slowly they retreat and again disappear as the rays of the sun are gradually shut off by the upturning curve of the earth.

The unequal distribution of precipitation in the climatic zones of western Peru has important hydrographic consequences. These will now be considered. In the preceding figure four types of stream profiles are displayed and each has its particular relation to the cloud bank. Stream 1 is formed wholly upon the coastal terraces beneath the cloud bank. It came into existence only after the uplift of the earth's crust that brought the wave-cut platforms above sea level. It is extremely youthful and on account first of the small seepage at its headquarters—it is elsewhere wholly without a tributary water supply—and, second, of the resistant granite that occurs along this part of the coast, it has very steep and irregular walls and an ungraded floor. Many of these "quebradas" are difficult to cross. A few of them have fences built across their floors to prevent the escape of cattle and burros that wander down from the grassy hills into the desert zone. Others are partitioned off into corrals by stone fences, the steep walls of the gorge preventing the escape of the cattle. To these are driven the market cattle, or mules and burros that are required for relays along the shore trail.

Stream 2 heads in the belt of rains. Furthermore it is a much older stream than 1, since it dates back to the time when the Coast Range was first formed. It has ample tributary slopes and a large number of small valleys. A trickle of water flows down to become lost in the alluvium of the lower part of the valley or to reappear in scattered springs. Where springs and seepage occur together, an olive grove or a garden marks the spot, a corral or two and a mud or stone or reed hut is near by, and there is a tiny oasis. Some of these dots of verdure become so dry during a prolonged drought that the people, long-established, move away. To others the people return periodically. Still others support permanent settlements.

Stream 3 has still greater age. Its only competitors are the feeble, almost negligible, streams that at long intervals flow east toward the dry zone. Hence it has cut back until it now heads in the desert. Its widely branched tributaries gather moisture from large tracts. There is running water in the valley floor even down in the terrace zone. At least there are many dependable springs and the permanent homes that they always encourage. A valley of this type is always marked by a well-defined trail that leads from settlement to settlement and eastward over the "pass" to the desert and the Andean towns.

Stream 4 is a so-called "antecedent" stream. It existed before the Coast Range was uplifted and cut its channel downward as the mountains rose in its path. The stretch where it crosses the mountains may be a canyon with a narrow, rocky, and uncultivable floor, so that the valley trails rise to a pass like that at the head of stream 3, and descend again to the settlements at the mouth of 4. There is in this last type an abundance of water, for the sources of the stream are in the zone of permanent snows and frequent winter rains of the lofty Cordillera of the Andes. The settlements along this stream are continuous, except where shut-ins occur—narrow, rocky defiles caused by more resistant rock

masses in the path of the stream. Here and there are villages.
The streams have fish. When the water rises the river may be
unfordable and people on opposite sides must resort to boats or
rafts.[4]

On windward mountain slopes there is always a belt of maximum precipitation whose elevation and width vary with the
strength of the wind, with the temperature, and with the topography. A strong and constant wind will produce a much more
marked concentration of the rainfall. The belt is at a low elevation in high latitudes and at a high elevation in low latitudes, with
many irregularities of position dependent upon the local and especially the minimum winter temperature. The topographic controls are important, since the rain-compelling elevation may scatter widely the localities of maximum precipitation or concentrate
them within extremely narrow limits. The human effects of these
climatic conditions are manifold. Wherever the heaviest rains
are, there, too, as a rule, are the densest forests and often the
most valuable kinds of trees. If the general climate be favorable
and the region lie near dense and advanced populations, exploitation of the forest and progress of the people will go hand in hand.
If the region be remote and some or all of the people in a primitive state, the forest may hinder communication and retard development, especially if it lie in a hot zone where the natural growth
of population is slow. . . . These are some of the considerations
we shall keep in mind while investigating the climate of the eastern border of the Peruvian Andes.

The belt of maximum precipitation on the eastern border of
the Andean Cordillera in Peru lies between 4,000 and 10,000 feet.
Judging by the temporary records of the expedition and especially

---

[4] In most of the coast towns the ford or ferry is an important institution and the
chimbadores or *baleadores* as they are called are expert at their trade: they know
the régime of the rivers to a nicety. Several settlements owe their origin to the
exigencies of transportation, permanent and periodic; thus before the development of
its irrigation system Camaná, according to General Miller (Memoirs, London, 1829,
Vol. 2, p. 27), was a hamlet of some 30 people who gained their livelihood through
ferrying freight and passengers across the Majes River.

by the types of forest growth, the heaviest rains occur around 8,000 feet. It is between these elevations that the densest part of the Peruvian *montaña* (forest) is found. The cold timber line is at 10,500 feet with exceptional extensions of a few species to

FIG. 93A—Cloud types and rainfall belts on the eastern border of the Peruvian Andes in the dry season, southern winter. The zone of maximum rainfall extends approximately from 4,000 to 10,000 feet elevation.

12,500 feet. In basins or deep secluded valleys near the mountain border, a dry timber line occurs at 3,000 feet with many variations in elevation due to the variable declivity and exposure of the slopes and degree of seclusion of the valleys. Elsewhere, the

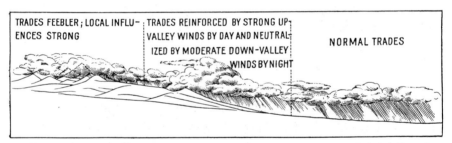

FIG. 93B—Cloud types and rainfall belts on the eastern border of the Peruvian Andes in the wet season, southern summer.

mountain forest passes without a break into the plains forest with change in type but with little change in density. The procumbent and suppressed trees of the cold timber line in regions of heavy winter snows are here absent, for the snows rarely reach below 14,000 feet and even at that elevation they are only light and temporary. The line of perpetual snow is at 15,000 feet. This permanent gap of several thousand feet vertical elevation between the zone of snow and the zone of forest permits the full extension of many pioneer forest species, which is to say, there is an irregular development of the cold timber line. It also permits the full use of the pasture belt above the timber (Fig. 97), hence permanent habitations exist but little below the snowline and a group of distinctive high-mountain folk enjoys a wide distribution. There is a seasonal migration here, but it is not wholesale; there are pastures snow-covered in the southern winter, but, instead of the complete winter burial of the Alpine meadows of our western mountains, we have here only a buried upper fringe. All the rest of the pasture belt is open for stock the year round.

This climatic distinction between the lofty grazing lands of the tropics and those of the temperate zones is far-reaching. Our mountain forests are not utilized from above but from below. Furthermore, the chief ways of communication lead around our forests, or, if through them, only for the purpose of putting one population group in closer touch with another. In the Peruvian Andes the largest population groups live above the forest, not below it or within it. It must be and is exploited from above.

Hence railways to the eastern valleys of Peru have two chief objects, (1) to get the plantation product to the dense populations above the forest and (2) to bring timber from the *montaña* to the treeless plateau. The mountain prospector is always near a habitation; the rubber prospector goes down into the forested valleys and plains far from habitations. The forest separates the navigable streams from the chief towns of the plateau; it does not lead down to rich and densely populated valley floors.

Students in eastern Peru should find it a little difficult to understand poetical allusions to silent and lonely highlands in contrast to the busy life of the valleys. To them Shelley's description of the view from the Euganean Hills of northern Italy,

> " Beneath is spread like a green sea
> The waveless plain of Lombardy, . . .
> Islanded by cities fair,"

might well seem to refer to a world that is upside down.

There is much variation in the forest types between the mountains and the plains. At the top of the forest zone the warm sunny slopes have a forest cover; the shady slopes are treeless. At the lower edge of the grassland, only the shady slopes are forested (Fig. 53B). Cacti of arboreal size and form grow on the lofty mountains far above the limits of the true forest; they also appear at 3,000 feet in modified form, large, rank, soft-spined, and in dense stands on the semi-arid valley floors below the dry timber line. Large tracts between 8,000 and 10,000 feet are covered with a forest growth distributed by species—here a dense stand of one type of tree, there another. This is the most accessible part of the Peruvian forest and along the larger valleys it is utilized to some extent. The number of species is more limited, however, and the best timber trees are lower down. Though often referred to as jungle, the lowlier growths at the upper edge of the forest zone have no resemblance to the true jungle that crowds the lowland forest. They are merely an undergrowth, generally open, though in some places dense. They are nowhere more dense than many examples from New England or the West.

Where deep valleys occur near the border of the mountains there is a semi-arid climate below and a wet climate above, with a correspondingly greater number of species within short distances of each other. This is a far more varied forest than at the upper edge of the timber zone or down on the monotonous plains. It has a higher intrinsic value than any other. That part of it between the Pongo and Yavero (1,200 to 4,000 feet) is very beautiful, with little undergrowth except a light ground-cover of ferns. The trees are from 40 to 100 feet in height with an average diameter of about 15 inches. It would yield from 3,000 to 5,000 board feet per acre exclusive of the palms. There are very few vines suspended from the forest crown and the trunks run clear from 30 to 60 feet above the ground. Were there plenty of labor and a good transportation line, these stands would have high economic value. Among the most noteworthy trees are the soft white cedar, strong and light; the amarillo and the sumbayllo, very durable in water; the black nogal, and the black balsam, straight and easy to work; the heavy yunquero, which turns pink when dry; the chunta or black palm, so hard and straight and easy to split

FIG. 94.

FIG. 95.

FIG. 94—Cloud belt at 11,000 feet in the Apurimac Canyon near Incahuasi. For a regional diagram and a climatic cross-section see Figs. 32 and 33.

FIG. 95—The tropical forest near Pabellon on the slopes of the Urubamba Valley. Elevation 3,000 feet (915 m.).

that wooden nails are made from it; and the rarer sandy matico, highly prized for dug-out canoes. Also from the chunta palm, hollow except for a few central fibers, easily removed, pipes are made to convey water. The cocobolo has a rich brown color and a glossy surface and is very rare, hence is much sought after for use in furniture making. Most of these woods take a brilliant polish and exhibit a richness and depth of color and a beauty of grain that are rare among our northern woods.

The plains forest northeast of the mountains is in the zone of moderate rainfall where there is one long dry season and one long wet season. When it is dry the daytime temperatures rise rapidly to such high levels that the relative humidity of the air falls below 50 per cent (Fig. 110). The effect on the vegetation is so marked that many plants pass into a distinctly wilted condition. On clear days the rapid fall in the relative humidity is astonishing. By contrast the air on the mountain border heats more slowly and has a higher relative humidity, because clouds form almost constantly in the ascending air currents and reflect and absorb a large part of the heat of the sun's rays. It is striking to find large tracts of cane and bamboo on the sand bars and on wet shady hillslopes in the slope belt, and to pass out of them in going to the plains with which we generally associate a swamp vegetation. They exist on the plains, but only in favored, that is to say wet, spots. Larger and more typical tracts grow farther north where the heavier rains of the Amazon basin fall.

The floods of the wet tropical season also have a restricting influence upon the tropical forest. They deliver such vast quantities of water to the low-gradient lowland streams that the plains rivers double, even treble, their width and huge pools and even temporary lakes form in the shallow depressions back of the natural levees. Of trees in the flooded areas there are only those few species that can grow standing in water several months each year. There are also cane and bamboo, ferns in unlimited numbers, and a dense growth of jungle. These are the haunts of the peccary, the red forest deer, and the jungle cat. Except along the narrow and tortuous animal trails the country is quite impassable. Thus for the sturdiest and most useful forest growth the one-wet-one-dry season zone of the plains has alternately too much and too little water. The rubber tree is most tolerant toward these conditions. Some of the best stands of rubber trees in Amazonia are in the southwestern part of the basin of eastern Peru and Bolivia, where there is the most typical development of the habitat marked by the seasonal alternation of floods and high temperatures.

When tropical agriculture is extended to the plains the long dry season will be found greatly to favor it. The southwestern quadrant of the Amazon basin, above referred to, is the best agricultural area within it. The northern limits of the tract are only a little beyond the Pongo. Thence northward the climate becomes wetter. Indeed the best tracts of all extend from Bolivia only a little way into southeastern Peru, and are coincident with the patchy grasslands that are there interspersed with belts of woodland and forest. Sugar-cane is favored by a climate that permits rapid growth with a heavy rainfall and a dry season is required for quality and for the harvest. Rice and a multitude of vegetable crops are also well suited to this type of climate. Even corn can be grown in large quantities.

At the present time tropical agriculture is almost wholly confined to the mountain valleys. The reasons are not wholly climatic, as the above enumeration of the advantages of the plains suggests. The consuming centers are on the plateau toward the west and limitation to mule pack transport always makes distance in a rough country a very serious problem. The valleys combine with the advantage of a short haul a climate astonishingly like the one just described. In fact it is even more extreme in its seasonal contrasts. The explanation is dependent upon precisely the same principles we have hitherto employed. The front range of the Andes and the course of the Urubamba run parallel for some distance. Further, the front range is in many places somewhat higher than the mountain spurs and knobs directly behind it. Even when these relations are reversed the front range still acts as a barrier to the rains for all the deep valleys behind it whose courses are not directly toward the plains. Thus, one of the largest valleys in Peru, the Urubamba, drops to 3,400 feet at Santa Ana and to 2,000 feet at Rosalina, well within the eastern scarp of the Andes. The mountains immediately about it are from 6,000 to 10,000 feet high. The result is a deep semi-arid pocket with only a patchy forest (Fig. 54, p. 79).[5] In places the degree of seclusion from the wind is so great that the scrub, cacti, and irrigation remind one strongly of the desert on the border of an oasis, only here the transition is toward forests instead of barren wastes. The dense forest, or *montaña,* grows in the zone of clouds and maximum precipitation between 4,000 and 10,000 feet. At the lower limit it descends a thousand feet farther on shady slopes than it does on sunny slopes. The continuous forest is so closely restricted to the cloud belt that in Fig. 99 the two limits may be seen in one photograph. All these sharply defined limits and contrasts are due to the fact that the broad valley, discharging through a narrow and remote gorge, is really to leeward of all the mountains around it. It is like a real desert basin except in a lesser degree of exclusion from the rains. If it were narrow and small the rains formed on the surrounding heights would be carried over into it. Rain on the hills and sunshine in the valley is actually the day-by-day weather of the dry season. In the wet season the sky is overcast, the rains are general, though lighter in the valley pocket, and plants there have then their season of most rapid growth. The dry season brings plants to maturity and is the time of harvest. Hence sugar and cacao plantations on a large scale, hence a varied life in a restricted area, hence a distinct geographic province unique in South America.

INTER-ANDEAN VALLEY CLIMATES

Not all the deep Andean valleys lie on or near the eastern border. Some, like the Apurimac and the Marañon, extend well

---

[5] A dry pocket in the Huallaga basin between 6° and 7° S. is described by Spruce (Notes of a Botanist on the Amazon and Andes, 2 vols., London, 1908). Tarapoto at an elevation of 1,500 feet above sea level, encircled by hills rising 2,000 to 3,000 feet higher, rarely experiences heavy rain though rain falls frequently on the hills.

into the interior of the Cordillera. Besides these deep remote valleys with their distinct climatic belts are basins, most of them with outlets to the sea—broad structural depressions occurring in some cases along large and in others along small drainage lines. The Cuzco basin at 11,000 feet and the Abancay basin at 6,000 to 8,000 feet are typical. Both have abrupt borders, narrow outlets, large bordering alluvial fans, and fertile irrigable soil. Their difference of elevation occurs at a critical level. Corn will ripen in the Cuzco basin, but cane will not. Barley, wheat, and potatoes are the staple crops in the one; sugar-cane, alfalfa, and fruit in the other. Since both are bordered by high pastures and by mineralized rocks, the deeper Abancay basin is more varied. If it were not so difficult to get its products to market by reason of its inaccessibility, the Abancay basin would be the more important. In both areas there is less rainfall on the basin floor than on the surrounding hills and mountains, and irrigation is practised, but the deeper drier basin is the more dependent upon it. Many small high basins are only within the limits of potato cultivation. They also receive proportionately more rain. Hence irrigation is unnecessary. According as the various basins take in one or another of the different product levels (Fig. 35) their life is meager and unimportant or rich and interesting.

The deep-valley type of climate has the basin factors more strongly developed. Below the Canyon of Choqquequirau, a topographic feature comparable with the Canyon of Torontoy, the Apurimac descends to 3,000 feet, broadens to several miles, and has large alluvial fans built into it. Its floor is really arid, with naked gravel and rock, cacti stands, and gnarled shrubs as the chief elements of the landscape. Moreover the lower part of the valley is the steeper. A former erosion level is indicated in Fig. 125. When it was in existence the slopes were more moderate than now and the valley broad and open. Thereupon came uplift and the incision of the stream to its present level. As a result, a steep canyon was cut in the floor of a mature valley. Hence the slopes are in a relation unlike that of most of the slopes in our most familiar landscapes. The gentle slopes are above, the steep be-

FIG. 96—Snow-capped mountain, Soirococha, north of Arma, Cordillera Vilcapampa. The blue glacier ice descends almost to the edge of a belt of extraordinary woodland growing just under the snowline. The glacier is seen to overhang the valley and to have built on the steep valley wall terminal moraines whose outer slopes are almost precipitous.

FIG. 97—Shrubby vegetation mixed with grass at 14,000 feet (4,270 m.) on the northern or sunny slopes of the Cordillera Vilcapampa above Pampaconas, a thousand feet below the snowline. The grass is remarkably profuse and supports the flocks and herds of a pastoral population.

Fig. 99.—The Urubamba Valley below Santa Ana. On the dry valley floor is a mixed growth of scattered trees, shrubs and grass, with shrubs predominating. Higher up a more luxuriant ravine vegetation appears. On the upper spurs true forest patches occupy the shady slopes. Finally, in the zone of clouds at the top of the picture is a continuous forest. See Fig. 17, for regional applications.

Fig. 98.—Dense ground cover, typical trees, epiphytes, and parasites of the tropical rain forest at 2,500-3,000 feet between Pongo de Mainique and Rosalina.

low. The break between the two, a topographic unconformity, may be distinctly traced.

Combined with these topographic features are certain climatic features of equal precision. Between 7,000 and 13,000 feet is a zone of clouds oftentimes marked out as distinctly as the belt of fog on the Peruvian coast.[6] Rarely does it extend across the valley. Generally it 'hangs as a white belt on the opposite walls. When the up-valley winds of day begin to blow it drifts up-valley, oftentimes to be dissolved as it strikes the warmer slopes of the upper valley, just as its settling under surface is constantly being dissolved in the warm dry air of the valley floor. Where the precipitation is heaviest there is a belt of woodland—dark, twisted trees, moss-draped, wet—a Druid forest. Below and above the woodland are grassy slopes. At Incahuasi a spur runs out and down until at last it terminates between two deep canyons. No ordinary wells could be successful. The ground water must be a thousand feet down, so a canal, a tiny thing only a few inches wide and deep, has been cut away up to a woodland stream. Thence the water is carried down by a contour-like course out of the woodland into the pasture, and so down to the narrow part of the spur where there is pasture but no springs or streams.

Corn fields surround the few scattered habitations that have been built just above the break or shoulder on the valley wall where the woodland terminates, and there are fine grazing lands. The trails follow the upper slopes whose gentler contours permit a certain liberty of movement. Then the way plunges downward over a staircase trail, over steep boulder-strewn slopes to the arid floor of a tributary where nature has built a graded route. And so to the still more arid floor of the main valley, where the ample and moderate slopes of the alluvial fans with their mountain streams permit plantation agriculture again to come in.

To these three climates, the western border type, the eastern

<hr>

[6] Speaking of Cómas situated at the headwaters of a source of the Perene amidst a multitude of *quebradas* Raimondi (op. cit., p. 109) says it "might properly be called the town of the clouds, for there is not a day during the year, at any rate towards the evening, when the town is not enveloped in a mist sufficient to hide everything from view."

border type, and the inter-Andean type, we have given chief attention because they have the most important human relations. The statistical records of the expedition as shown in the curves and the discussion that accompanies them give attention to those climatic features that are of theoretical rather than practical interest, and are largely concerned with the conventional expression of the facts of weather and climate. They are therefore combined in the following chapter which is devoted chiefly to a technical discussion of the meteorology as distinguished from the climatology of the Peruvian Andes.

CHAPTER X

METEOROLOGICAL RECORDS FROM THE PERUVIAN ANDES

INTRODUCTION

THE data in this chapter, on the weather and climate of the Peruvian Andes, were gathered under the usual difficulties that accompany the collection of records at camps scarcely ever pitched at the same elevation or with the same exposure two days in succession. Some of them, and I may add, the best, were contributed by volunteer observers at fixed stations. The observations are not confined to the field of the Yale Peruvian Expedition of 1911, but include also observations from Professor Hiram Bingham's Expeditions of 1912 and 1914-15, together with data from the Yale South American Expedition of 1907. In addition I have used observations supplied by the Morococha Mining Company through J. P. Little. Some hitherto unpublished observations from Cochabamba, Bolivia, gathered by Herr Krüger at considerable expense of money for instruments and of time from a large business, are also included, and he deserves the more credit for his generous gift of these data since they were collected for scientific purposes only and not in connection with enterprises in which they might be of pecuniary value. My only excuse to Herr Krüger for this long delay in publication (they were put into my hands in 1907) is that I have wanted to publish his data in a dignified form and also to use them for comparison with the data of other climatic provinces.

A further word to the reader seems necessary before he examines the following curves and tables. It would be somewhat audacious to assume that these short-term records have far-reaching importance. Much of their value lies in their organization with respect to the data already published on the climate of Peru. But since this would require a delay of several years in their publication it seems better to present them now in their simplest form. After all, the professional climatologist, to whom they are

157

chiefly of interest, scarcely needs to have such organization supplied to him. Then, too, we hope that there will become available in the next ten or fifteen years a vastly larger body of climatological facts from this region. When these have been collected we may look forward to a volume or a series of volumes on the "Climate of Peru," with full statistical tables and a complete discussion of them. That would seem to be the best time for the reproduction of the detailed statistics now on hand. It is only necessary that there shall be sufficient analysis of the data from time to time to give a general idea of their character and to indicate in what way the scope of the observations might profitably be extended. I have, therefore, taken from the available facts only such as seem to me of the most importance because of their unusual character or their special relations to the boundaries of plant provinces or of the so-called "natural regions" of geography.

Machu Picchu [1]

The following observations are of special interest in that they illustrate the weather during the southern winter and spring at the famous ruins of Machu Picchu in the Canyon of Torontoy. The elevation is 8,500 feet. The period they cover is too short to give more than a hint of the climate or of the weather for the year. It extends from August 20, 1912, to November 6, 1912 (79 days).

ANALYTICAL TABLE OF WIND DIRECTIONS, MACHU PICCHU, 1912

Direction of wind	Number of Observations					
	Aug. 20 7 a. m.	— 1 p. m.	Sept. 30 7 p. m.	Oct. 1 7 a. m.	— 1 p. m.	Nov. 6 7 p. m.
N.	5	2	5	2	—	—
N. W.	9	10	14	4	6	11
W.	—	1	2	2	2	4
S. W.	—	—	1	1	1	6
S.	—	—	1	—	—	2
S. E.	4	2	1	—	—	3
E.	6	3	3	12	4	4
N. E.	8	7	6	4	1	3
CALM	—	—	2	5	3	3

[1] Observer: E. C. Erdis of the 1912 and 1914-15 Expeditions.

Direction of wind	Percentages of Total Observations [2]					
	Aug. 20 7 a. m.	— 1 p. m.	Sept. 30 7 p. m.	Oct. 1 7 a. m.	— 1 p. m.	Nov. 6 7 p. m.
N.	15.6	8.0	14.2	6.7	——	——
N. W.	28.1	40.0	40.0	13.3	35.3	30.7
W.	——	4.0	5.7	6.7	11.8	11.1
S. W.	——	——	2.8	3.3	5.9	16.7
S.	——	——	2.8	——	——	5.5
S. E.	12.5	8.0	2.8	——	——	8.3
E.	18.8	12.0	8.6	40.0	23.5	11.1
N. E.	25.0	28.0	17.1	13.3	5.9	8.3
CALM	——	——	5.7	16.7	17.6	8.3

The high percentage of northwest winds during afternoon hours is due to the up-valley movement of the air common to almost all mountain borders. The air over a mountain slope is heated more than the free air at the same elevation over the plains (or

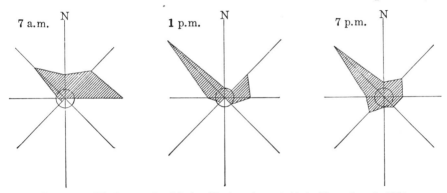

Fig. 100—Wind roses for Machu Picchu, August 20 to November 6, 1912.

lower valley); hence a barometric gradient towards the mountain becomes established. At Machu Picchu the Canyon of Torontoy trends northwest, making there a sharp turn from an equally sharp northeast bend directly upstream. The easterly components are unrelated to the topography. They represent the trades. If a wind rose were made for still earlier morning hours these winds would be more faithfully represented. That an easterly and northeasterly rather than a southeasterly direction should be assumed by the trades is not difficult to believe when we consider the trend of the Cordillera—southeast to northwest. The observa-

---

[2] Percentages given because the number of observations varies.

tions from here down to the plains all show that there is a distinct change in wind direction in sympathy with the larger features of the topography, especially the deep valleys and canyons, the trades coming in from the northeast.

CLOUDINESS

It will be seen that the sky was overcast or a fog lay in the valley 53 per cent of the time at early morning hours. Even at noon the sky was at no time clear, and it was more than 50 per cent clear only 18 per cent of the time. Yet this is the so-called "dry" season of the valleys of the eastern Andes. The rainfall record is in close sympathy. In the 79 days' observations rain is recorded on 50 days with a greater proportion from mid-September to the end of the period (November 6), a distinct transition toward the wet period that extends from December to May. The approximate distribution of the rains by hours of observation (7 A. M., 1 P. M., 7 P. M.) was in the ratio 4:3:6. Also the greatest number of heavy showers as well as the greatest number of showers took place in the evening. The rainfall was apparently unrelated to wind direction in the immediate locality, though undoubtedly associated with the regional movement of the moist plains air toward the mountains. All these facts regarding clouds and rain plainly show the location of the place in the belt of maximum precipitation. There is, therefore, a heavy cover of vegetation. While the situation is admirable for defence, the murky skies and frequent fogs somewhat offset its topographic surroundings as a lookout.

ANALYTICAL TABLE OF THE STATE OF THE SKY, MACHU PICCHU, 1912

	Morning		Total		Noon		Total		Evening		Total	
	Aug.-Sept.	Oct.-Nov.	Days	%	Aug.-Sept.	Oct.-Nov.	Days	%	Aug.-Sept.	Oct.-Nov.	Days	%
Foggy	3.0	14.0	17.0	28.4	1.0	——	1.0	2.6	1.0	2.0	3.0	4.3
Overcast	12.0	3.0	15.0	25.0	6.0	8.0	14.0	36.8	13.0	11.0	24.0	34.8
50-100% cloudy	4.0	10.0	14.0	23.3	9.0	7.0	16.0	42.2	8.0	15.0	23.0	33.3
0-50% cloudy	6.0	4.0	10.0	16.7	5.0	2.0	7.0	18.4	9.0	4.0	13.0	18.8
Clear	3.0	1.0	4.0	6.6	0.0	0.0	0.0	0.0	3.0	3.0	6.0	8.8

Santa Lucia [3]

Santa Lucia is a mining center in the province of Puno (16° S.), at the head of a valley here running northeast towards Lake Titicaca. Its elevation, 15,500 feet above sea level, confers on it unusual interest as a meteorological station. A thermograph has been installed which enables a closer study of the temperature to be made than in the case of the other stations. It is unfortunate, however, that the observations upon clouds, wind directions, etc., should not have been taken at regular hours. The time ranges from 8.30 to 11.30 for morning hours and from 2.30 to 5.30 for afternoon. The observations cover portions of the years 1913 and 1914.

TEMPERATURE

Perhaps the most striking features of the weather of Santa Lucia are the highly regular changes of temperature from night to day or the uniformly great diurnal range and the small differences of temperature from day to day or the low diurnal variability. For the whole period of nearly a year the diurnal variability never exceeds 9.5° F. (5.3° C.) and for days at a time it does not exceed 2-3° F. (1.1°-1.7° C.). The most frequent variation, occurring on 71 per cent of the total number of days, is from 0-3° F., and the mean for the year gives the low variability of 1.9° F. (1.06° C.). These facts, illustrative of a type of weather comparable in *uniformity* with low stations on the Amazon plains, are shown in the table following as well as in the accompanying curves.

FREQUENCY OF THE DIURNAL VARIABILITY, SANTA LUCIA, 1913-14

Degrees F.	May	June	July	Aug.	Sept.	Oct.	Nov.	Dec.	Jan.	Feb.	March	Total No. of days
0	—	2	6	3	4	6	2	—	1	—	2	26
0-1	2	7	7	5	6	4	8	12	14	9	5	79
1-2	11	5	7	11	7	8	5	5	4	9	13	85
2-3	2	8	8	9	3	7	7	5	5	4	6	64
3-4	4	4	2	1	4	1	3	6	2	4	2	33
4-5	1	3	1	—	2	1	3	—	2	1	1	15
Over 5	—	1	—	2	4	4	2	2	3	1	—	19
Days per month	20	30	31	31	30	31	30	30	31	28	29	321

[3] Observer: Señor Valdivia. For location of Santa Lucia see Fig. 66.

If we take the means of the diurnal variations by months we have a still more striking curve showing how little change there is between successive days. June and December are marked by humps in the curve. They are the months of extreme weather when for several weeks the temperatures drop to their lowest or climb to their highest levels. Moreover, there is at these lofty stations no pronounced lag of the maximum and minimum temperatures for the year behind the times of greatest and least heating such as we have at lower levels in the temperate zone. Thus we have the highest temperature for the year on December 2, 70.4° F. (21.3° C.), the lowest on June 3, 0.2° F. (—17.7° C.). The daily maxima and minima have the same characteristic. Radiation is active in the thin air of high stations and there is a very direct relation between the times of greatest heat received and greatest heat contained. The process is seen at its best immediately after the sun is obscured by clouds. In five minutes I have observed the temperature drop 20° F. (11.1° C.) at 16,000 feet (4,877 m.); and a drop of 10° F. (5.6° C.) is common anywhere above 14,000 feet (4,267 m.). In the curves of daily maximum and minimum temperatures we have clearly brought out the uniformity with which the maxima of high-level stations rise to a mean level during the winter months (May-August). Only at long intervals is there a short series of cloudy days when the maximum is 10°-12° F. (5.6°-6.7° C.) below the normal and the minimum stands at abnormally high levels. Since clouds form at night in quite variable amounts—in contrast to the nearly cloudless days—there is a far greater variability among the minimum temperatures. Indeed the variability of the winter minima is greater than that of the summer minima, for at the latter season the nightly cloud cover imposes much more stable atmospheric temperatures. The summer maxima have a greater degree of variability. Several clear days in succession allow the temperature to rise from 5°-10° F. (2.8°-5.6° C.) above the winter maxima. But such extremes are rather strictly confined to the height of the summer season—December and January. For the rest of the summer the maxima rise only a few degrees above those of the winter. This feature of the climate combines with a December maximum of rainfall to limit the period of most rapid plant growth to two months. Barley sown in late November could scarcely mature by the end of January, even if growing on the Argentine plains and much less at an elevation which carries the night temperatures below freezing at least once a week and where the mean temperature hovers about 47° F. (8.3° C.). The proper conditions for barley growing are not encountered above 13,000 to 13,500 feet and the farmer cannot be certain that it will ripen above 12,500 feet in the latitude of Santa Lucia.

The curve of mean monthly temperatures expresses a fact of great importance in the plant growth at high situations in the Andes—the sharp break between the winter and summer seasons. There are no real spring and autumn seasons. This is especially well shown in the curve for non-periodic mean monthly range of temperature for the month of October. During the half of the year that the sun is in the southern hemisphere the sun's noonday rays strike Santa Lucia at an angle that varies between 0° and 16° from the vertical. The days and nights are of almost equal length and though there is rapid radiation at night there is also rapid insolation by day. When the sun is in the northern hemisphere the days are shortened from one to two hours and the angle of insolation decreased, whence the total amount of heat received is so diminished that the mean monthly temperature lies only a little above freezing point. In winter the quiet pools beside the springs freeze over long before dark as the hill shadows grow down into the high-level valleys, and by morning ice also covers the brooks and marshes. Yet the sun and wind-cured *ichu* grass lives here, pale green in summer, straw-yellow in winter. The tola bush also grows rather abundantly. But we are almost at the upper limit of the finer grasses and a few hundred feet higher carries one into the realm of the snowline vegetation, mosses and lichens and a few sturdy flowering plants.

For convenience in future comparative studies the absolute extremes are arranged in the following table:

ABSOLUTE MONTHLY EXTREMES, SANTA LUCIA, 1913-14

Date	Highest	Lowest	Date
May [4] (12)	62° F.	9° F.	May (25, 26)
June (4 days)	60° F.	0.2° F.	June (3)
July (4 days, 31)	60° F.	5° F.	July (8)
Aug. (8, 26)	62° F.	4° F.	Aug. (4, 5)
Sept. (several days)	62° F.	7° F.	Sept. (4 days)
Oct. (24)	63° F.	10° F.	Oct. (12, 13)
Nov. (11) [5]	63° F.	24.0° F.	Nov. (29)
Dec. (2)	70.4° F.	22.2° F.	Dec. (14)
Jan. (19)	69.5° F.	26.5° F.	Jan. (3, 15)
Feb. (16,18)	63.2° F.	30.5° F.	Feb. (23)
March (8)	68.4° F.	28.5° F.	March (6)

RAINFALL

The rainfall record for Santa Lucia is for the year beginning November, 1913. For this period the precipitation amounts to 24.9 inches of which over 85 per cent fell in the rainy season from November to March. Most of the rain fell during the violent afternoon tempests that characterize the summer of these high altitudes.

The rainfall of Santa Lucia for this first year of record approximates closely to the yearly mean of 23.8 inches for the station of Caylloma in the adjacent province of that name. Caylloma is the center of a mining district essentially similar to Santa Lucia though the elevation of its meteorological station, 14,196 feet (4,330 m.), is lower. It is one of the few Peruvian stations for which a comparatively long series of records is available. The *Boletín de la Sociedad Geográfica de Lima* [6] contains a résumé of rainfall and temperature for seven years, 1896-7 to 1902-3. Later data may be found in subsequent volumes of the same publication but they have not been summarized or in any way prepared for analysis and they contain several typographical errors. A graphic representation of the monthly rainfall for the earlier period is here reproduced from the *Boletín de minas del Perú.* [7] The

---

[4] Observations began on May 12.

[5] For the first half of the month only; no record for the second half.

[6] Boletín de la Sociedad Geográfica de Lima, Vol. 13, pp. 473-480, Lima, 1903.

[7] Boletín del Cuerpo de Ingenieros de Minas del Perú, No. 34, Lima, 1905, also reproduced in No. 45, 1906.

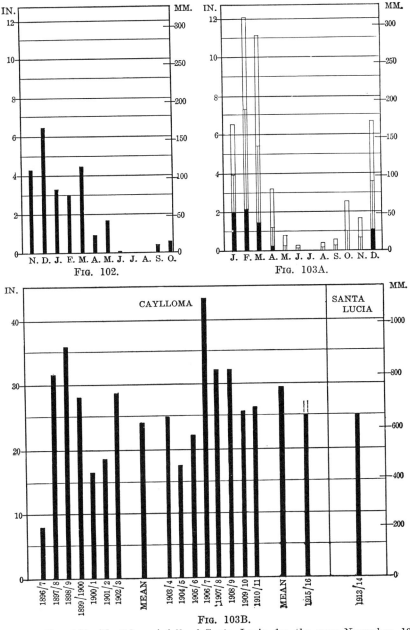

Fig. 102—Monthly rainfall of Santa Lucia for the year November, 1913, to October, 1914. No rain fell in July and August.

Fig. 103A—Maximum, mean and minimum monthly rainfall of Caylloma for the period 1896-7 to 1902-3. July was absolutely rainless. Caylloma is situated immediately east of the crest of the Maritime Cordillera in a position similar to that of Santa Lucia (see Fig. 66).

Fig. 103B—Annual rainfall of Caylloma for the periods 1896-7 to 1902-3; 1903-4 to 1910-11 and for 1915-6 (incomplete: May and June, months of low rainfall, are missing). Means for the respective seven and eight year periods are shown and the rainfall of Santa Lucia for the single observation year is inserted for comparison.

amount of precipitation fluctuates considerably from year to year. For the earlier period, with a mean of 23.8 inches the minimum (1896-7) was 8 inches and the maximum (1898-9) 36 inches. For the later period, 1903-4 to 1910-11, with a mean of 29.5 inches the minimum (1904-5) was 17.5 inches and the maximum (1906-7) was 43 inches.

RAINFALL, SANTA LUCIA, NOV. 1913 TO OCT. 1914

	No of fine days	No. of rainy days	Max. for single day	Total rainfall in inches
November	9	21	1.150	4.264 [8]
December	16	15	.700	6.439
January	17	14	.610	3.313
February	9	17	.910	2.975
March	11	20	1.102	4.381
April	17	13	0.31	0.92
May	8	23	0.35	1.63
June	27	3	0.05	0.07
July	31	0	0.00	0.00
August	31	0	0.00	0.00
September	23	7	0.05	0.35
October	21	10	0.14	0.56
Total				24.902

WIND

An analysis of the wind at Santa Lucia shows an excess of north and south winds over those of all other directions. The wind-rose for the entire period of observation (Fig. 104) clearly expresses this fact. When this element is removed we observe a strongly seasonal distribution of the wind. The winter is the time of north and south winds. In summer the winds are chiefly from the northeast or the southwest. Among single months, August and February show this fact clearly as well as the less decisive character of the summer (February) wind.

The mean wind velocity for the month of February was 540 meters per minute for the morning and 470 meters per minute for the afternoon. The higher morning rate, an unusual feature of

---

[8] The record is copied literally without regard to the absurdity of the second and third decimal places.

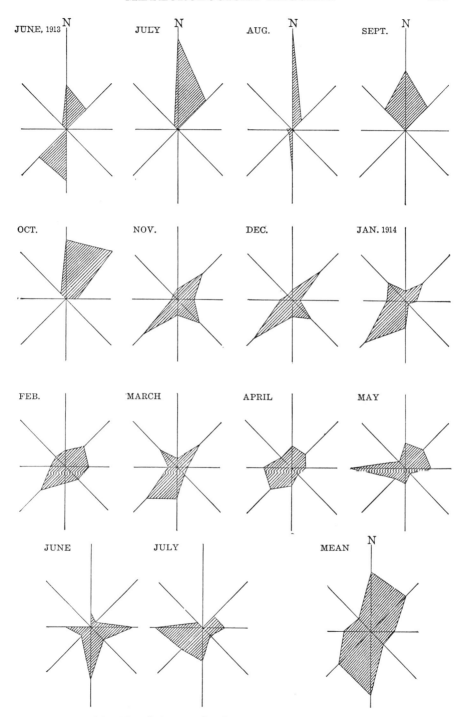

Fig. 104—Monthly wind roses for Santa Lucia, June, 1913, to July, 1914, and composite rose for the whole period of observation.

the weather of high stations, or indeed of wind-phenomena in general, is due, however, to exceptional changes in wind strength on two days of the month, the 16th and 25th, when the velocity decreased from a little less than a thousand meters per minute in the morning to 4 and 152 meters respectively in the afternoon. More typical is the March record for 1914 at Santa Lucia, when the wind was *always* stronger in the afternoon than in the morning, their ratios being 550 to 510.

CLOUD

The greater strength of the afternoon wind would lead us to suppose that the cloudiness, which in the trade-wind belt, is to so great an extent dependent on the wind, is greatest in the afternoon. The diagrams bring out this fact. Rarely is the sky quite clear after the noon hour. Still more striking is the contrast between the morning and afternoon if we combine the two densest shadings of the figures. Light, high-lying cirrus clouds are most characteristic of early morning hours. They produce some very striking sky effects just before sunrise as they catch the sun's rays aloft. An hour or two after sunrise they disappear and small cumulus clouds begin to form. These grow rapidly as the winds begin and by afternoon become bulky and numerous. In the wet season they grow into the nimbus and stratus types that precede a sudden downpour of water or a furious hailstorm. This is best seen from the base of a mountain range looking towards the crest, where the cloud- and rain-making processes of this type are most active.

CLOUD ANALYSIS, SANTA LUCIA

Type of cloud	Nov. a. m.	Nov. p. m.	Dec. a. m.	Dec. p. m.	Jan. a. m.	Jan. p. m.	Feb. a. m.	Feb. p. m.	March a. m.	March p. m.	Total a. m.	Total p. m.
Cirrus	6	2	15	2	9	2	5	3	6	3	41	12
Cirro-stratus	—	—	—	—	—	—	—	—	—	—	—	—
Cirro-cumulus	4	4	7	11	3	5	6	8	17	10	37	38
Cumulus	3	4	4	7	10	9	15	13	5	13	37	46
Strato-cumulus	2	6	3	10	7	14	2	3	—	3	14	36
Stratus	—	—	—	1	—	—	—	1	1	2	2	4
Nimbus	—	—	—	—	—	—	—	—	—	—	—	—
Clear	—	—	2	—	2	1	—	—	2	—	6	1

UNUSUAL WEATHER PHENOMENA, SANTA LUCIA, 1913-14

The following abstracts are selected because they give some important features of the weather not included in the preceding tables and graphs. Of special interest are the strong contrasts

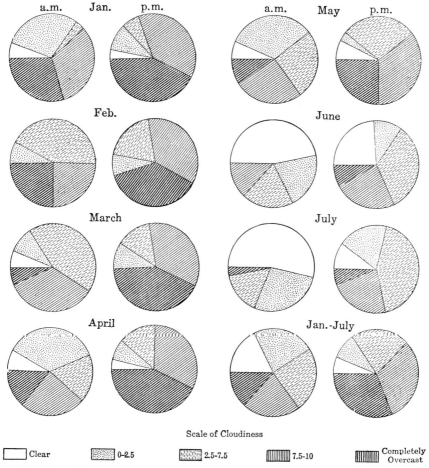

Fig. 105—Monthly cloudiness of Santa Lucia from January to July, 1914. Mean cloudiness for the whole period is also shown.

between the comparatively high temperatures of midday and the sudden "tempests" accompanied by rain or hail that follow the strong convectional movements dependent upon rapid and unequal heating. The furious winds drive the particles of hail like shot. It is sometimes impossible to face them and the pack train must be halted until the storm has passed. Frequently they leave the ground white with hailstones. We encountered one after another of these "tempestades" on the divide between Lambrama and Antabamba in 1911. They are among the most impetuous little storms I have ever experienced. The longest of them raged on the divide from two-o'clock until dark, though in the valleys the sun was shining. Fortunately, in this latitude they do not turn into heavy snowstorms as in the Cordillera of northwestern Argentina, where the passes are now and then blocked for weeks at a time and loss of human life is no infrequent occurrence.[9] They do, however, drive the shepherds down from the highest slopes to the mid-valley pastures and make travel uncomfortable if not unsafe.

ABSTRACT FROM DAILY WEATHER OBSERVATIONS, SANTA LUCIA, 1913-14

NOVEMBER

" Tempest " recorded 11 times, distant thunder and lightning 9 times.
Unusual weather records: " clear sky, scorching sun, good weather " (Nov. 29); " morning sky without a single cloud, weather agreeable " (Nov. 30).

DECEMBER

Clear morning sky 6 times. Starry night or part of night 7 times.
Beginning of rain and strong wind frequently observed at 5-6 P. M.
" Tempest " mentioned 19 times—5 times at midnight, 8 times at 5-6 P. M.

JANUARY

Clear morning sky 5 times. Starry night 3 times.
Rain, actual or threatening, characteristic of afternoons.
" Tempest," generally about 5-6 P. M., 7 times.
Sun described 4 times as scorching and, when without wind, heat as stifling.
Weather once " agreeable."

FEBRUARY

Constant cloud changes, frequent afternoon or evening rains.
" Tempest," generally 4 P. M. and later, 16 times.

---

[9] In the Eastern Cordillera, however, snowstorms may be more serious. **Prior to** the construction of the Urubamba Valley Road by the Peruvian government **the three** main routes to the Santa Ana portion of the valley proceeded via the passes of Salcantay, Panticalla, and Yanahuara respectively. Frequently all are completely snow-blocked and fatalities are by no means unknown. In 1864 for instance nine persons succumbed on the Yanahuara pass (Raimondi, op. cit., p. 109).

Twice clear morning skies, once starry night.

Scorching sun and stifling heat on one occasion.

" Tempest," generally in late afternoon and accompanied by hail, 19 times.

Observed 3 or 4 times a strong " land breeze" (terral) of short duration (15-20 mins.) and at midnight.

MOROCOCHA

Morococha, in the Department of Ancachs, Peru, lies in 76° 11′ west longitude and 11° 45′ south latitude and immediately east of the crest line of the Maritime Cordillera. It is 14,300 feet above sea level, and is surrounded by mountains that extend from 1,000 to 3,000 feet higher. The weather records are of special interest in comparison with those of Santa Lucia. Topographically the situations of the two stations are closely similar hence we may look for climatic differences dependent on the latitudinal difference. This is shown in the heavier rainfall of Morococha, 4° nearer the equatorial climatic zone. (For location see Fig. 66.)

The meteorological data for 1908-09 were obtained from records kept by the Morococha Mining Company for use in a projected hydro-electric installation. Other data covering the years 1906-11 have appeared in the bulletins of the *Sociedad Geográfica de Lima*. These are not complete but they have supplied rainfall data for the years 1910-11;[10] those for 1906 and 1907 have been obtained from the *Boletín de Minas*.[11]

TEMPERATURE

The most striking facts expressed by the various temperature curves are the shortness of the true winter season—its restriction to June and July—and its abrupt beginning and end. This is well known to anyone who has lived from April to October or November at high elevations in the Central Andes. Winter comes on suddenly and with surprising regularity from year to year during the last few days of May and early June. In the last week of July or the first week of August the temperatures make an equally sudden rise. During 1908 and 1909 the mean temperature reached the freezing point but once each year—July 24 and July 12 re-

---

[10] Boletín de la Sociedad Geográfica de Lima, Vol. 27, 1911; Vol. 28, 1912.

[11] Boletín del Cuerpo de Ingenieros de Minas del Perú, No. 65, 1908.

spectively. The absolute minimum for the two years was – 22° C.
July of 1908 and June of 1909 are also the months of smallest
diurnal variability, showing that the winter temperatures are
maintained with great regularity. Like all tropical high-level stations, Morococha exhibits winter maxima that are very high as
compared with the winter maxima of the temperate zone. In both
June and July of 1908 and 1909 the maximum was maintained for
about a week above 55° F. (12.8° C.), and in 1909 above 60° F.
(15.6° C.), the mean maximum for the year being only 4.7° F.
higher. For equal periods, however, the maxima fell to levels
about 10° F. below those for the period from December to
May, 1908.

It is noteworthy that the lowest maximum for 1909 was in
October, 44° F. (6.7° C.); and that other low maxima but little
above those of June and July occur in almost all the other months
of the year. While 1909 was in this respect an exceptional year,
it nevertheless illustrates a fact that may occur in any month of
any year. Its occurrence is generally associated with cloudiness.
One of the best examples of this is found in the January maximum
curve for 1909, where in a few days the maxima fell 12° F. Cloud
records are absent, hence a direct comparison cannot be made, but
a comparison of the maximum temperature curve with the graphic
representation of mean monthly rainfall, will emphasize this relation of temperature and cloudiness. February was the wettest
month of both 1908 and 1909. In sympathy with this is the large
and sharp drop from the January level of the maxima—the highest
for the year—to the February level. The mean temperatures are
affected to a less degree because the cloudiness retards night radiation of heat, thus elevating the maxima. Thus in 1908 the lowest
minimum for both January and February was 28.4° F. (—2° C.).
For 1909 the minima for January and February were 27.5° F.
(—2.5° C.) and 29.3° F. (—1.5° C.) respectively.

The extent to which high minima may hold up the mean temperature is shown by the fact that the mean monthly temperature for January, 1908, was lower than for February. Single
instances illustrate this relation equally well. For example, on

March 5th, 1908, there occurred the heaviest rainfall of that year. The maximum and minimum curves almost touch. The middle of April and late September, 1909, are other illustrations. The relationship is so striking that I have put the two curves side by side and have had them drawn to the same scale.

FREQUENCY OF THE DIURNAL VARIABILITY, MOROCOCHA, 1908 AND 1909

1908

Degrees F.	J.	F.	M.	A.	M.	J.	J.	A.	S.	O.	N.	D.	Total No. of days
0	—	3	2	3	—	—	2	1	3	1	1	3	19
0-1	6	5	6	10	9	10	13	10	8	6	6	5	94
1-2	4	1	3	7	5	3	7	7	8	6	6	4	61
2-3	6	1	3	4	9	2	2	4	4	7	7	4	53
3-4	5	3	2	3	3	4	2	9	4	5	3	5	48
4-5	2	3	1	1	2	5	5	—	1	1	6	3	30
Over 5	3	4	3	2	3	6	—	—	2	5	1	5	34
Days per month	26	20	20	30	31	30	31	31	30	31	30	29	339

1909

Degrees F.	J.	F.	M.	A.	M.	J.	J.	A.	S.	O.	N.	D.	Total No. of days	Mean for 1908-1909
0	6	1	4	2	1	2	4	4	3	6	2	1	36	27.5
0-1	9	8	5	6	6	7	8	13	9	4	11	10	96	95
1-2	4	6	8	3	11	14	3	3	5	3	9	6	75	68
2-3	3	7	4	8	4	3	6	6	4	6	1	3	55	54
3-4	4	5	3	6	4	4	4	3	6	3	2	5	49	48.5
4-5	1	1	5	1	2	—	2	1	1	2	—	2	18	24
Over 5	4	—	2	4	3	—	4	1	2	7	5	3	35	34.5
Days per month	31	28	31	30	31	30	31	31	30	31	30	30	364	351.5

RAINFALL

The annual rainfall of Morococha is as follows:

```
1906..........28 inches..........(  712 mm.)
1907..........40    "    ..........(1,011 mm.)
12 1908..........57    "    ..........(1,450 mm.)
1909..........45    "    ..........(1,156 mm.)
1910..........47    "    ..........(1,195 mm.)
1911..........25    "    ..........(  622 mm.)
```

[12] This figure is approximate: some days' records were missing from the first three months of the year and the total was estimated on a proportional basis.

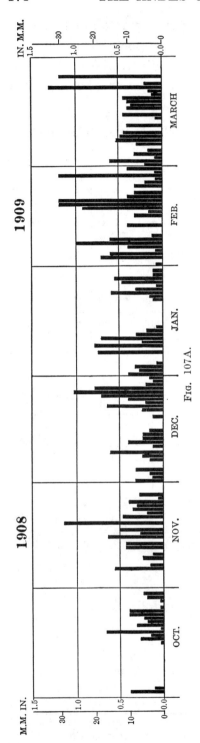

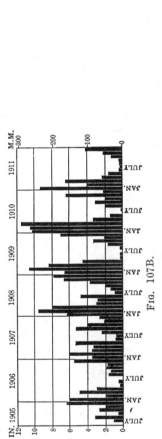

FIG. 107—Rainfall of Morococha. Fig. 107A shows daily rainfall during the rainy (summer) season, 1908-1909. Fig. 107B shows monthly rainfall from July, 1905, to December, 1911, and Fig. 107C the annual and mean rainfall for the same period.

The mean for the above six years amounts to 40 inches (1,024 mm.). This is a value considerably higher than that for Caylloma or Santa Lucia. The greater rainfall of Morococha is probably due in part to its more northerly situation. An abnormal feature of the rainfall of 1908, the rainiest year, is the large amount that fell in June. Ordinarily June and July, the coldest months, are nearly or quite rainless. The normal concurrence of highest temperatures and greatest precipitation is of course highly favorable to the plant life of these great altitudes. Full advantage can be taken of the low summer temperatures if the growing temperatures are concentrated and are accompanied by abundant rains. Since low temperatures mean physiologic dryness, whether or not rains are abundant, the dryness of the winter months has little effect in restricting the range of Alpine species.

The seasonal distribution of rain helps the plateau people as well as the plateau plants. The transportation methods are primitive and the trails mere tracks that follow the natural lines of topography and drainage. Coca is widely distributed, likewise corn and barley which grow at higher elevations, and wool must be carried down to the markets from high-level pastures. In the season of rains the trails are excessively wet and slippery, the streams are often in flood and the rains frequent and prolonged. On the other hand the insignificant showers of the dry or non-growing season permit the various products to be exchanged over dry trails.

The activities of the plateau people have had a seasonal expression from early times. Inca chronology counted the beginning of the year from the middle of May, that is when the dry season was well started and it was inaugurated with the festivals of the Sun. With the exception of June when the people were entirely busied in the irrigation of their fields, each month had its appropriate feasts until January, during which month and February and March no feasts were held. April, the harvest month, marked the recommencement of ceremonial observances and a revival of social life.[13]

---

[13] Christoval de Molina, The Fables and Rites of the Yncas, Hakluyt Soc. Publs., 1st Ser., No. 48, 1873.

In Spanish times the ritualistic festivals, incorporated with
fairs, followed the seasonal movement. Today progress in transportation has caused the decadence of many of the fairs but others
still survive. Thus two of the most famous fairs of the last century, those of Vilque (province of Puno) and Yunguyo (province
of Chucuito), were held at the end of May and the middle of
August respectively. Copacavana, the famous shrine on the
shores of Titicaca, still has a well-attended August fair and
Huari, in the heart of the Bolivian plateau, has an Easter fair
celebrated throughout the Andes.

COCHABAMBA

Cochabamba, Bolivia, lies 8,000 feet above sea level in a broad
basin in the Eastern Andes. The Cerro de Tunari, on the northwest, has a snow and ice cover for part of the year. The tropical
forests lie only a single long day's journey to the northeast. Yet
the basin is dry on account of an eastern front range that keeps
out the rain-bearing trade winds. The Rio Grande has here cut
a deep valley by a roundabout course from the mountains to the
plains so that access to the region is over bordering elevations.
The basin is chiefly of structural origin.

The weather records from Cochabamba are very important. I
could obtain none but temperature data and they are complete for
1906 only. Data for 1882-85 were secured by von Boeck [14] and they
have been quoted by Sievers and Hann. The mean annual temperature for 1906 was 61.9° F. (16.6° C.), a figure in close agreement with von Boeck's mean of 60.8° F. (16° C.). The monthly
means indicate a level of temperature favorable to agriculture.
The basin is in fact the most fertile and highly cultivated area of
its kind in Bolivia. Bananas, as well as many other tropical and
subtropical plants, grow in the central plaza. The nights of mid-
winter are uncomfortably cool; and the days of midsummer are

---

[14] See Meteorologische Zeitschrift, Vol. 5, p. 195, 1888. Also cited by J. Hann in
Handbuch der Climatologie, Vol. 2, Stuttgart, 1897; W. Sievers, Süd- und Mittelamerika,
Leipzig and Vienna, 1914, p. 334.

uncomfortably hot but otherwise the temperatures are delightful. The absolute extremes for 1906 were 81.5° F. (27.5° C.) on December 11, and 39.9° F. (4.4° C.) on July 15 and 16. The (uncorrected) readings of von Boeck give a greater range. High minima rather than high maxima characterize the summer. The curve for 1906 shows the maxima for June and July cut off strikingly by an abrupt drop of the temperature and indicates a rather close restriction of the depth of the season to these two months, which are also those of greatest diurnal range.

The rainfall of about 18 inches is concentrated in the summer season, 85 per cent falling between November and March. During this time the town is somewhat isolated by swollen streams and washed out trails: hence here, as on the plateau, there is a distinct seasonal distribution of the work of planting, harvesting, moving goods, and even mining, and of the general commerce of the towns. There is an approach to our winter season in this respect and in respect of a respite from the almost continuously high temperatures of summer. The daytime temperatures of summer are however mitigated by the drainage of cool air from the surrounding highlands. This, indeed, prolongs the period required for the maturing of plants, but there are no harmful results because freezing temperatures are not reached, even in winter.

MONTHLY TEMPERATURES, COCHABAMBA, 1906

Month	Mean Min.	Mean Max.	Mean Range	Daily Mean
January	55.7	72.25	16.65	63.3
February	**61.2**	71.3	**10.1**	65.5
March	59.8	72.6	12.8	65.5
April	55.06	70.8	15.74	62.2
May	50.9	68.7	17.8	59.1
June	47.1	65.6	18.5	55.6
July	**44.8**	**64.9**	20.1	**54.1**
August	49.9	68.0	18.1	58.2
September	55.6	73.2	17.6	63.7
October	56.1	73.4	17.3	64.0
November	58.1	**75.7**	17.6	**66.2**
December	58.6	73.9	15.3	65.8

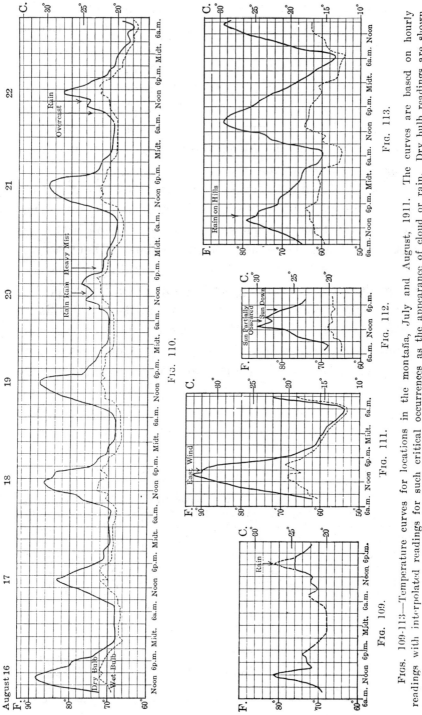

FIG. 110.

FIG. 113.

FIG. 112.

FIG. 111.

FIG. 109.

FIGS. 109-113.—Temperature curves for locations in the montaña, July and August, 1911. The curves are based on hourly readings with interpolated readings for such critical occurrences as the appearance of cloud or rain. Dry bulb readings are shown by solid lines, wet bulb by dotted lines, and breaks in the continuity of the observations by heavy broken lines. Fig. 109 is for Pongo de Mainique, August 20 and 21; Fig. 110 for Yavero; Fig. 111 for Santo Anato, August 11 and 12; Fig. 112 for Sahuayaco, August 29, and Fig. 113 for Santa Ana, July 30 to August 1.

FIG. 114.

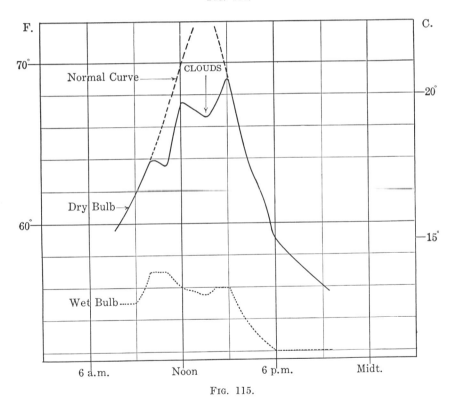

FIG. 115.

FIG. 114—Typical afternoon cloud composition at Santa Ana during the dry season.

FIG. 115—Temperature curve for Abancay drawn from data obtained by hourly readings on September 27, 1911. Dry bulb readings are shown by a heavy solid line, wet bulb readings by a dotted line. The heavy broken line shows the normal curve when the sky is unobscured by cloud. The reduction in temperature with cloud is very marked.

FREQUENCY OF DIURNAL VARIABILITY AT COCHABAMBA, 1906

Degrees F.	J.	F.	M.	A.	M.	J.	J.	A.	S.	O.	N.	D.	Total No. of days
0	1	3	10	12	6	10	9	6	9	6	3	4	79
0-1	5	—	3	5	3	3	—	4	—	3	1	1	28
1-2	10	10	13	11	15	7	14	11	15	10	14	13	143
2-3	7	11	3	1	5	8	7	4	3	6	7	6	68
3-4	6	2	2	1	2	2	1	6	3	4	3	5	37
4-5	—	—	—	—	—	—	—	—	—	1	1	1	3
Over 5	2	2	—	—	—	—	—	—	—	1	1	1	7

A series of curves shows the daily march of temperature at various locations along the seventy-third meridian. Figs. 109 to 113 are for the Urubamba Valley. Respectively they relate to Pongo de Mainique, 1,200 feet elevation (365 m.), the gateway to the eastern plains; Yavero, 1,600 feet (488 m.), where the tributary of this name enters the main stream; Santo Anato 1,900 feet (580 m.); Sahuayaco, 2,400 feet (731 m.), and Santa Ana, 3,400 feet (1,036 m.), one of the outposts of civilization beyond the Eastern Cordillera. The meteorological conditions shown are all on the same order. They are typical of dry season weather on the dry floor of a montaña valley. The smooth curves of clear days are marked by high mid-day temperatures and great diurnal range. Santo Anato is a particularly good illustration: the range for the 24 hours is 38° F. (21.1° C.). This site, too, is remarkable as one of the most unhealthful of the entire valley. The walls of the valley here make a sharp turn and free ventilation of the valley is obstructed. During the wet season tertian fever prevails to a degree little known east of the Cordillera, though notorious enough in the deep valleys of the plateau. The curves show relative humidity falling to a very low minimum on clear days. At Santo Anato and Santa Ana, for example, it drops below 30 per cent during the heat of the day. Afternoon cloudiness, however, is a common feature even of the dry season. A typical afternoon cloud formation is shown in Fig. 114. The effect on temperature is most marked. It is well shown in the curve for August 20 and 22 at Yavero. Cloudiness and precipita-

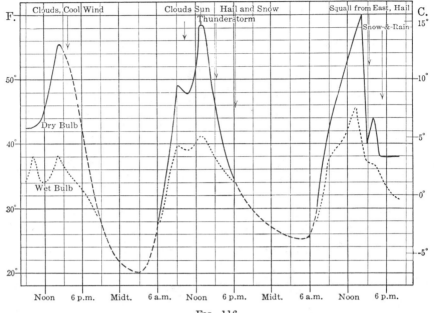

FIG. 116.

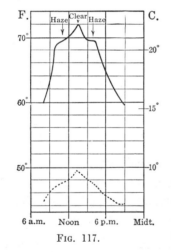

FIG. 117.

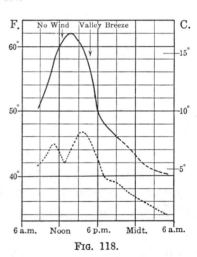

FIG. 118.

FIGS. 116-118—Temperature curves for locations in the Maritime Cordillera and its western valleys, October, 1911. For construction of curves see Figs. 109-113. Fig. 116 is for Camp 13 on the northern slope of the Maritime Cordillera (which here runs from east to west), October 13-15; Fig. 117 for Cotahuasi, October 26; Fig. 118 for Salamanca, October 31.

tion increase during the summer months. At Santa Ana the rainfall for the year 1894-95 amounted to 50 inches, of which 60 per cent fell between December and March. For a discussion of topographic features that have some highly interesting climatic effects in the eastern valleys of Peru see Chapter VI.

Abancay, 8,000 feet (2,440 m.), in one of the inter-Andean basins, is situated in the zone of marked seasonal precipitation.

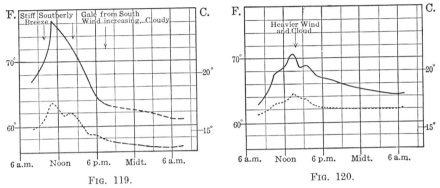

FIG. 119.

FIG. 120.

FIGS. 119-120—Temperature curves for the Coast Desert, November, 1911. Fig. 119 is for Aplao, November 4 and 5; and Fig. 120 for Camaná, November 9 and 10. For construction of curves see Figs. 109 to 113.

The single day's record shows the characteristic effect of cloud reducing the maximum temperature of the day and maintaining the relative humidity.

Camp 13, 15,400 feet (4,720 m.), lies near the crest of the Maritime Cordillera a little south of Antabamba. Afternoon storms are one of its most significant features. Cotahuasi, 9,100 feet (2,775 m.) is near the head of a west-coast valley. Its low humidity is worthy of note. That for Salamanca, 12,700 feet (3,870 m.), is similar but not so marked.

Aplao, 3,100 feet (945 m.), and Camaná at the seacoast are stations in the west-coast desert. The interior location of the former gives it a greater range of temperature than Camaná, yet even here the range is small in comparison with the diurnal extremes of the montaña, and the tempering effect of the sea-breeze is clearly apparent. Camaná shows a diurnal temperature range of under 10° F. and also the high relative humidity, over 70 per cent, characteristic of the coast.

PART II

PHYSIOGRAPHY OF THE PERUVIAN ANDES

CHAPTER XI

THE PERUVIAN LANDSCAPE

FROM the west coast the great Andean Cordillera appears to have little of the regularity suggested by our relief maps. Steep and high cliffs in many places form the border of the land and obstruct the view; beyond them appear distant summits rising into the zone of clouds. Where the cliffs are absent or low, one may look across a sun-baked, yellow landscape, generally broken by irregular foothills that in turn merge into the massive outer spurs and ranges of the mountain zone. The plain is interrupted by widely separated valleys whose green lowland meadows form a brilliant contrast to the monotonous browns and yellows of the shimmering desert. In rare situations the valley trenches enable one to look far into the Cordillera and to catch memorable glimpses of lofty peaks capped with snow.

If the traveler come to the west-coast landscape from the well-molded English hills or the subdued mountains of Vermont and New Hampshire with their artistic blending of moderate profiles, he will at first see nothing but disorder. The scenery will be impressive and, in places, extraordinary, but it is apparently composed of elements of the greatest diversity. All the conceivable variations of form and color are expressed, with a predominance of bold rugged aspects that give a majestic appearance to the mountain-bordered shore. One looks in vain for some sign of a quiet view, for some uniformity of features, for some landscape that will remind him of the familiar hills of home. The Andes are aggressive mountains that front the sea in formidable spurs or desert ranges. Could we see in one view their entire elevation

from depths of over 20,000 feet beneath sea level to snowy summits, a total altitude of 40,000 feet (12,200 m.), their excessive
boldness would be more apparent. No other mountains in the
world are at once so continuously lofty and so near a coast which
drops off to abyssal depths.

The view from the shore is, however, but one of many which
the Andes exhibit. Seen from the base the towering ranges display a stern aspect, but, like all mountains, their highest slopes
and spurs must be crossed and re-crossed before the student is
aware of other aspects of a quite different nature. The Andes
must be observed from at least three situations: from the floors
of the deep intermontane valleys, from the intermediate slopes
and summits, and from the uppermost levels as along the range
crests and the highest passes. Strangely enough it is in the summit views that one sees the softest forms. At elevations of 14,000
to 16,000 feet (4,270 to 4,880 m.), where one would expect rugged
spurs, serrate chains, and sharp needles and horns, one comes frequently upon slopes as well graded as those of a city park—grass-
covered, waste-cloaked, and with gentle declivity (Figs. 121-124).

The graded, waste-cloaked slopes of the higher levels are interpreted as the result of prolonged denudation in an erosion
cycle which persisted through the greater part of the Tertiary
period, and which was closed by uplifts aggregating at least several thousands of feet. Above the level of the mature slopes rise
the ragged profiles and steep, naked declivities of the snow-capped
mountains which bear residual relations to the softer forms at
their bases. They are formed upon rock masses of greater
original elevation and of higher resistance to denudation. Though
they are dominating topographic features, they are much less extensive and significant than the tame landscape which they surmount.

Below the level of the mature slopes are topographic features
of equal prominence: gorges and canyons up to 7,000 feet deep.
The deeply intrenched streams are broken by waterfalls and almost continuous rapids, the valley walls are so abrupt that one
may, in places, roll stones down a 4,000-foot incline to the river

F<small>IG</small>. 121.

F<small>IG</small>. 122.

F<small>IG</small>. 121—Looking north from the hill near Anta in the Anta basin north of Cuzco. Typical composition of slopes and intermont basins in the Central Andes. Alluvial fill in the foreground; mature slopes in the background; in the extreme background the snow-capped crests of the Cordillera Vilcapampa.

F<small>IG</small>. 122—Showing topographic conditions before the formation of the deep canyons in the Maritime Cordillera. The view, looking across a tributary canyon of the Antabamba river, shows in the background the main canyon above Huadquirca. Compare with Fig. 60.

Fig. 124—Dissected mature slopes north of Anta in the Anta basin north of Cuzco.

Fig. 123—Mature slopes between Ollantaytambo and Urubamba.

bed, and the tortuous trail now follows a stream in the depths of a profound abyss, now scales the walls of a labyrinthine canyon.

The most striking elements of scenery are not commonly the most important in physiography. The oldest and most significant surface may be at the top of the country, where it is not seen by the traveler or where it cannot impress him, except in contrast to features of greater height or color. The layman frequently seizes on a piece of bad-land erosion or an outcrop of bright-colored sandstone or a cliff of variegated clays or

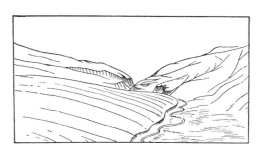

FIG. 125—Mature upper and young lower slopes at the outlet of the Cuzco basin.

a snow-covered mountain as of most interest. All we can see of a beautiful snow-clad peak is mere entertainment compared with what subdued waste-cloaked hill-slopes may show. We do not wish to imply that everywhere the tops of the Andes are meadows, that there are no great scenic features in the Peruvian mountains, or that they are not worth while. But we do wish to say that the bold features are far less important in the interpretation of the landscape.

Amid all the variable forms of the Peruvian Cordillera certain strongly developed types recur persistently. That their importance and relation may be appreciated we shall at once name them categorically and represent them in the form of a block diagram (Fig. 126). The principal topographic types are as follows:

1. An extensive system of high-level, well-graded, mature slopes, below which are:

2. Deep canyons with steep, and in places, cliffed sides and narrow floors, and above which are:

3. Lofty residual mountains composed of resistant, highly deformed rock, now sculptured into a maze of serrate ridges and sharp commanding peaks.

4. Among the forms of high importance, yet causally unrelated to the other closely associated types, are the volcanic cones and plateaus of the western Cordillera.

5.   At the valley heads are a full complement of glacial features, such as cirques, hanging valleys, reversed slopes, terminal moraines, and valley trains.

6.   Finally there is in all the valley bottoms a deep alluvial fill formed during the glacial period and now in process of dissection.

Though there are in many places special features either remotely related or quite unrelated to the principal enumerated types, they belong to the class of minor forms to which relatively small attention will be paid, since they are in general of small extent and of purely local interest.

The block diagram represents all of these features, though of

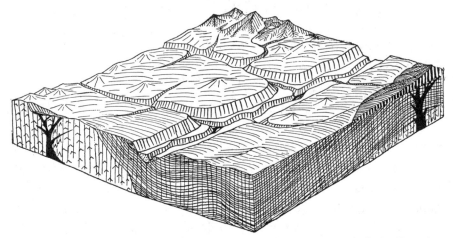

Fig. 126—Block diagram of the typical physiographic features of the Peruvian Andes.

necessity somewhat more closely associated than they occur in nature. Reference to the photographs, Figs. 121-124, will make it clear that the diagram is somewhat ideal; on the other hand the photographs together include all the features which the diagram displays. In descending from any of the higher passes to the valley floor one passes in succession down a steep, well-like cirque at a glaciated valley head, across a rocky terminal moraine, then down a stair-like trail cut into the steep scarps which everywhere mark the descent to the main valley floors, over one after another of the confluent alluvial fans that together constitute a large part of the valley fill, and finally down the steep sides of the inner valley to the boulder-strewn bed of the ungraded river.

We shall now turn to each group of features for description and explanation, selecting for first consideration the forms of widest development and greatest significance—the high-level mature slopes lying between the lofty mountains which rise above them and the deep, steep-walled valleys sunk far below them. These are the great pasture lands of the Cordillera; their higher portions constitute the typical *puna* of the Indian shepherds. In many sections it is possible to pasture the vagrant flocks almost anywhere upon the graded slopes, confident that the *ichu,* a tufted forage grass, will not fail and that scattered brooks and springs will supply the necessary water. At nightfall the flocks are driven down between the sheltering walls of a canyon or in the lee of a cliff near the base of a mountain, or, failing to reach either of these camps, the shepherd confines his charge within the stone walls of an isolated corral.

In those places where the graded soil-covered slopes lie within the zone of agriculture—below 14,000 feet—they are cultivated, and if the soil be deep and fertile they are very intensively cultivated. Between Anta and Urubamba, a day's march north of Cuzco, the hill slopes are covered with wheat and barley fields which extend right up to the summits (Fig. 134). In contrast are the uncultivated soil-less slopes of the mountains and the bare valley walls of the deeply intrenched streams. The distribution of the fields thus brings out strongly the principal topographic relations. Where the softer slopes are at too high a level, the climatic conditions are extreme and man is confined to the valley floors and lower slopes where a laborious system of terracing is the first requirement of agriculture.

The appearance of the country after the mature slopes had been formed is brought out in Fig. 122. The camera is placed on the floor of a still undissected, mature valley which shows in the foreground of the photograph. In the middle distance is a valley whose great depth and steepness are purposely hidden; beyond the valley are the smoothly graded, catenary curves, and interlocking spurs of the mature upland. In imagination one sees the valleys filled and the valley slopes confluent on the former (now imaginary) valley floor which extends without important change of expression to the border of the Cordillera. No extensive cliffs occur on the restored surface, and none now occur on large tracts of the still undissected upland. Since the mature slopes represent a long period of weathering and erosion, their surfaces were covered with a deep layer of soil. Where glaciation at the higher levels and vigorous erosion along the canyons have taken place, the former soil cover has been removed; elsewhere it is an important feature. Its presence lends a marked softness and beauty to these lofty though subdued landscapes.

The graded mountain slopes were not all developed (1) at the same elevation, nor (2) upon rock of the same resistance to denudation, nor (3) at the same distance from the major streams, nor (4) upon rock of the same structure. It follows that they will not all display precisely the same form. Upon the softer rocks at the lowest levels near the largest streams the surface was worn down to extremely moderate slopes with a local relief of not more than several hundred feet. Conversely, there are quite unreduced portions whose irregularities have mountainous proportions, and between these extremes are almost all possible variations. Though the term *mature* in a broad way expresses the stage of development which the land had reached, *post mature* should be applied to those portions which suffered the maximum reduction and now exhibit the softest profiles. At no place along the 73rd meridian was denudation carried to the point of even local peneplanation. All of the major and some of the minor divides bear residual elevations and even approximately plane surfaces do not exist.

Among the most important features of the mature slopes are (1) their great areal extent—they are exhibited throughout the whole Central Andes, (2) their persistent development upon rocks of whatever structure or degree of hardness, and (3) their present great elevation in spite of moderate grades indicative of their development at a much lower altitude. Mature slopes of equivalent form are developed in widely separated localities in the Central Andes: in every valley about Cochabamba, Bolivia, at 10,000 feet (3,050 m.); at Crucero Alto in southern Peru at 14,600 feet

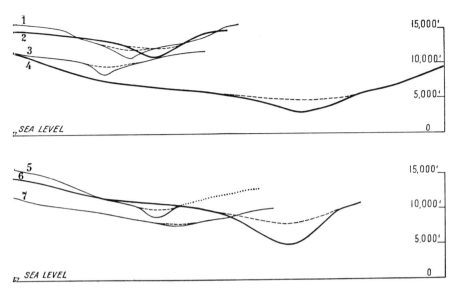

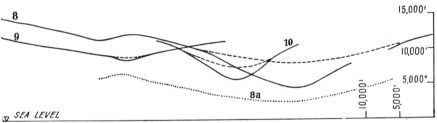

FIG. 127—Topographic profiles across typical valleys of southern Peru. They are drawn to scale and the equality of gradient of the gentler upper slopes is so close that almost any curve would serve as a composite of the whole. These curves form the basis of the diagram, Fig. 128, whereby the amount of elevation of the Andes in late geologic time may be determined. The approximate locations of the profiles are as follows: 1, Antabamba; 2, Chuquibambilla; 3, upland south of Antabamba; 4, Apurimac Canyon above Pasaje; 5, Abancay; 6, Arma (Cordillera Vilcapampa); 7, divide above Huancarama; 8, Huascatay; 9, Huascatay, farther downstream; 10, Rio Pampas. The upper valley in 8 is still undissected; 7 is practically the same; 8a is at the level which 8 must reach before its side slopes are as gentle as at the end of the preceding interrupted cycle.

(4,450 m.); several hundred miles farther north at Anta near Cuzco, 11,000 feet to 12,000 feet (3,600 to 3,940 m.), and Fig. 129 shows typical conditions in the Vilcabamba Valley along the route of the Yale Peruvian Expedition of 1911. The characteristic slopes so clearly represented in these four photographs are the most persistent topographic elements in the physiography of the Central Andes.

The rock masses upon which the mature slopes were formed range from soft to hard, from stratified shales, slates, sandstones, conglomerates, and limestones to volcanics and intrusive granites. While these variations impose corresponding differences of form, the graded quality of the slopes is rarely absent. In some places the highly inclined strata are shown thinly veiled with surface débris, yet so even as to appear artificially graded. The rock in one place is hard granite, in another a moderately hard series of lava flows, and again rather weak shales and sandstones.

Proof of the rapid and great uplift of certain now lofty mountain ranges in late geologic time is one of the largest contributions of physiography to geologic history. Its validity now rests upon a large body of diversified evidence. In 1907 I crossed the Cordillera Sillilica of Bolivia and northern Chile and came upon clear evidences of recent and great uplift. The conclusions presented at that time were tested in the region studied in 1911, 500 miles farther north, with the result that it is now possible to state more precisely the dates of origin of certain prominent topographic forms, and to reconstruct the conditions which existed before the last great uplift in which the Central Andes were born. The relation to this general problem of the forms under discussion will now be considered.

The gradients of the mature slopes, as we have already seen, are distinctly moderate. In the Anta region, over an area several hundred square miles in extent, they run from several degrees to 20° or 30°. Ten-degree slopes are perhaps most common. If the now dissected slopes be reconstructed on the basis of many clinometer readings, photographs, and topographic maps, the result is a series of profiles as in Fig. 127. If, further, the restored slopes be coördinated over an extensive area the gradients of the resulting valley floors will run from 3° to 10°. Finally, if these valley floors be extended westward to the Pacific and eastward to the Amazon basin, they will be found about 5,000 feet above sea level and 4,000 feet above the eastern plains. (For explanation of method and data employed, see the accompanying figures 127-128). It is, therefore, a justifiable conclusion that since the

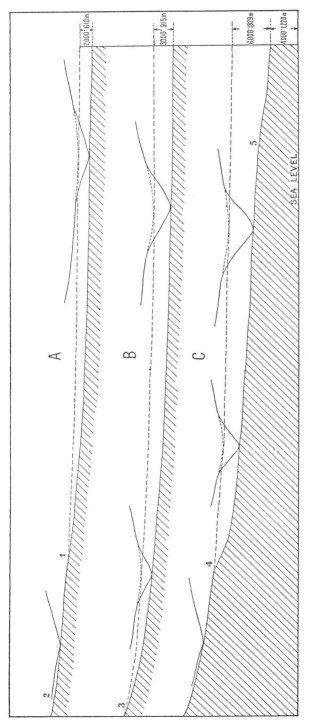

Fɪɢ. 128—Composition of slopes and profiles in the Peruvian Andes. By superimposing the cross profiles of typical valleys as shown in Fig. 127 a restoration is possible of the longitudinal profiles of the earlier cycle of erosion. The difference in elevation of the two profiles gives less than the minimum amount of uplift that must have occurred. Case A represents a valley in which recent cutting has not yet reached the valley head. Below the point I the profile has been steepened and lowered by erosion in the current cycle. Above point I the profile is still in the stage it reached in the preceding cycle. In case B the renewed erosion of the current cycle has reached to the valley head. Case C represents conditions similar to those in the preceding cases save that the stream is typical of those that lie nearest the steep flexed or faulted margins of the Cordillera and discharge to the low levels of the desert pampa on the west or the tropical plains on the east.

formation of the slopes the Andes have been uplifted at least a mile, or, to put it in another way, the Andes at the time of formation of the mature slopes were at least a mile lower than they are at present.

Further proof of recent and great uplift is afforded by the deeply intrenched streams. After descending the long graded slopes one comes upon the cliffed canyons with a feeling of consternation. The effect of powerful erosion, incident upon uplift, is heightened by the ungraded character of the river bed. Falls and rapids abound, the river profiles suggest tumultuous descents, and much time will elapse before the river beds have the regular and moderate gradients of the streams draining the mature surface before uplift as shown in the profiles by the dotted lines representing the restored valley floors of the older cycle. Since the smooth-contoured landscape was formed great changes have taken place. The streams have changed from completely graded to almost completely ungraded profiles; in place of a subdued landscape we now have upland slopes intersected by mile-deep canyons; the high-level slopes could not have been formed under existing conditions, for they are being dissected by the present streams.

Since the slopes of the land in general undergo progressive changes in the direction of flatter gradients during a given geographical cycle, it follows that with the termination of one cycle and the beginning of another, two sets of slopes will exist and that the gradients of the two will be unlike. The result is a break in the descent of the slopes from high to low levels to which the name "topographic unconformity" is now applied. It will be a prominent feature of the landscape if the higher, older, and flatter gradients have but little declivity, and the gradients of the lower younger slopes are very steep. In those places where the relief of the first cycle was still great at the time of uplift, the erosion forms of the second cycle may not be differentiated from those of the first, since both are marked by steep gradients. In the Central Andes the change in gradient between the higher and lower slopes is generally well marked. It occurs at variable heights above the valley floors, though rarely more than 3,000 feet above them. In the more central tracts, far from the main streams and their associated canyons, dissection in the present erosion cycle has not yet been initiated, the mature slopes are still intact, and a topographic unconformity has not yet been developed. The higher slopes are faced with rock and topped with slowly moving waste. Ascent of the spur end is by steep zigzag trails; once the top is gained the trail runs along the gentler slopes without special difficulties.

It is worth noting at this point that the surface of erosion still older than the mature slopes herewith described appears not to have been developed along the seventy-third meridian of Peru, or if developed at one time, fragments of it no longer remain. The last well-developed remnant is southwest of Cuzco, Fig. 130. I have elsewhere described the character and geographic distribution of this oldest recognizable surface of the Central Andes.[1] Southern Peru and Bolivia and northern Chile display its features in what seems an unmistakable manner. The best locality yet found is in the Desaguadero Valley between Ancoaqui and Concordia. There one may see thousands of feet of strongly inclined sediments of varying resistance beveled by a well-developed surface of erosion whose preserval is owing to a moderate rainfall and to location in an interior basin.[2]

The highest surface of a region, if formed during a prolonged period of erosion, becomes a surface of reference in the determination of the character and amount of later crustal deformations, having somewhat the same functions as a key bed in stratigraphic geology. Indeed, concrete physiographic facts may be the *only* basis for arguments as to both epeirogenic and orogenic movements. The following considerations may show in condensed form the relative value of physiographic evidence:

1. If movements in the earth's crust are predominantly *down-*

[1] The Physiography of the Central Andes, Am. Journ. Sci., Vol. 40, 1909, pp. 197-217 and 373-402.

[2] Results of an Expedition to the Central Andes, Bull. Am. Geog. Soc., Vol. 46, 1914. Figs. 28 and 29.

ward, sedimentation may be carried on continuously and a clear geologic record may be made.

2. Even if crustal movements are alternately downward and upward, satisfactory conclusions may be drawn from both (a) the nature of the buried surfaces of erosion, and (b) the alternating character of the sediments.

3. If, however, the deformative processes effect steady or intermittent uplifts, there may be no sediments, at least within the limits of the positive crustal units, and a geologic record must be derived not from sedimentary deposits but from topographic forms. We speak of the *lost intervals* represented by stratigraphic breaks or unconformities and commonly emphasize our ignorance concerning them. The longest, and, from the human standpoint, the most important, break in the sedimentary record is that of the present wherever degradation is the predominant physiographic process. Unlike the others the *lost interval* of the present is not lost, if we may so put it, but is in our possession, and may be definitely described as a concrete thing. It is the physiography of today.

Even where long-buried surfaces of erosion are exposed to view, as in northern Wisconsin, where the Pre-Cambrian paleoplain projects from beneath the Paleozoic sediments, or, as in New Jersey and southeastern Pennsylvania, where the surface developed on the crystalline rocks became by depression the floor of the Triassic and by more recent uplift and erosion has been exposed to view,—even in such cases the exposures are of small extent and give us at best but meager records. In short, many of the breaks in the geologic record are of such long duration as to make imperative the use of physiographic principles and methods. The great Appalachian System of eastern North America has been a land area practically since the end of the Paleozoic. In the Central Andes the "lost interval," from the standpoint of the sedimentary record, dates from the close of the Cretaceous, except in a few local intermont basins partially filled with Tertiary or Pleistocene deposits. Physiographic interpretations, therefore, serve the double purpose of supplying a part of the geologic record while at the same time forming a basis for the scientific study of the surface distribution of living forms.

The geologic dates of origin of the principal topographic forms of the Central Andes may be determined with a fair degree of accuracy. Geologic studies in Peru and Bolivia have emphasized the wide distribution of the Cretaceous formations. They consist principally of thick limestones above and sandstones and conglomerates below, and thus represent extensive marine submergence of the earth's crust in the Cretaceous where now there are very lofty mountains. The Cretaceous deposits are everywhere strongly deformed or uplifted to a great height, and all have been deeply eroded. They were involved, together with other and much older sediments, in the erosion cycle which resulted in the development of the widely extended series of mature slopes already described. From low scattered island elevations projecting above sea level, as in the Cretaceous period, the Andes were transformed by compression and uplift to a rugged mountain belt subjected to deep and powerful erosion. The products of erosion were in part swept into the adjacent seas, in part accumulated on the floors of intermont basins, as in the great interior basins of Titicaca and Poopó.

Since the early Tertiary strata are themselves deformed from once simple and approximately horizontal structures and subjected to moderate tilting and faulting, it follows that mountainmaking movements again affected the region during later Tertiary. They did not, however, produce extreme effects. They did stimulate erosion and bring about a reorganization of all the slopes with respect to the new levels.

This agrees closely with a second line of evidence which rests upon an independent basis. The alluvial fill which lies upon all the canyon and valley floors is of glacial origin, as shown by its interlocking relations with morainal deposits at the valley heads. It is now in process of dissection and since its deposition in the Pleistocene had been eroded on the average about 200 feet. Clearly, to form a 3,000-foot canyon in hard rock requires much more time than to deposit and again partially to excavate an alluvial fill several hundred feet deep. Moreover, the glacial material is coarse throughout, and was built up rapidly and dissected rapidly. In most cases, furthermore, coarse material at the bottom of the glacial series rests directly upon the rock of a narrow and ungraded valley floor. From these and allied facts it is concluded that there is no long time interval represented by the transitions from degrading to aggrading processes and back again. The early Pleistocene, therefore, seems quite too short a period in which to produce the bold forms and effect the deep erosion which marks the period between the close of the mature cycle and the beginnings of deposition in the Pleistocene.

The alternative conclusion is that the greater part of the canyon cutting was effected in the late Tertiary, and that it continued into the early Pleistocene until further erosion was halted by changed climatic conditions and the augmented delivery of land waste to all the streams. The final development of the well-graded high-level slopes is, therefore, closely confined to a small portion of the Tertiary. The closest estimate which the facts support appears to be Miocene or early Pliocene. It is clear, however, that only the culmination of the period can be definitely assigned. Erosion was in full progress at the close of the Cretaceous and by middle Tertiary had effected vast changes in the landscape. The Tertiary strata are marked by coarse basal deposit and by thin and very fine top deposits. Though their deformed condition indicates a period of crustal disturbance, the Tertiary beds give no indication of wholesale transformations. They indicate chiefly tilting and moderate and normal faulting. The previously developed effects of erosion were, therefore, not radically modified. The surface was thus in large measure prepared by erosion in the early Tertiary for its final condition of maturity reached during the early Pliocene.

It seems appropriate, in concluding this chapter, to summarize in its main outlines the physiography of southern Peru, partly to condense the extended discussion of the preceding paragraphs, and partly to supply a background for the three chapters that follow. The outstanding features are broad plateau areas separated by well-defined "Cordilleras." The plateau divisions are not everywhere of the same origin. Those southwest of Cuzco (Fig. 130), and in the Anta Basin (Fig. 124), northwest of Cuzco, are due to prolonged erosion and may be defined as peneplane surfaces uplifted to a great height. They are now bordered on the one hand by deep valleys and troughs and basins of erosion and deformation; and, on the other hand, by residual elevations that owe their present topography to glacial erosion superimposed upon the normal erosion of the peneplane cycle. The residuals form true mountain chains like the Cordillera Vilcanota and Cordillera Vilcapampa; the depressions due to erosion or deformation or both are either basins like those of Anta and Cuzco or valleys of the canyon type like the Urubamba canyon; the plateaus are broad rolling surfaces, the *punas* of the Peruvian Andes.

There are two other types of plateaus. The one represents a mature stage in the erosion cycle instead of an ultimate stage; the other is volcanic in origin. The former is best developed about Antabamba (Figs. 122 and 123), where again deep canyons and residual ranges form the borders of the plateau remnants. The latter is well developed above Cotahuasi and in its simplest form is represented in Fig. 133. Its surface is the top of a vast accumulation of lavas in places over a mile thick. While rough in detail it is astonishingly smooth in a broad view (Fig. 29). Above it rise two types of elevations: first, isolated volcanic cones of great extent surrounded by huge lava flows of considerable relief; and second, discontinuous lines of peaks where volcanic cones of less extent are crowded closely together. The former type is displayed on the Coropuna Quadrangle, the latter on the Cotahuasi and La Cumbre Quadrangles.

So high is the elevation of the lava plateau, so porous its soil, so dry the climate, that a few through-flowing streams gather the drainage of a vast territory and, as in the Grand Canyon country of our West, they have at long intervals cut profound canyons. The Arma has cut a deep gorge at Salamanca; the Cotahuasi runs in a canyon in places 7,000 feet deep; the Majes heads at the edge of the volcanic field in a steep amphitheatre of majestic proportions.

Finally, we have the plateaus of the coastal zone. These are plains with surfaces several thousand feet in elevation separated by gorges several thousand feet deep. The Pampa de Sihuas is an illustration. The post-maturely dissected Coast Range separates it from the sea. The pampas are in general an aggradational product formed in a past age before uplift initiated the present canyon cycle of erosion. Other plateaus of the coastal zone are erosion surfaces. The Tablazo de Ica appears to be of this type. That at Arica, Chile, near the southern boundary of Peru, is demonstrably of this type with a border on which marine planation has in places given rise to a broad terrace effect.[3]

---

[3] The Physiography of the Central Andes, by Isaiah Bowman; Am. Journ. Sci., Vol. 28, 1909, pp. 197-217 and 373-402. See especially, *ibid.*, Fig. 11, p. 216.

Fig. 129.

Fig. 130.

Fig. 129—Composition of slopes at Puquiura, Vilcabamba Valley, elevation 9,000 feet (2,740 m.). The second prominent spur entering the valley on the left has a flattish top unrelated to the rock structure. Like the spurs on the right its blunt end and flat top indicate an earlier erosion cycle at a lower elevation.

Fig. 130—Inclined Paleozoic strata truncated by an undulating surface of erosion at 15,000 feet, southwest of Cuzco.

FIG. 131—Terraced valley slopes at Huaynacotas, Cotahuasi Valley, at 11,500 feet (3,500 m.). Solimana is in the background. On the floor of the Cotahuasi Canyon fruit trees grow. At Huaynacotas corn and potatoes are the chief products. The section is composed almost entirely of lava. There are over a hundred major flows aggregating 5,000 to 7,000 feet thick.

CHAPTER XII

THE WESTERN ANDES: THE MARITIME CORDILLERA OR CORDILLERA OCCIDENTAL

THE Western or Maritime Cordillera of Peru forms part of the great volcanic field of South America which extends from Argentina to Ecuador. On the walls of the Cotahuasi Canyon (Fig. 131), there are exposed over one hundred separate lava flows piled 7,000 feet deep. They overflowed a mountainous relief, completely burying a limestone range from 2,000 to 4,000 feet high. Finally, upon the surface of the lava plateau new mountains were formed, a belt of volcanoes 5,000 feet (1,520 m.) high and from 15,000 to 20,000 feet (4,570 to 6,100 m.) above the sea. There were vast mud flows, great showers of lapilli, dust, and ashes, and with these violent disturbances also came many changes in the drainage. Sixty miles northeast of Cotahuasi the outlet of an unnamed deep valley was blocked, a lake was formed, and several hundred feet of sediments were deposited. They are now wasting rapidly, for they lie in the zone of alternate freezing and thawing, a thousand feet and more below the snowline. Some of their bad-land forms look like the solid bastions of an ancient fortress, while others have the delicate beauty of a Japanese temple.

Not all the striking effects of vulcanism belong to the remote geologic past. A day's journey northeast of Huaynacotas are a group of lakes only recently hemmed in by flows from the small craters thereabouts. The fires in some volcanic craters of the Peruvian Andes are still active, and there is no assurance that devastating flows may not again inundate the valleys. In the great Pacific zone or girdle of volcanoes the earth's crust is yet so unstable that earthquakes occur every year, and at intervals of a few years they have destructive force. Cotahuasi was greatly damaged in 1912; Abancay is shaken every few years; and the violent earthquakes of Cuzco and Arequipa are historic.

On the eastern margin of the volcanic country the flows thin out and terminate on the summit of a limestone (Cretaceous) plateau. On the western margin they descend steeply to the narrow west-coast desert. The greater part of the lava dips beneath the desert deposits; there are a few intercalated flows in the deposits themselves, and the youngest flows—limited in number—have extended down over the inner edge of the desert.

The immediate coast of southern Peru is not volcanic. It is composed of a very hard and ancient granite-gneiss which forms a narrow coastal range (Fig. 171). It has been subjected to very long and continued erosion and now exhibits mature erosion forms of great uniformity of profile and declivity.

From the outcrops of older rocks beneath the lavas it is possible to restore in a measure the pre-volcanic topography of the Maritime Cordillera. In its present altitude it ranges from several thousand to 15,000 feet above sea level. The unburied topography has been smoothed out; the buried topography is rough (Figs. 29 and 166). The contact lines between lavas and buried surfaces in the deep Majes and Cotahuasi valleys are in places excessively serrate. From this, it seems safe to conclude that the period of vulcanism was so prolonged that great changes in the unburied relief were effected by the agents of erosion. Thus, while the dominant process of volcanic upbuilding smoothed the former rough topography of the Maritime Cordillera, erosion likewise measurably smoothed the present high extra-volcanic relief in the central and eastern sections. The effect has been to develop a broad and sufficiently smooth aspect to the summit topography of the entire Andes to give them a plateau character. Afterward the whole mountain region was uplifted about a mile above its former level so that at present it is also continuously lofty.

The zone of most intense volcanic action does not coincide with the highest part of the pre-volcanic topography. If the pre-volcanic relief were even in a very general way like that which would be exhibited if the lavas were now removed, we should have to say that the chief volcanic outbursts took place on the western flank of an old and deeply dissected limestone range.

The volume of the lavas is enormous. They are a mile and a half thick, nearly a hundred miles wide, and of indefinite extent north and south. Their addition to the Andes, therefore, *has greatly broadened the zone of lofty mountains.* Their passes are from 2,000 to 3,000 feet higher than the passes of the eastern Andes. They have a much smaller number of valleys sufficiently deep to enjoy a mild climate. Their soil is far more porous and dry. Their vegetation is more scanty. They more than double the difficulties of transportation. And, finally, their all but unpopulated loftier expanses are a great vacant barrier between farms in the warm valleys of eastern Peru and the ports on the west coast.

The upbuilding process was not, of course, continuous. There were at times intervals of quiet, and some of them were long enough to enable streams to become established. Buried valleys may be observed in a number of places on the canyon walls, where subsequently lava flows displaced the streams and initiated new drainage systems. In these quiet intervals the weathering agents attacked the rock surfaces and formed soil. There were at least three or four such prolonged periods of weathering and erosion wherein a land surface was exposed for many thousands of years, stream systems organized, and a cultivable soil formed. No evidence has been found, however, that man was there to cultivate the soil.

The older valleys cut in the quiet period are mere pygmies beside the giant canyons of today. The present is the time of dominant erosion. The forces of vulcanism are at last relatively quiet. Recent flows have occurred, but they are limited in extent and in effects. They alter only the minor details of topography and drainage. Were it not for the oases set in the now deep-cut canyon floors, the lava plateau of the Maritime Cordillera would probably be the greatest single tract of unoccupied volcanic country in the world.

The lava plateau has been dissected to a variable degree. Its high eastern margin is almost in its original condition. Its western margin is only a hundred miles from the sea, so that the streams have steep gradients. In addition, it is lofty enough to have a moderate rainfall. It is, therefore, deeply and generally dissected. Within the borders of the plateau the degree of dissection depends chiefly upon position with respect to the large streams. These were in turn located in an accidental manner. The repeated upbuilding of the surface by the extensive outflow of liquid rock obliterated all traces of the earlier drainage. In the Cotahuasi Canyon the existing stream, working down through a mile of lavas, at last uncovered and cut straight across a mountain spur 2,000 feet high. Its course is at right angles to that pursued by the stream that once drained the spur. It is noteworthy that the Cotahuasi and adjacent streams take northerly courses and join Atlantic rivers. The older drainage was directly west to the Pacific. Thus, vulcanism not only broadened the Andes and increased their height, but also moved the continental divide still nearer the west coast.

The glacial features of the western or Maritime Cordillera are of small extent, partly because vulcanism has added a considerable amount of material in post-glacial time, partly because the climate is so exceedingly dry that the snowline lies near the top of the country. The slopes of the volcanic cones are for the most part deeply recessed on the southern or shady sides. Above 17,500 feet (5,330 m.) the process of snow and ice excavation still continues, but the tracts that exceed this elevation are confined to the loftiest peaks or their immediate neighborhood. There is a distinct difference between the glacial forms of the eastern or moister and the western or dryer flanks of this Cordillera. Only peaks like Coropuna and Solimana near the western border now bear or ever bore snowfields and glaciers. By contrast the eastern aspect is heavily glaciated. On La Cumbre Quadrangle, there is a huge glacial trough at 16,000 feet (4,876 m.), and this extends with ramifications up into the snowfields that formerly included the highest country. Prolonged glacial erosion produced a full set of topographic forms characteristic of the work of Alpine glaciers. Thus, each of the main mountain chains that make up the Andean system has, like the system as a whole, a relatively more-dry and a relatively less-dry aspect.   The snowline is, therefore, canted from west to east on each chain as well as on the system.   However, this effect is combined with a solar effect in an unequal way. In the driest places the solar factor is the more efficient and the snowline is there canted from north to south.

CHAPTER XIII

THE EASTERN ANDES: THE CORDILLERA VILCAPAMPA

THE culminating range of the eastern Andes is the so-called Cordillera Vilcapampa. Its numerous, sharp, snow-covered peaks are visible in every summit view from the central portion of the Andean system almost to the western border of the Amazon basin. Though the range forms a water parting nearly five hundred miles long, it is crossed in several places by large streams that flow through deep canyons bordered by precipitous cliffs. The Urubamba between Torontoy and Colpani is the finest illustration. For height and ruggedness the Vilcapampa mountains are among the most noteworthy in Peru. Furthermore, they display glacial features on a scale unequaled elsewhere in South America north of the ice fields of Patagonia.

GLACIERS AND GLACIAL FORMS

One of the most impressive sights in South America is a tropical forest growing upon a glacial moraine. In many places in eastern Bolivia and Peru the glaciers of the Ice Age were from 5 to 10 miles long—almost the size of the Mer de Glace or the famous Rhone glacier. In the Juntas Valley in eastern Bolivia the tree line is at 10,000 feet (3,050 m.), but the terminal moraines lie several thousand feet lower. In eastern Peru the glaciers in many places extended down nearly to the tree line and in a few places well below it. In the Cordillera Vilcapampa vast snowfields and glacier systems were spread out over a summit area as broad as the Southern Appalachians. The snowfields have since shrunk to the higher mountain recesses; the glaciers have retreated for the most part to the valley heads or the cirque floors; and the lower limit of perpetual snow has been raised to 15,500 feet.

FIG. 132.

FIG. 133.

FIG. 132—Recessed volcanoes in the right background and eroded tuffs, ash beds, and lava flows on the left. Maritime Cordillera above Cotahuasi.

FIG. 133—The summit of the great lava plateau above Cotahuasi on the trail to Antabamba. The lavas are a mile and a half in thickness. The elevation is 16,000 feet. Hence the volcanoes in the background, 17,000 feet above sea level, are mere hills on the surface of the lofty plateau.

Fig. 134.

Fig. 135.

Fig. 134—Southwestern aspect of the Cordillera Vilcapampa between Anta and Urubamba from Lake Huaipo. Rugged summit topography in the background, graded post-mature slopes in the middle distance, and solution lake in limestone in the foreground.

Fig. 135—Summit view, Cordillera Vilcapampa. There are fifteen glaciers represented in this photograph. The camera stands on the summit of a minor divide in the zone of nivation.

These features are surprising because neither Whymper [1] nor Wolf [2] mentions the former greater extent of the ice on the volcanoes of Ecuador, only ten or twelve degrees farther north. Moreover, Reiss [3] denies that the hypothesis of universal climatic change is supported by the facts of a limited glaciation in the High Andes of Ecuador; and J. W. Gregory [4] completely overlooks published proof of the existence of former more extensive glaciers elsewhere in the Andes:

" . . . the absence not only of any traces of former more extensive glaciation from the tropics, as in the Andes and Kilimandjaro, but also from the Cape." He says further: "In spite of the extensive glaciers now in existence on the higher peaks of the Andes, there is practically no evidence of their former greater extension." (!)

Whymper spent most of his time in exploring recent volcanoes or those recently in eruption, hence did not have the most favorable opportunities for gathering significant data. Reiss was carried off his feet by the attractiveness of the hypothesis [5] relating to the effect of glacial denudation on the elevation of the snowline. Gregory appeared not to have recognized the work of Hettner on the Cordillera of Bogotá and of Sievers [6] and Acosta on the Sierra Nevada de Santa Marta in northern Colombia.

The importance of the glacial features of the Cordillera Vilcapampa developed on a great scale in very low latitudes in the southern hemisphere is twofold: first, it bears on the still unsettled problem of the universality of a colder climate in the Pleistocene, and, second, it supplies additional data on the relative depression of the snowline in glacial times in the tropics.   Snow-

---

[1] Travels Amongst the Great Andes of the Equator, 1892.

[2] Geografia y Geologia del Ecuador, 1892.

[3] Das Hochgebirge der Republik Ecuador, Vol. 2, 2 Ost-Cordillera, 1902, p. 162.

[4] Contributions to the Geology of British East Africa; Pt. 1, The Glacial Geology of Mount Kenia, Quart. Journ. Geol. Soc., Vol. 50, 1894, p. 523.

[5] See especially A. Penck (Penck and Brückner), Die Alpen im Eiszeitalter, 1909, Vol. 1, p. 6, and I. C. Russell, Glaciers of Mount Rainier, 18th Ann. Rep't, U. S. Geol. Surv., 1896-97, Sect. 2, pp. 384-385.

[6] Die Sierra Nevada de Santa Marta und die Sierra de Perijá, Zeitschrift der Gesellschaft für Erdkunde zu Berlin, Vol. 23, 1888, pp. 1-158.

clad mountains near the equator are really quite rare. Mount
Kenia rising from a great jungle on the equator, Kilimandjaro
with its two peaks, Kibo and Mawenzi, two hundred miles farther
south, and Ingomwimbi in the Ruwenzori group thirty miles north
of the equator, are the chief African examples. A few mountains
from the East Indies, such as Kinibalu in Borneo, latitude 6° north,
have been found glaciated, though now without a snow cover. In
higher latitudes evidences of an earlier extensive glaciation have
been gathered chiefly from South America, whose extension 13°
north and 56° south of the equator, combined with the great height
of its dominating Cordillera, give it unrivaled distinction in the
study of mountain glaciation in the tropics.

Furthermore, mountain summits in tropical lands are delicate
climatic registers. In this respect they compare favorably with
the inclosed basins of arid regions, where changes in climate are
clearly recorded in shoreline phenomena of a familiar kind. Lofty
mountains in the tropics are in a sense inverted basins, the lower
snowline of the past is like the higher shoreline of an interior
basin; the terminal moraines and the alluvial fans in front of them
are like the alluvial fans above the highest strandline; the present
snow cover is restricted to mountain summits of small areal extent, just as the present water bodies are restricted to the lowest
portions of the interior basin; and successive retreatal stages are
marked by terminal moraines in the one case as they are marked
in the other by flights of terraces and beach ridges.

I made only a rapid reconnaissance across the Cordillera Vilcapampa in the winter season, and cannot pretend from my limited
observations to solve many of the problems of the field. The data
are incorporated chiefly in the chapter on Glacial Features.
In this place it is proposed to describe only the more prominent
glacial features, leaving to later expeditions the detailed descrip-
tions upon which the solution of some of the larger problems must
depend.

At Choquetira three prominent stages in the retreat of the ice
are recorded. The lowermost stage is represented by the great fill
of morainic and outwash material at the junction of the Choque-

tira, and an unnamed valley farther south at an elevation of 11,500 feet (3,500 m.). A mile below Choquetira a second moraine appears, elevation 12,000 feet (3,658 m.), and immediately above the village a third at 12,800 (3,900 m.). The lowermost moraine is well dissected, the second is ravined and broken but topographically distinct, the third is sharp-crested and regular. A fourth though minor stage is represented by the moraine at the snout of the living glacier and still less important phases are represented in some valleys—possibly the r e c o r d   o f   post-glacial changes of climate. Each main moraine is marked by an important amount of outwash, the first and third moraines being associated with the greatest masses. The material in the moraines represents only a part of that removed to form the successive steps in the valley profile. The lowermost one has an enormous volume, since it is the oldest and

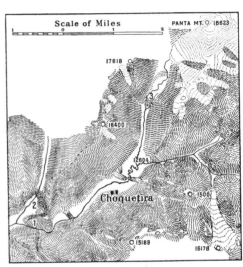

Fig. 136—Glacial sculpture on the southwestern flank of the Cordillera Vilcapampa. Flat-floored valleys and looped terminal moraines below and glacial steps and hanging valleys are characteristic. The present snowfields and glaciers are shown by dotted contours.

was built at a time when the valley was full of waste. It is fronted by a deep fill, over the dissected edge of which one may descend 800 feet in half an hour. It is chiefly alluvial in character, whereas the next higher one is composed chiefly of bowlders and is fronted by a pronounced bowlder train, which includes a remarkable perched bowlder of huge size. Once the valley became cleaned out the ice would derive its material chiefly by the slower process of plucking and abrasion, hence would build much smaller moraines during later recessional stages, even though the stages were of equivalent length.

There is a marked difference in the degree of dissection of the moraines. The lowermost and oldest is so thoroughly dissected as to exhibit but little of its original surface. The second has been greatly modified, but still possesses a ridge-like quality and marks the beginning of a noteworthy flattening of the valley gradient. The third is as sharp-crested as a roof, and yet was built so long ago that the flat valley floor behind it has been modified by the meandering stream. From this point the glacier retreated up-valley several miles (estimated) without leaving more than the thinnest veneer on the valley floor. The retreat must, therefore, have been rapid and without even temporary halts until the glacier reached a position near that occupied today. Both the present ice tongues and snowfields and those of a past age are emphasized by the presence of a patch of scrub and woodland that extends on the north side of the valley from near the snowline down over the glacial forms to the lower valley levels.

The retreatal stages sketched above would call for no special comment if they were encountered in mountains in northern latitudes. They would be recognized at once as evidence of successive periodic retreats of the ice, due to successive changes in temperature. To understand their importance when encountered in very low latitudes it is necessary to turn aside for a moment and consider two rival hypotheses of glacial retreat. First we have the hypothesis of periodic retreat, so generally applied to terminal moraines and associated outwash in glaciated mountain valleys. This implies also an advance of the ice from a higher position, the whole taking place as a result of a climatic change from warmer to colder and back again to warmer.

But evidences of more extensive mountain glaciation in the past do not in themselves prove a change in climate over the whole earth. In an epoch of fixed climate a glacier system may so deeply and thoroughly erode a mountain mass, that the former glaciers may either diminish in size or disappear altogether. As the work of excavation proceeds, the catchment basins are sunk to, and at last below, the snowline; broad tributary spurs whose snows nourish the glaciers, may be reduced to narrow or skeleton ridges with little snow to contribute to the valleys on either hand; the

Fig. 137.

Fig. 138.

Fig. 137—Looking up a spurless flat-floored glacial trough near the Chucuito pass in the Cordillera Vilcapampa from 14,200 feet (4,330 m.). Note the looped terminal and lateral moraines on the steep valley wall on the left. A stone fence from wall to wall serves to inclose the flock of the mountain shepherd.

Fig. 138—Terminal moraine in the glaciated Choquetira Valley below Choquetira. The people who live here have an abundance of stones for building corrals and stone houses. The upper edge of the timber belt (cold timber line) is visible beyond the houses. Elevation 12,100 feet (3,690 m.).

glaciers retreat and at last disappear. There would be evidences of glaciation all about the ruins of the former loftier mountain, but there would be no living glaciers. And yet the climate might remain the same throughout.

It is this "topographic" hypothesis that Reiss and Stübel accept for the Ecuadorean volcanoes. Moreover, the volcanoes of Ecuador are practically on the equator—a very critical situation when we wish to use the facts they exhibit in the solution of such large problems as the contemporaneous glaciation of the two hemispheres, or the periodic advance and retreat of the ice over the whole earth. This is not the place to scrutinize either their facts or their hypothesis, but I am under obligations to state very emphatically that the glacial features of the Cordillera Vilca-pampa require the climatic and not the topographic hypothesis. Let us see why.

The differences in degree of dissection and the flattening gradient up-valley that we noted in a preceding paragraph leave no doubt that each moraine of the bordering valleys in the Vilca-pampa region, represents a prolonged period of stability in the conditions of topography as well as of temperature and precipita-tion. If change in topographic conditions is invoked to explain retreat from one position to the other there is left no explanation of the periodicity of retreat which has just been established. If a period of cold is inaugurated and glaciers advance to an ulti-mate position, they can retreat only through change of climate effected either by general causes or by topographic development to the point where the snowfields become restricted in size. In the case of climatic change the ice changes are periodic. In the case of retreat due to topographic change there should be a steady or non-periodic falling back of the ice front as the catchment basins decrease in elevation and the snow-gathering ridges tribu-tary to them are reduced in height.

Further, the matterhorns of the Cordillera Vilcapampa are not bare but snow-covered, vigorous glaciers several miles in length and large snowfields still survive and the divides are not arêtes but broad ridges. In addition, the last two moraines, composed of very loose material, are well preserved. They indicate clearly that the time since their formation has witnessed no wholesale topographic change. If (1) no important topographic changes have taken place, and (2) a vigorous glacier lay for a long period back of a given moraine, and (3) *suddenly retreated several miles and again became stable,* we are left without confidence in the application of the topographic hypothesis to the glacial

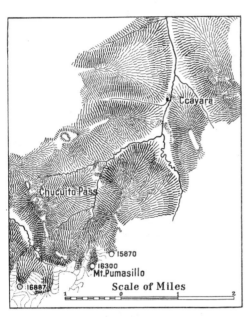

features of the Vilcapampa region. Glacial retreat may be suddenly begun in the case of a late stage of topographic development, but it should be an orderly retreat marked by a large number of small moraines, or at least a plentiful strewing of the valley floor with débris.

The number of moraines in the various glaciated valleys of the Cordillera Vilcapampa differ, owing to differences in elevation and to the variable size of the catchment basins. All valleys, however, display the

Fig. 139—Glacial features on the eastern slopes of the Cordillera Vilcapampa.

same sudden change from moraine to moraine and the same characteristics of gradient. In all of them the lowermost moraine is always more deeply eroded than the higher moraines, in all of them glacial erosion was sufficiently prolonged greatly to modify the valley walls, scour out lake basins, or broad flat valley floors, develop cirques, arêtes, and pinnacled ridges in limited number. In some, glaciation was carried to the point where only skeleton divides remained, in most places broad massive ridges or mountain knots persist. In spite of all these differences successive moraines were formed, separated by long stretches either thinly covered with till or exposing bare rock.

In examining this group of features it is important to recognize the essential fact that though the number of moraines varies from valley to valley, the differences in character between the moraines at low and at high elevations in a single valley are constant. It is also clear that everywhere the ice retreated and advanced periodically, no matter with what topographic features it was associated, whether those of maturity or of youth in the glacial cycle. We, therefore, conclude that topographic changes had no significant part to play in the glacial variations in the Cordillera Vilcapampa.

The country west of the Cordillera Vilcapampa had been reduced to early topographic maturity before the Ice Age, and then uplifted with only moderate erosion of the masses of the interfluves. That on the east had passed through the same sequence of events, but erosion had been carried much farther. The reason for this is found in a strong climatic contrast. The eastern is the windward aspect and receives much more rain than the western. Therefore, it has more streams and more rapid dissection. The result was that the eastern slopes were cut to pieces rapidly after the last great regional uplift; the broad interfluves were narrowed to ridges. The region eastward from the crest of the Cordillera to the Pongo de Mainique looks very much like the western half of the Cascade Mountains in Oregon the summit tracts of moderate declivity are almost all consumed.

The effect of these climatic and topographic contrasts is manifested in strong contrasts in the position and character of the glacial forms on the opposite slopes of the range. At Pampaconas on the east the lowermost terminal moraine is at least a thousand feet below timber line. Between Vilcabamba pueblo and Puquiura the terminal moraine lies at 11,200 feet (3,414 m.). By contrast the largest Pleistocene glacier on the western slope, nearly twelve miles long, and the largest along the traverse, ended several miles below Choquetira at 11,500 feet (3,504 m.) elevation, or just at the timber line. Thus, the steeper descents of the eastern side of the range appear to have carried short glaciers to levels far lower than those attained by the glaciers of the western slope.

It seems at first strange that the largest glaciers were west of the divide between the Urubamba and the Apurimac, that is, on the relatively dry side of the range. The reason lies in a striking combination of topographic and climatic conditions. Snow is a mobile form of precipitation that is shifted about by the wind like a sand dune in the desert. It is not required, like water, to begin a downhill movement as soon as it strikes the earth. Thus, it is a noteworthy fact that snow drifting across the divides may ultimately cause the largest snowfields to lie where the least snow actually falls. This is illustrated in the Bighorns of Wyoming and others of our western ranges. It is, however, not the wet snow near the snowline, but chiefly the dry snow of higher altitudes that is affected. What is now the dry or leeward side

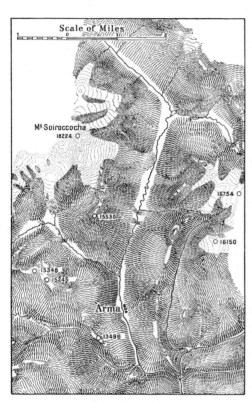

FIG. 140—Glacial sculpture in the heart of the Cordillera Vilcapampa. In places the topography has so high a relief that the glaciers seem almost to overhang the valleys. See Figs. 96 and 179 for photographs.

of the Cordillera appears in glacial times to have actually received more snow than the wet windward side.

The topography conspired to increase this contrast. In place of many streams, direct descents, a dispersion of snow in many valleys, as on the east, the western slopes had indirect descents, gentler valley profiles, and that higher degree of concentration of drainage which naturally goes with topographic maturity. For example, there is nothing in the east to compare with the big spurless valley near the pass above Arma. The side walls were so extensively trimmed that the valley was turned into a trough. The floor was smoothed and deepened and all the tributary glaciers were either left high up on the bordering slopes or entered the main valley with very steep profiles; their lateral and terminal moraines now hang in festoons on the steep side walls. Moreover, the range crest is trimmed from the west so that the serrate skyline is a feature rarely seen from eastern viewpoints. This may not hold true for more than a small part of the Cordillera. It was probably emphasized here less by the contrasts already noted than by the geologic structure. The eastward-flowing glaciers descended over dip slopes on highly inclined sandstones, as at Pampaconas. Those flowing westward worked either in a jointed granite or on the outcropping *edges* of the sandstones, where the quarrying process known as glacial plucking permitted the development of excessively steep slopes.

There are few glacial steps in the eastern valleys. The western valleys have a marvelous display of this striking glacial feature. The accompanying hachure maps show them so well that little description is needed. They are from 50 to 200 feet high. Each one has a lake at its foot into which the divided stream trickles over charming waterfalls. All of them are clearly associated with a change in the volume of the glacier that carved the valley. Wherever a tributary glacier entered, or the side slopes increased notably in area, a step was formed. By retreat some of them became divided, for the process once begun, would push the step far up valley after the manner of an extinguishing waterfall.

The retreat of the steps, the abrasion of the rock, and the sapping of the cirques at the valley heads excavated the upper valleys so deeply that they are nearly all, as W. D. Johnson has put it, "down at the heel." Thus, above Arma, one plunges suddenly from the smooth, grassy glades of the strongly glaciated valley head down over the outer slopes of the lowermost terminal moraine to the steep lower valley. Above the moraine are fine pastures, in the steep valley below are thickets and rocky defiles. There are long quiet reaches in the streams of the glaciated valley heads besides pretty lakes and marshes. Below, the stream is swift, almost torrential. Arma itself is built upon alluvial deposits of glacial origin. A mile farther down the valley is constricted and steep-walled—really a canyon.

Though the glaciers have retreated to the summit region, they are by no means nearing extinction. The clear blue ice of the glacier descending from Mt. Soiroccocha in the Arma Valley seems almost to hang over the precipitous valley border. In curious contrast to its suggestion of cold and storm is the patch of dark green woodland which extends right up to its border. An earthquake might easily cause the glacier to invade the woodland. Some of the glaciers between Choquetira and Arma rest on terminal moraines whose distal faces are from 200 to 300 feet high. The ice descending southeasterly from Panta Mt. is a good illustration. Earlier positions of the ice front are marked by equally large moraines. The one nearest that engaged by the living glacier confines a large lake that discharges through a gap in the moraine and over a waterfall to the marshy floor of the valley.

Retreat has gone so far, however, that there are only a few large glacier systems. Most of the tributaries have withdrawn toward their snowfields. In place of the twenty distinct glaciers now lying between the pass and the terminal moraine below Choquetira, there was in glacial times one great glacier with twenty minor tributaries. The cirques now partly filled with damp snow must then have been overflowing with dry snow above and ice below. Some of the glaciers were over a thousand feet thick; a few were nearly two thousand feet thick, and the cirques that fed them held snow and ice at least a half mile deep. Such a remarkably complete set of glacial features only 700 miles from the equator is striking evidence of the moist climate on the windward eastern part of the great Andean Cordillera, of the universal change in climate in the glacial period, and of the powerful dominating effects of ice erosion in this region of unsurpassed Alpine relief.

The main axis of the Cordillera Vilcapampa consists of granite in the form of a batholith between crystalline schists on the one hand (southwest), and Carboniferous limestones and sandstones and Silurian shales and slates on the other (northeast). It is not a domal uplift in the region in which it was observed in 1911, but

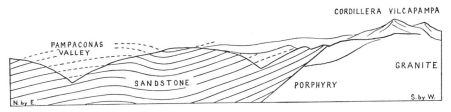

Fig. 141—Composite geologic section on the northeastern border of the Cordillera Vilcapampa, in the vicinity of Pampaconas, to show the deformative effects of the granite intrusion. There is a limited amount of limestone near the border of the Cordillera. Both limestone and sandstone are Carboniferous. See Appendix B. See also Figs. 142 and 146. The section is about 15 miles long.

an axial intrusion, in places restricted to a narrow belt not more than a score of miles across. As we should expect from the variable nature of the invaded material, the granite belt is not uniform in width nor in the character of its marginal features. In places the intrusion has produced strikingly little alteration of the country rock; in other localities the granite has been injected into the original material in so intimate a manner as almost completely to alter it, and to give rise to a very broad zone of highly metamorphosed rock. Furthermore, branches were developed so that here and there tributary belts of granite extend from the main mass to a distance of many miles. Outlying batholiths occur whose common petrographic character and similar manner of occurrence leave little doubt that they are related abyssally to a common plutonic mass.

The Vilcapampa batholith has two highly contrasted borders, whether we consider the degree of metamorphism of the country rock, the definition of the border, or the resulting topographic forms. On the northeastern ridge at Colpani the contact is so sharp that the outstretched arms in some places embrace typical granite on the one hand and almost unaltered shales and slates on the other. Inclusions or xenoliths of shale are common, however, ten and fifteen miles distant, though they are prominent features in a belt only a few miles wide. The lack of more intense contact effects is a little remarkable in view of the altered character of

the inclusions, all of which are crystalline in contrast to the fissile shales from which they are chiefly derived. Inclusions within a few inches of the border fall into a separate class, since they show in general but trifling alteration and preserve their original cleavage planes. It appears that the depth of the intrusion must have been rela-

FIG. 142—The deformative effects of the Vilcapampa intrusion on the northeastern border of the Cordillera. The deformed strata are heavy-bedded sandstones and shales and the igneous rocks are chiefly granites with bordering porphyries. Looking northwest near Puquiura. For conditions near Pampaconas, looking in the opposite direction, see Fig. 141. For conditions on the other side of the Cordillera see Fig. 146.

tively slight or the intrusion sudden, or both shallow and sudden, conditions which produce a narrow zone of metamorphosed material and a sharp contact.

The relation between shale and granite at Colpani is shown in Fig. 143. Projections of granite extend several feet into the shale and slate and generally end in blunt barbs or knobs. In a few places there is an intimate mixture of irregular slivers and blocks of crystallized sediments in a granitic groundmass, with sharp lines of demarcation between igneous and included material. The contact is vertical for at least several miles. It is probable that other localities on the con-

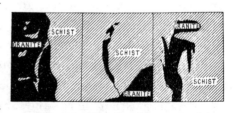

FIG. 143—Relation of granite intrusion to schist on the northeastern border of the Vilcapampa batholith near the bridge of Colpani, lower end of the granite Canyon of Torontoy. The sections are from 15 to 25 feet high and represent conditions at different levels along the well-defined contact.

tact exhibit much greater modification and invasion of the weak shales and slates, but at Colpani the phenomena are both simple and restricted in development.

The highly mineralized character of the bordering sedimentary strata, and the presence of numbers of complementary dikes, nearly identical in character to those in the parent granite now exposed by erosion over a broad belt roughly parallel to the contact, supplies a basis for the inference that the granite may underlie the former at a slight depth, or may have had far greater metamorphic effects upon its sedimentary roof than the intruded granite has had upon its sedimentary rim.

The physiographic features of the contact belt are of special interest. No available physiographic interpretation of the topography of a batholith includes a discussion of those topographic and drainage features that are related to the lithologic character of the intruded rock, the manner of its intrusion, or the depth of erosion since intrusion. Yet each one of these factors has a distinct topographic effect. We shall, therefore, turn aside for a moment from the detailed discussion of the Vilcapampa region to an examination of several physiographic principles and then return to the main theme for applications.

It is recognized that igneous intrusions are of many varieties and that even batholithic invasions may take place in rather widely different ways. Highly heated magmas deeply buried beneath the earth's surface produce maximum contact effects, those nearer the surface may force the strata apart without extreme lithologic alterations of the displaced beds, while through the stoping process a sedimentary cover may be largely absorbed and the magmas may even break forth at the surface as in ordinary vulcanism. If the sedimentary beds have great vertical variation in resistance, in attitude, and in composition, there may be afforded an opportunity for the display of quite different effects at different levels along a given contact, so that a great variety of physical conditions will be passed by the descending levels of erosion. At one place erosion may have exposed only the summit of the batholith, at another the associated dikes and sheets and ramifying branches may be exposed as in the zone of fracture, at a third point the original zone of flowage may be reached with characteristic marginal schistosity, while at still greater depths there may be uncovered a highly metamorphosed rim of resistant sedimentary rock.

The mere enumeration of these variable structural features is sufficient to show how variable we should expect the associated land forms to be. Were the forms of small extent, or had they but slight distinction upon comparison with other erosional effects, they would be of little concern. They are, on the contrary, very extensively developed; they affect large numbers of lofty mountain ranges besides still larger areas of old land masses subjected to extensive and deep erosion, thus laying bare many batholiths long concealed by a thick sedimentary roof.

The differences between intruded and country rock dependent upon these diversified conditions of occurrence are increased or diminished according to the history of the region after batholithic invasion takes place. Regional metamorphism may subsequently induce new structures or minimize the effects of the old. Joint systems may be developed, the planes widely spaced in one group of rocks giving rise to monolithic masses very resistant to the agents of weathering, while those of an adjacent group may be so closely spaced as greatly to hasten the rate of denudation. There may be developed so great a degree of schistosity in one rock as to give rise (with vigorous erosion) to a serrate topography; on the other hand the forms developed on the rocks of a batholith may be massive and coarse-textured.

To these diversifying conditions may be added many others involving a large part of the field of dynamic geology. It will perhaps suffice to mention two others: the stage of erosion and the special features related to climate. If a given intrusion has been accompanied by an important amount of uplift or marginal compression, vigorous erosion may follow, whereupon a chance will be offered for the development of the greatest contrast in the degree of boldness of topographic forms developed upon rocks of unequal resistance. Ultimately these contrasts will diminish in intensity, as in the case of all regional differences of relief, with progress toward the end of the normal cycle of erosion. If peneplanation ensue, only feeble topographic differences may mark

Fig. 144—Cliffed canyon wall in the Urubamba Valley between Huadquiña and Torontoy. There is a descent of nearly 2,000 feet shown in the photograph, and it is developed almost wholly along successive joint planes.

Fig. 145—Another aspect of the canyon wall of Fig. 144. The almost sheer descents are in contrast with the cliff-and-platform type of topography characteristic of the Grand Canyon of the Colorado.

the line of contact which was once a prominent topographic feature. With reference to the effects of climate it may be said simply that a granite core of batholithic origin may extend above the snowline or above timber line or into the timbered belt, whereas the invaded rock may occur largely below these levels with obvious differences in both the rate and the kind of erosion affecting the intruded mass.

If we apply the foregoing considerations to the Cordillera Vilcapampa, we shall find some striking illustrations of the principles involved. The invasion of the granite was accompanied by moderate absorption of the displaced rock, and more especially by the marginal pushing aside of the sedimentary rim. The immediate effect must have been to give both intruded rock and country rock greater height and marked ruggedness. There followed a period of regional compression and torsion, and the development of widespread joint systems with strikingly regular features. In the Silurian shales and slates these joints are closely spaced; in the granites they are in many places twenty to thirty feet apart. The shales, therefore, offer many more points of attack and have weathered down into a smooth-contoured topography boldly overlooked along the contact by walls and peaks of granite. *In some cases a canyon wall a mile high is developed entirely on two or three joint planes inclined at an angle no greater than 15°.* The effect in the granite is to give a marked boldness of relief, nowhere more strikingly exhibited than at Huadquiña, below Colpani, where the foot-hill slopes developed cn shales and slates suddenly become moderate. The river flows from a steep and all but uninhabited canyon into a broad valley whose slopes are dotted with the terraced *chacras,* or farms, of the mountain Indians.

The Torontoy granite is also homogeneous while the shales and slates together with their more arenaceous associates occur in alternating belts, a diversity which increases the points of attack and the complexity of the forms. Tending toward the same result is the greater hardness of the granite. The tendency of the granite to develop bold forms is accelerated in lofty valleys disposed about snow-clad peaks, where glaciers of great size once existed, and where small glaciers still linger. The plucking action of ice has an excellent chance for expression, since the granite may be quarried cleanly without the production of a large amount of spoil which would load the ice and diminish the intensity of its plucking action.

As a whole the Central Andes passed through a cycle of erosion in late Tertiary time which was interrupted by uplift after the general surface had been reduced to a condition of topographic maturity. Upon the granites mature slopes are not developed except under special conditions (1) of elevation as in the small batholith above Chuquibambilla, and (2) where the granite is itself bordered by resistant schists which have upheld the surface over a broad transitional belt. Elsewhere the granite is marked by exceedingly rugged forms: deep steep-walled canyons, precipitous cirques, matterhorns, and bold and extended escarpments of erosion. In the shale belt the trails run from valley to valley in every direction without special difficulties, but in the granite they follow the rivers closely or cross the axis of the range by carefully selected routes which generally reach the limit of perpetual snow. Added interest attaches to these bold topographic forms because of the ruins now found along the canyon walls, as at Torontoy, or high up on the summit of a precipitous spur, as at Machu Picchu near the bridge of San Miguel.

The Vilcapampa batholith is bordered on the southwest by a series of ancient schists with which the granite sustains quite different relations. No sharp dividing line is visible, the granite extending along the planes of foliation for such long distances as in places to appear almost interbedded with the schists. The relation is all the more striking in view of the trifling intrusions effected in the case of the seemingly much weaker shales on the opposite contact. Nor is the metamorphism of the invaded rock limited to simple intrusion. For several miles beyond the zone of intenser effects the schists have been enriched with quartz to such an extent that their original darker color has been changed to light gray or dull white. At a distance they may even appear as homogeneous and light-colored as the granite. At distant points the schists assume a darker hue and take on the characters of a rather typical mica schist.

It is probable that the Vilcapampa intrusion is one of a family of batholiths which further study may show to extend over a much larger territory. The trail west of Abancay was followed quite closely and accidentally crosses two small batholiths of peculiar interest. Their limits were not closely followed out, but

Fig. 146—Deformative effects on limestone strata of the granite intrusion on the southwestern border of the Vilcapampa batholith above Chuquibambilla. Fig. 147 is on the same border of the batholith several miles farther northwest. The granite mass on the right is a small outlier of the main batholith looking south. The limestone is Cretaceous. See Appendix C for locations.

were accurately determined at a number of points and the remaining portion of the contact inferred from the topography. In the case of the larger area there may indeed be a connection westward with a larger mass which probably constitutes the ranges distant some five to ten miles from the line of traverse.

These smaller intrusions are remarkable in that they appear to have been attended by little alteration of either invading or invaded rock, though the granites were observed to become distinctly more acid in the contact zone. Space was made for them by displacing the sedimentary cover and by a marked shortening of the sedimentary rim through such structures as overthrust faults and folds. The contact is observable in a highly metamorphosed belt about twenty feet wide, and for several hundred feet more the granite has absorbed the limestone in small amounts with the production of new minerals and the development of a distinctly lighter color. The deformative effects of the batholithic invasion are shown in their gross details in Figs. 141, 142, and 146; the finer details of structure are represented in Fig. 147, which is drawn from a measured outcrop above Chuquibambilla.

It will be seen that we have here more than a mere crinkling, such as the mica schists of the Cordillera Vilcapampa display. The diversified sedimentary series is folded and faulted on a large scale with broad structural undulations visible for miles along the abrupt valley walls. Here and there, however, the strata become weaker generally through the thinning of the beds and the more rapid alternation of hard and soft layers, and for short distances

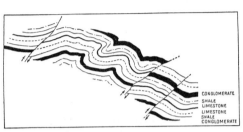

they have absorbed notable amounts of the stresses induced by the igneous intrusions. In such places not only the structure but the composition of the rock shows the effects of the intrusion. Certain shales in the section are carbonaceous and in all observed cases the organic matter has been transformed to anthracite, a

FIG. 147—Overthrust folds in detail on the southwestern border of the Vilcapampa batholith near Chuquibambilla. The section is fifteen feet high. Elevation, 13,100 feet (4,000 m.). For comparison with the structural effects of the Vilcapampa intrusion on the northeast see Fig. 142.

condition generally associated with a certain amount of minute mashing and a cementation of both limestone and sandstone.

The granite becomes notably darker on approach to the northeastern contact near Colpani; the proportion of ferro-magnesian minerals in some cases is so large as to give a distinctly black color in sharp contrast to the nearly white granite typical of the central portion of the mass. Large masses of shale foundered in the invading magma, and upon fusion gave rise to huge black masses impregnated with quartz and in places smeared or injected with granite magma. Everywhere the granite is marked by numbers of black masses which appear at first sight to be aggregations of dark minerals normal to the granite and due to differentiation processes at the time of crystallization. It is, however, noteworthy that these increase rapidly in number on approach to the contact, until in the last half-mile they appear to grade into the shale inclusions. It may, therefore, be doubted that they are aggregations. From their universal distribution, their uniform character, and their marked increase in numbers on approach to lateral contacts, it may reasonably be inferred that they represent foundered masses of country rock. Those distant from present contacts are in almost all cases from a few inches to a foot in diameter, while on approach to lateral contacts they are in places ten to twenty feet in width, as if the smaller areas represented the last remnants of large inclusions engulfed in the magma near the upper or roof contact. They are so thoroughly injected with silica and also with typical granite magma as to make their reference to the country rock less secure on petrographical than on purely distributional grounds.

A parallel line of evidence relates to the distribution of complementary dikes throughout the granite. In the main mass of the batholith the dikes are rather evenly distributed as to kind with a slight preponderance of the dark-colored group. Near the contact, however, aplitic dikes cease altogether and great numbers of melanocratic dikes appear. It may be inferred that we have in this pronounced condition suggestions of strong influence upon the final processes of invasion and cooling of the granite magma, on the part of the country rock detached and absorbed by the invading mass. It might be supposed that the indicated change in the character of the complementary dikes could be ascribed to possible differentiation of the granite magma whereby a darker facies would be developed toward the Colpani contact. It has, however, been pointed out already that the darkening of the granite in this direction is intimately related to a marked increase in the number of inclusions, leaving little doubt that the thorough digestion of the smaller masses of detached shales is responsible for the marked increase in the number and variety of the ferro-magnesian and special contact minerals.

Upon the southwestern border of the batholith the number of aplitic dikes greatly increases. They form prominent features, not only of the granite, but also of the schists, adding greatly to the strong contrast between the schist of the border zone and that outside the zone of metamorphism. In places in the border schists, these are so numerous that one may count up to twenty in a single view, and they range in size from a few inches to ten or fifteen feet. The greater fissility of the schists as contrasted with the shales on the opposite or eastern margin of the batholith caused them to be relatively much more passive in relation to the granite magma. They were not so much torn off and incorporated in the magma, as they were thoroughly injected and metamorphosed. Added to this is the fact that they are petrographically more closely allied to the granite than are the shales upon the northeastern contact.

CHAPTER XIV

THE COASTAL TERRACES

ALONG the entire coast of Peru are upraised and dissected terraces of marine origin. They extend from sea level to 1,500 feet above it, and are best displayed north of Mollendo and in the desert south of Payta. The following discussion relates to that portion of the coast between Mollendo and Camaná.

At the time of the development of the coastal terraces the land was in a state of temporary equilibrium, for the terraces were cut to a mature stage as indicated by the following facts: (1) the terraces have great width—from one to five and more miles; (2) their inner border is straight, or, where curves exist, they are broad and regular; (3) the terrace tops are planed off smoothly so that they now have an even gradient and an almost total absence of rock stacks or unreduced spurs; (4) the mature slopes of the Coast Range, strikingly uniform in gradient and stage of development (Fig. 148), are perfectly organized with respect to the inner edge of the terrace. They descend gradually to the terrace margin, showing that they were graded with respect to sea level when the sea stood at the inner edge of the highest terrace.

From the composition and even distribution of the thick-bedded Tertiary deposits of the desert east of the Coast Range, it is concluded that the precipitation of Tertiary time was greater than that of today (see p. 261). Therefore, if the present major streams reach the sea, it may also be concluded that those of an earlier period reached the sea, provided the topography indicates the perfect adjustment of streams to structure. Lacustrine sediments are absent throughout the Tertiary section. Such through-flowing streams, discharging on a stable coast, would also have mature valleys as a consequence of long uninterrupted erosion at a fixed level. The Majes river must have cut through the Coast Range at Camaná then as now. Likewise the Vitor at Quilca must have cut straight across the Coast Range. An examination of the surface leading down from the Coast Range to the upper edge of these valleys fully confirms this deduction. Flowing and well-graded slopes descend to the brink of the inner valley in each case, where they give way to the gorge walls that continue the descent to the valley floor.

Confirmatory evidence is found in the wide Majes Valley at Cantas and Aplao. (See the Aplao Quadrangle for details.) Though the observer is first impressed with the depth of the valley, its width is more impressive still. It is also clear that two periods of erosion are represented on its walls. Above Aplao the valley walls swing off to the west in a great embayment quite inexplicable on structural grounds; in fact the floor of the embayment is developed across the structure, which is here more disordered than usual. The same is true below Cantas, as seen from the trail, which drops over two scarps to get to the valley floor. The upper, widely opened valley is correlated with the latter part of the period in which were formed the mature terraces of the coast and the mature slopes bordering the larger valleys where they cross the Coast Range.

After its mature development the well-graded marine terrace was upraised and dissected. The deepest and broadest incisions in it were made where the largest streams crossed it. Shallower and narrower valleys were formed where the smaller streams that headed in the Coast Range flowed across it. Their depth and breadth was in general proportional to the height of that part of the Coast Range in which their headwaters lay and to the size of their catchment basins.

When the dissection of the terrace had progressed to the point where about one-third of it had been destroyed, there came depression and the deposition of Pliocene or early Pleistocene sands, gravels, and local clay beds. Everywhere the valleys were partly or wholly filled and over broad stretches, as in the vicinity of stream mouths and upon lower portions of the terrace, extensive deposits were laid down. The largest deposits lie several hours'

Fig. 148.

Fig. 149.

Fig. 148—The Coast Range between Mollendo and Arequipa at the end of June, 1911. There is practically no grass and only a few dry shrubs. The fine network over the hill slopes is composed of interlacing cattle tracks. The cattle roam over these hills after the rains which come at long intervals. (See page 141 for description of the rains and the transformations they effect. For example, in October, 1911, these hills were covered with grass.)

Fig. 149—The great marine terrace at Mollendo. See Fig. 150 for profile.

ride south of Camaná, where locally they attain a thickness of several hundred feet. Their upper surface was well graded and they show a prolonged period of deposition in which the former coastal terrace was all but concealed.

The uplift of the coast terrace and its subsequent dissection bring the physical history down to the present. The uplift was not uniform; three notches in the terrace show more faintly upon the granite-gneiss where the buried rock terrace has been swept clean again, more strongly upon the softer superimposed sands. They lie below the 700-foot contour and are insignificant in appearance beside the slopes of the Coast Range or the ragged bluff of the present coast.

The effect of the last uplift of the coast was to impel the Majes River again to cut down its lower course nearly to sea level. The Pliocene terrace deposits are here entirely removed over an area several leagues wide. In their place an extensive delta and alluvial fan have been formed. At first the river undoubtedly cut down to base level at its mouth and deposited the cut material on the sea floor, now shoal, for a considerable distance from shore. We should still find the river in that position had other agents not intervened. But in the Pleistocene a great quantity of waste was swept into the Majes Valley, whereupon aggradation began; and in the middle and lower valley it has continued down to the present.

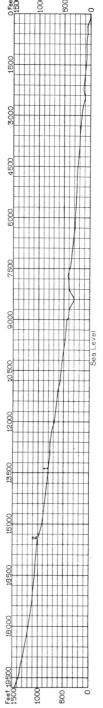

Fig. 150—Profile of the coastal terraces at Mollendo. At 1, in a tributary gorge, fossiliferous clay occurs at 800 feet elevation above the sea. At 2 is a characteristic change of profile marking a drop from a higher to a lower terrace. On the extreme left is the highest terrace, just under 1,500 feet (460 m.).

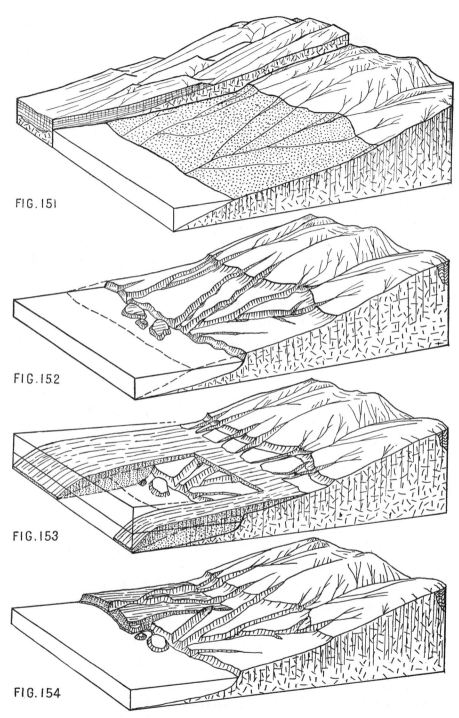

FIG. 151

FIG. 152

FIG. 153

FIG. 154

FIGS. 151-154—These four diagrams represent the physical history and the corresponding physiographic development of the coastal region of Peru between Camaná and Mollendo. The sedimentary beds in the background of the first diagram are hypothetical and are supposed to correspond to the quartzites of the Majes Valley at Aplao.

The effect has been not only the general aggradation of the valley floor, but also the development of a combined delta and superimposed alluvial fan at the valley mouth. The seaward extension of the delta has been hastened by the gradation of the shore between the bounding headlands, thus giving rise to marine marshes in which every particle of contributed waste is firmly held. The plain of Camaná, therefore, includes parts of each of the following: a delta, a superposed alluvial fan, a salt-water marsh, a fresh-water marsh, a series of beaches, small amounts of piedmont fringe at the foot of Pliocene deposits once trimmed by the river and by waves, and extensive tracts of indefinite fill. (See the Camaná Quadrangle for details.)

With the coastal conditions now before us it will be possible to attempt a correlation between the erosion features and the deposits of the coast and those of the interior. An understanding of the comparisons will be facilitated by the use of diagrams, Figs. 151-154, and by a series of concise summary statements. From the relations of the figure it appears that:

1. The Tertiary deposits bordering the Majes Valley east of the Coast Range were in process of deposition when the sea planed the coastal terrace (Fig. 151).

2. A broad mature marine terrace without stacks or sharply alternating spurs and reëntrants (though the rock is a very resistant granite) is correlated with the mature grades of the Coast Range, with which they are integrated and with the mature profiles of the main Cordillera.

3. Such a high degree of topographic organization requires the dissection in the *late* stages of the erosion cycle of at least the inner or eastern border of the piedmont deposits of the desert, largely accumulated during the *early* stages of the cycle.

4. Since the graded slopes of the Coast Range on the one side descend to a former shore whose elevation is now but 1,500 feet above sea level, and since only ten to twenty miles inland on the other side of the range, the same kind of slope extends beneath Tertiary deposits 4,000 feet above sea level, it appears that aggradation of the outer (or western) part of the Tertiary deposits

on the eastern border of the Coast Range continued down to the end of the cycle of erosion, though

5. There must have been an outlet to the sea, since, as we have already seen, the water supply of the Tertiary was greater than that of today and the present streams reach the sea. Moreover, the mature upper slopes and the steep lower slopes of the large valleys make a pronounced topographic unconformity, showing two cycles of valley development.

6. Upon uplift of the coast and dissection of the marine terraces at the foot of the Coast Range, the streams cut deep trenches on the floors of their former valleys (Fig. 152) and removed (a) large portions of the coast terrace, and (b) large portions of the Tertiary deposits east of the Coast Range.

7. Depression of the coastal terrace and its partial burial meant the drowning of the lower Majes Valley and its partial filling with marine and later with terrestrial deposits. It also brought about the partial filling by stream aggradation of the middle portion of the valley, causing the valley fill to abut sharply against the steep valley walls. (See Fig. 155.)

8. Uplift and dissection of both the terrace and its overlying sediments would be accompanied by dissection of the former valley fill, provided that the waste supply was not increased and that the uplift was regional and approximately equal throughout— not a bowing up of the coast on the one hand, or an excessive bowing up of the mountains on the other. But the waste supply has not remained constant, and the uplift has been greater in the Cordillera than on the coast. Let us proceed to the proof of these two conclusions, since upon them depends the interpretation of the later physical history of the coastal valleys.

It is known that the Pleistocene was a time of augmented waste delivery. At the head of the broadly opened Majes Valley there was deposited a huge mass of extremely coarse waste several hundred feet deep and several miles long. Forward from it, interstratified with its outer margin, and continuing the same alluvial grade, is a still greater mass of finer material which descends to lower levels. The fine material is deposited on the floor

FIG. 156—Canyon of the Majes River through the Coast Range north of Camaná. The rock is a granite-gneiss capped by rather flat-lying sedimentaries.

FIG. 155—Steep walls in the Majes Valley below Cantas and the abrupt termination against them of a deep alluvial fill.

of a valley cut into Tertiary strata, hence it is younger than the Tertiary. It is now, and has been for some time past, in process of dissection, hence it was not formed under present conditions of climate and relief. It is confidently assigned to the Pleistocene, since this is definitely known to have been a time of greater precipitation and waste removal on the mountains, and deposition on the plains and the floors of mountain valleys. Such a conclusion appears, even on general grounds, to be but a shade less reliable than if we were able to find in the upper Majes Valley, as in so many other Andean valleys, similar alluvial deposits interlocked with glacial moraines and valley trains.

In regard to the second consideration—the upbowing of the Cordillera—it may be noted that the valley and slope profiles of the main Cordillera shown on p. 191, when extended toward the margin of the mountain belt, lie nearly a mile above the level of the sea on the west and the Amazon plains on the east. The evidence of regional bowing thus afforded is checked by the depths of the mountain valleys and the stream profiles in them. The streams are now sunk from one to three thousand feet below their former level. Even in the case of three thousand feet of erosion the stream profiles are still ungraded, the streams themselves are almost torrential, and from one thousand to three thousand feet of vertical cutting must still be accomplished before the profiles will be as gentle and regular as those of the preceding cycle of erosion, in which were formed the mature slopes now lying high above the valley floors.

Further evidence of bowing is afforded by the attitude of the Tertiary strata themselves, more highly inclined in the case of the older Tertiary, less highly inclined in the case of the younger Tertiary. It is noteworthy that the gradient of the present valley floor is distinctly less than that of the least highly inclined strata. This is true even where aggradation is now just able to continue, as near the nodal point of the valley, above Aplao, where cutting ceases and aggradation begins. (See the Aplao Quadrangle for change of function on the part of the stream a half mile above Cosos). Such a progressive steepening of gradients in the direction of the oldest deposits, shows very clearly a corresponding progression in the growth of the Andes at intervals throughout the Tertiary.

Thus we have aggradation in the Tertiary at the foot of the growing Andes; aggradation in the Pliocene or early Pleistocene on the floor of a deep valley cut in earlier deposits; aggradation in the glacial epoch; and aggradation now in progress. Basin deposits within the borders of the Peruvian Andes are relatively rare. The profound erosion implied by the development, first of a mature topography across this great Cordillera, and second of many deep canyons, calls for deposition on an equally great scale on the mountain borders. The deposits of the western border are a mile thick, but they are confined to a narrow zone between the Coast Range and the Cordillera. Whatever material is swept beyond the immediate coast is deposited in deep ocean water, for the bottom falls off rapidly. The deposits of the eastern border of the Andes are carried far out over the Amazon lowland. Those of earlier geologic periods were largely confined to the mountain border, where they are now upturned to form the front range of the Andes. The Tertiary deposits of the eastern border are less restricted, though they appear to have gathered chiefly in a belt from fifty to one hundred miles wide.

The deposits of the western border were laid down by short streams rising on a divide only 100 to 200 miles from the Pacific. Furthermore, they drain the dry leeward slopes of the Andes. The deposits of the wet eastern border were made by far larger streams that carry the waste of nearly the whole Cordillera. Their shoaling effect upon the Amazon depression must have been a large factor in its steady growth from an inland sea to a river lowland.

CHAPTER XV

PHYSIOGRAPHIC AND GEOLOGIC DEVELOPMENT

GENERAL FEATURES

In the preceding chapter we employed geologic facts in the determination of the age of the principal topographic forms. These facts require further discussion in connection with their closest physiographic allies if we wish to show how the topography of today originated. There are many topographic details that have a fundamental relation to structure; indeed, without a somewhat detailed knowledge of geology only the broader and more general features of the landscape can be interpreted. In this chapter we shall therefore refer not to the scenic features as in a purely topographic description, but to the rock structure and the fossils. A complete and technical geologic discussion is not desirable, first, because it should be based upon much more detailed geologic field work, and second because after all our main purpose is not to discuss the geologic features *per se,* but the physiographic background which the geologic facts afford. I make this preliminary observation partly to indicate the point of view and partly to emphasize the necessity, in a broad, geographic study, for the reconstruction of the landscapes of the past.

The two dominating ranges of the Peruvian Andes, called the Maritime Cordillera and the Cordillera Vilcapampa, are composed of igneous rock—the one volcanic lava, the other intrusive granite. The chief rock belts of the Andes of southern Peru are shown in Fig. 157. The Maritime Cordillera is bordered on the west by Tertiary strata that rest unconformably upon Palaeozoic quartzites. It is bordered on the east by Cretaceous limestones that grade downward into sandstones, shales, and basal conglomerates. At some places the Cretaceous deposits rest upon old schists, at others upon Carboniferous limestones and related strata, upon small granite intrusives and upon old and greatly altered volcanic rock.

The Cordillera Vilcapampa has an axis of granitic rock which was thrust upward through schists that now border it on the west and slates that now border it on the east. The slate series forms a broad belt which terminates near the eastern border of the Andes, where the mountains break down abruptly to the river plains of the Amazon Basin. The immediate border on the east is formed of vertical Carboniferous limestones. The narrow foothill belt is composed of Tertiary sandstones that grade into loose sands and conglomerates. The inclined Tertiary strata were leveled by erosion and in part overlain by coarse and now dissected river gravels, probably of Pleistocene age. Well east of the main border are low ranges that have never been described. They could not be reached by the present expedition on account of lack of time. On the extreme western border of that portion of the Peruvian Andes herein described, there is a second distinct border chain, the Coast Range. It is composed of granite and once had considerable relief, but erosion has reduced its former bold forms to gentle slopes and graded profiles.

The continued and extreme growth of the Andes in later geologic periods has greatly favored structural and physiographic studies. Successive uplifts have raised earlier deposits once buried on the mountain flanks and erosion has opened canyons on whose walls and floors are the clearly exposed records of the past. In addition there have been igneous intrusions of great extent that have thrust aside and upturned the invaded strata exposing still further the internal structures of the mountains. From sections thus revealed it is possible to outline the chief events in the history of the Peruvian Andes, though the outline is still necessarily broad and general because based on rapid reconnaissance. However, it shows clearly that the landscape of the present represents but a temporary stage in the evolution of a great mountain belt. At the dawn of geologic history there were chains of mountains where the Andes now stand. They were swept away and even their roots deeply submerged under invading seas. Re-

Fig. 157—Outline sketch showing the principal rock belts of Peru along the seventy-third meridian. They are: *1*, Pleistocene and Recent gravels and sands, the former partly indurated and slightly deformed, with the degree of deformation increasing toward the mountain border (south). *2*, Tertiary sandstones, inclined from 15° to 30° toward the north and unconformably overlain by Pleistocene gravels. *3*, fossil-bearing Carboniferous limestones with vertical dip. *4*, non-fossiliferous slates, shales, and slaty schists (Silurian) with great variation in degree of induration and in type of structure. South of the parallel of 13° is a belt of Carboniferous limestones and sandstones bordering (*5*) the granite axis of the Cordillera Vilcapampa. For its structural relations to the Cordillera see Figs. 141 and 142. *6*, old and greatly disturbed volcanic agglomerates, tuffs and porphyries, and quartzitic schists and granite-gneiss. *7*, principally Carboniferous limestones north of the axis of the Central Ranges and Cretaceous limestones south of it. Local granite batholiths in the axis of the Central Ranges. *8*, quartzites and slates predominating with thin limestones locally. South of *8* is a belt of shale, sandstone, and limestone with a basement quartzite appearing on the valley floors. *9*, a portion of the great volcanic field of the Central Andes and characteristically developed in the Western or Maritime Cordillera, throughout northern Chile, western Bolivia, and Peru. At Cotahuasi (see also Fig. 20) Cretaceous limestones appear beneath the lavas. *10*, Tertiary sandstones of the coastal desert with a basement of old volcanics and quartzites appearing on the valley walls. The valley floor is aggraded with Pleistocene and Recent alluvium. *11*, granite-gneiss of the Coast Range. *12*, late Tertiary or Pleistocene sands and gravels deposited on broad coastal terraces. For rock structure and character see the other figures in this chapter. For a brief designation of index fossils and related forms see Appendix B. For the names of the drainage lines and the locations of the principal towns see Figs. 20 and 204.

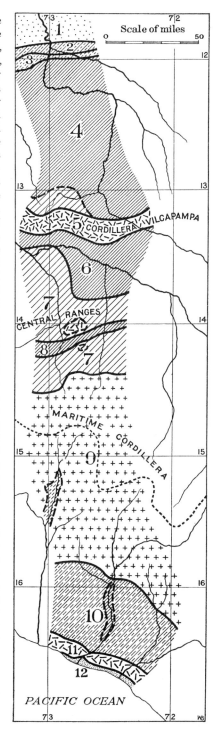

peated uplifts of the earth's crust reformed the ancient chains or created new ones out of the rock waste derived from them. Each new set of forms, therefore, exhibits some features transmitted from the past. Indeed, the landscape of today is like the human race—inheriting much of its character from past generations. For this reason the philosophical study of topographic forms requires at least a broad knowledge of related geologic structures.

SCHISTS AND SILURIAN SLATES [1]

The oldest series of rocks along the seventy-third meridian of Peru extends eastward from the Vilcapampa batholith nearly to the border of the Cordillera, Fig. 157. It consists of (1) a great mass of slates and shales with remarkable uniformity of composition and structure over great areas, and (2) older schists and siliceous members in restricted belts. They are everywhere thoroughly jointed; near the batholith they are also mineralized and altered from their original condition; in a few places they have been intruded with dikes and other form of igneous rock.

The slates and shales underlie known Carboniferous strata on their eastern border and appear to be a physical continuation of the fossiliferous slates of Bolivia; hence they are provisionally referred to the Silurian, though they may possibly be Devonian. Certainly the known Devonian exceeds in extent the known Silurian in the Central Andes but its lithological character is generally quite unlike the character of the slates here referred to the Silurian. The schists are of great but unknown age. They are unconformably overlain by known Carboniferous at Puquiura in the Vilcapampa Valley (Fig. 158), and near Chuquibambilla on the opposite side of the Cordillera Vilcapampa. The deeply weathered fissile mica schists east of Pasaje (see Appendix C for all locations) are also unconformably overlain by conglomerate and sandstone of Carboniferous age. While the schists vary considerably in lithological appearance and also in structure, they are everywhere the lowest rocks in the series and may with confidence

---

[1] For a list of the fossils that form the basis of the age determinations in this chapter see Appendix B.

be referred to the early Palaeozoic, while some of them may date from the Proteriozoic.

The Silurian beds are composed of shale, sandstone, shaly sandstone, limestone, and slate with some slaty schist, among which the shales are predominent and the limestones least important. Near their contact with the granite the slate series is composed of alternating beds of sandstone and shale arranged in beds from one to three feet thick. At Santa Ana they become

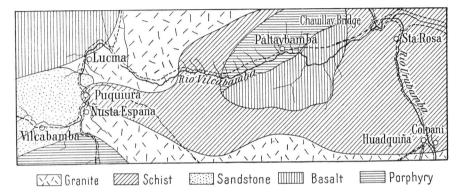

Granite   Schist   Sandstone   Basalt   Porphyry

Fig. 158—Geologic sketch map of the lower Urubamba Valley. A single traverse was made along the valley, hence the boundaries are not accurate in detail. They were sketched in along a few lateral traverses and also inferred from the topography. The country rock is schist and the granite intruded in it is an arm of the main granite mass that constitutes the axis of the Cordillera Vilcapampa. The structure and to some degree the extent of the sandstone on the left are represented in Figs. 141 and 142.

more fissile and slaty in character and in several places are quarried and used for roofing. At Rosalina they consist of almost uniform beds of shale so soft and so minutely and thoroughly jointed as to weather easily. Under prolonged erosion they have, therefore, given rise to a well-rounded and soft-featured landscape. Farther down the Urubamba Valley they again take on the character of alternating beds of sandstone and shale from a few feet to fifteen and more feet thick. In places the metamorphism of the series has been carried further—the shales have become slates and the sandstones have been altered to extremely resistant quartzites. The result is again clearly shown in the topography of the valley wall which becomes bold, inclosing the river in narrow "pongos" or canyons filled with huge bowlders and dangerous rapids. The hills become mountains, ledges appear, and even the heavy forest cover fails to smooth out the natural ruggedness of the landscape.

It is only upon their eastern border that the Silurian series includes calcareous beds, and all of these lie within a few thousand yards of the contact with the Carboniferous limestones and shales. At first they are thin paper-like layers; nearer the top they are a few inches wide and finally attain a thickness of ten or twelve feet. The available limestone outcrops were rigorously examined for fossils but none were found, although they are lavishly distributed throughout the younger Carboniferous beds just above them. It is also remarkable that though the Silurian age of these beds is reasonably inferred they are not separated from the Carboniferous by an unconformity, at least we could find none in this locality. The later beds disconformably overlie the earlier beds, although the sharp differences in lithology and fossils make it easy to locate the line of separation. The limestone beds of the Silurian series are extremely compact and unfossiliferous. At least in this region those of Carboniferous age are friable and the fossils varied and abundant. The Silurian beds are everywhere strongly inclined and throughout the eastern half or third of their outcrop in the Urubamba Valley they are nearly vertical.

In view of the enormous thickness of the repeated layers of shale and sandstone this series is of great interest. Added importance attaches to their occurrence in a long belt from the eastern edge of the Bolivian highlands northward through Peru and possibly farther. From the fact that their disturbance has been on broad lines over wide areas with extreme metamorphism, they are to be separated from the older mica-schists and the crumpled chlorite schists of Puquiura and Pasaje. Further reasons for this distinction lie in their lithologic difference and, to a more important degree, in the strong unconformity between the Carboniferous and the schists in contrast to the disconformable relations shown between the Carboniferous and Silurian fifty miles away at Pongo de Mainique. The mashing and crumpling that the schists have experienced at Puquiura is so intense, that were they a part of the Silurian series the latter should exhibit at least a slight unconformity in relation to the Carboniferous limestones deposited upon them.

If our interpretation of the relation of the schists to the slates and shales be correct, we should have a mountain-making period introduced in pre-Silurian time, affecting the accumulated sediments and bringing about their metamorphism and crumpling on a large scale. From the mountains and uplands thus created on the schists, sediments were washed into adjacent waters and accumulated as even-bedded and extensive sheets of sands and muds (the present slates, shales, quartzites, etc.). Nowhere do the sediments of the slate series show a conglomeratic phase; they are remarkably well-sorted and consist of material disposed with great regularity. Though they are coarsest at the bottom the lower beds do not show cross-bedding, ripple marking, or other signs of shallow-water conditions. Toward the upper part of the series these features, especially the ripple-marking, make their appearance. During the deposition of the last third of the series, and again just before the deposition of the limestone, the beds took on a predominantly arenaceous character associated with ripple marks and cross-bedding characteristic of shallow-water deposits.

In the persistence of arenaceous sediments throughout the series and the distribution of the ripple marks through the upper third of the beds, we have a clear indication that the degree of shallowness was sufficient to bring the bottom on which the sediments accumulated into the zone of current action and possibly wave action. It is also worth considering whether the currents involved were not of similar origin to those now a part of the great counter-clockwise movements in the southern seas. If so, their action would be peculiarly effective in the wide distribution of the sediment derived from a land mass on the eastern edge of a continental coast, since they would spread out the material to a greater and greater degree as they flowed into more southerly latitudes. Among geologic agents a broad ocean current of relatively uniform flow would produce the most uniform effects throughout a geologic period, in which many thousand feet of clastic sediments were being accumulated. A powerful ocean current would also work on flats (in contrast to the gradient required by near-shore processes), and at the same time be of such deep and steady flow as to result in neither ripple marks nor cross-bedding.

The increasing volume of shallow-water sediments of uniform character near the end of the Silurian, indicates great crustal stability at a level which brought about neither a marked gain nor loss of material to the region. At any rate we have here no Devonian sediments, a characteristic shared by almost all the great sedimentary formations of Peru. At the beginning of the Carboniferous the water deepened, and great heavy-bedded limestones appear with only thin shale partings through a vertical distance of several hundreds of feet. The enormous volume of Silurian sediments indicates the deep and prolonged erosion of the land masses then existing, a conclusion further supported (1) by the extensive development of the Silurian throughout Bolivia as well as Peru, (2) by the entire absence of coarse material whether at the top or bottom of the section, and (3) by the very limited extent of older rock now exposed even after repeated and irregular uplift and deep dissection. Indeed, from the latter very striking fact, it may be reasonably argued that in a general way the relief of the country was reduced to sea level at the close of the Silurian. Over the perfected grades of that time there would then be afforded an opportunity for the effective transportation of waste to the extreme limits of the land.

Further evidence of the great reduction of surface during the Silurian and Devonian is supplied by the extensive development of the Carboniferous strata. Their outcrops are now scattered across the higher portions of the Andean Cordillera and are prevailingly calcareous in their upper portions. Upon the eastern border of the Silurian they indicate marine conditions from the opening of the period, but at Pasaje in the Apurimac Valley they are marked by heavy beds of basal conglomerate and sandstone, and an abundance of ripple marking and other features associated with shallow-water and possibly near-shore conditions.

Carboniferous strata are distributed along the seventy-third meridian and rival in extent the volcanic material that forms the western border of the Andes.   They range in character from basal conglomerates, sandstones, and shales of limited development, to enormous beds of extremely resistant blue limestone, in general well supplied with fossils.   On the eastern border of the

FIG. 159—Topographic and structural section at the northeastern border of the Peruvian Andes.   The slates are probably Silurian, the fossiliferous limestones are known Carboniferous, and the sandstones are Tertiary grading up to Pleistocene.

Andes they are abruptly terminated by a great fault, the continuation northward of the marginal fault recognized in eastern Bolivia by Minchin[2] and farther north by the writer.[3]   Coarse red sandstones with conglomeratic phase abut sharply and with moderate inclination against almost vertical sandstones and limestones of Carboniferous age.   The break between the vertical limestones and the gently inclined sandstones is marked by a prominent scarp nearly four thousand feet high (Fig. 159), and the limestone itself forms a high ridge through which the Urubamba has cut a narrow gateway, the celebrated Poṅgo de Mainique.

At Pasaje, on the western side of the Apurimac, the Carboniferous again appears resting upon the old schists described on p. 236. It is steeply upturned, in places vertical, is highly conglomeratic, and in a belt a half-mile wide it forms true badlands topography.

[2] Eastern Bolivia and the Gran Chaco, Proc. Royal Geogr. Soc., Vol. 3, 1881, pp. 401-420.

[3] The Physiography of the Central Andes, Am. Journ. Sci., Vol. 28, 1909, p. 395.

It is succeeded by evenly bedded sandstones of fine and coarse composition in alternate beds, then follow shales and sandstones and finally the enormous beds of limestone that characterize the series. The structure is on the whole relatively simple in this region, the character and attitude of the beds indicating their accumulation in a nearly horizontal position. Since the basal conglomerate contains only pebbles and stones derived from the subjacent schists and does not contain granites like those in the Cordillera Vilcapampa batholith on the east it is concluded that the

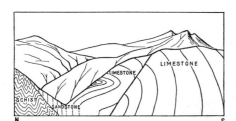

batholithic invasion was accompanied by the compression and tilting of the Carboniferous beds and that the batholith itself is post-Carboniferous. From the ridge summits above Huascatay and in the deep valleys thereabouts the Carboniferous strata may be seen to extend far toward the west, and also to have great extent north and south. Because of

FIG. 160—The deformative effects of the granite intrusion of the Cordillera Vilcapampa are here shown as transmitted through ancient schists to the overlying conglomerates, sandstones, and limestones of Carboniferous age, in the Apurimac Valley at Pasaje.

their dissected, bare, and, therefore, well-exposed condition they present exceptional opportunities for the study of Carboniferous geology in central Peru.

Carboniferous strata again appear at Puquiura, Vilcapampa, and Pampaconas. They are sharply upturned against the Vilcapampa batholith and associated volcanic material, chiefly basalt, porphyry, and various tuffs and related breccias. The Carboniferous beds are here more arenaceous, consisting chiefly of alternating beds of sandstone and shale. The lowermost beds, as at Pongo de Mainique, are dominantly marine, fossiliferous limestone beds having a thickness estimated to be over two miles.

From Huascatay westward and southward the Carboniferous is in part displaced by secondary batholiths of granite, in part cut off or crowded aside by igneous intrusions of later date, and in still larger part buried under great masses of Tertiary volcanic material. Nevertheless, it remains the dominating rock type over the whole stretch of country from Huascatay to Huancarama. In the northwestern part of the Abancay sheet its effect on the landscape may be observed in the knife-like ridge extending from west to east just above Huambo. Above Chuquibambilla it again outcrops, resting upon a thick resistant quartzite of unknown age, Fig. 162. It is strongly developed about Huadquirca and Antabamba and, still associated with a quartzite floor, it finally disappears under the lavas of the

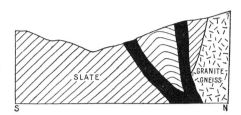

FIG. 161—Types of deformation north of Lambrama near Sotospampa. A dark basaltic rock has invaded both granite-gneiss and slate. Sills and dikes occur in great numbers. The topographic depression in the profile is the Lambrama Valley. See the Lambrama Quadrangle.

great volcanic field on the western border of the Andes. Figs. 141 and 142 show its relation to the invading granite batholiths and Fig. 162 shows further structural features as developed about Antabamba where the great volcanic field of the Maritime Cordillera begins.

Both the enormous thickness of the Carboniferous limestone series and the absence of clastic members over great areas in the

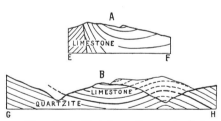

FIG. 162—Sketch sections at Antabamba to show (a) deformed limestones on the upper edge of the geologic map, Fig. 163 A; and (b) the structural relations of limestone and quartzite. See also Fig. 163.

upper portion of the series prove the widespread extent of the Carboniferous seas and their former occurrence in large interlimestone tracts from which they have since been eroded. At Puquiura they extend far over the schist, in fact almost completely conceal it; at Pasaje they formerly covered the micaschists extensively, their erosion in both cases being conditioned by the pronounced uplift and marginal deformation which accompanied the development of the Vilcapampa batholith.

The degree of deformation of the Carboniferous sediments varies between simple uplift through moderate folding and complex disturbances resulting in nearly vertical attitudes. The simplest structures are represented at Pasaje, where the uplift of the intruded schists, marginal to the Vilcapampa batholith, has produced an enormous monoclinal fold exposing the entire section from basal conglomerates and sandstones to the thickest limestone. Above Chuquibambilla the limestones have

C   D

Fig. 163—Geologic sketch section to show the relation of the volcanic flows of Fig. 164 to the sandstones and quartzites beneath.

been uplifted and very gently folded by the invasion of granite associated with the main batholith and several satellitic batholiths of limited extent. A higher degree of complexity is shown at Pampaconas (Fig. 141), where the main monoclinal fold is traversed almost at right angles by secondary folds of great amplitude. The limestones are there carried to the limit of the winter snows almost at the summit of the Cordillera. The crest of each secondary anticline rises to form a group of conspicuous peaks and tabular ridges. Higher in the section, as at Puquiura, the sandstones are thrown into a series of huge anticlines and synclines, apparently by the marginal compression brought about at the time of the intrusion of the granite core of the range. At Pongo de Mainique the whole of the visible Carboniferous is practically vertical, and is cut off by a great fault marking the abrupt eastern border of the Cordillera.

It is noteworthy that the farther east the Carboniferous extends the more dominantly marine it becomes, though marine beds of great thickness constitute a large part of the series in whatever location. From Huascatay westward the limestones become more and more argillaceous, and finally give way altogether to an enormous thickness of shales, sandstones, and thin conglomerates. These were observed to extend with strong inclination westward out of the region studied and into and under the volcanoes crowning the western border of the Cordillera. Along the line of traverse opportunity was not afforded for further study of this aspect of the series, since our route led generally along the strike rather than along the dip of the beds. It is interesting to note, however, that these observations as to the increasing amounts of clastic material in a westward direction were afterwards confirmed by Señor José Bravo, the Director of the Bureau of Mines at Lima, who had found Carboniferous land plants in shales at Pacasmayo, the only fossils of their kind found in Peru. For-merly it had been supposed that non-marine Carboniferous was not represented in Peru. From the varied nature of the flora, the great thickness of the shales in which the specimens were col-lected, and the fact that the dominantly marine Carbonifer-ous elsewhere in Peru is of great extent, it is concluded that the land upon which the plants grew had a considerable area and probably extended far west of the present coast line. Since its emergence it has passed through several orogenic move-ments. These have resulted in the uplift of the marine portion of the Carboniferous, while the terrestrial deposits seem to have

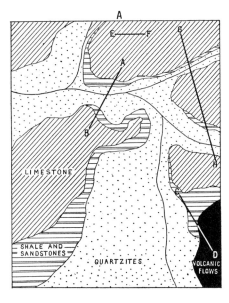

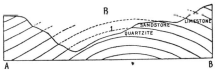

FIG. 164—Geologic sketch map and section, Antabamba region. The Anta-bamba River has cut through almost the entire series of bedded strata.

all but disappeared in the down-sunken blocks of the ocean floor, west of the great fault developed along the margin of the Cordil-lera. The following figures are graphic representations of this hypothesis.

The wide distribution of the Carboniferous sediments and especially the limestones, together with the uniformity of the fos-sil faunas, makes it certain that the sea extended entirely across

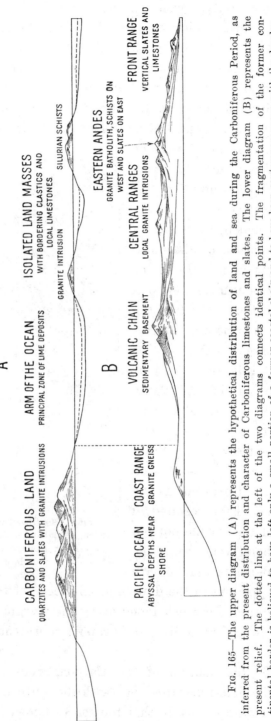

Fig. 165—The upper diagram (A) represents the hypothetical distribution of land and sea during the Carboniferous Period, as inferred from the present distribution and character of Carboniferous limestones and slates. The lower diagram (B) represents the present relief. The dotted line at the left of the two diagrams connects identical points. The fragmentation of the former continental border is believed to have left only a small portion of a former coastal chain and to have been contemporaneous with the development of ocean abysses near the present shore.

the region now occupied by the Andes. However, from the relation of the Carboniferous to the basal schists, and the most conservative extension of the known Carboniferous, it may be inferred that the Carboniferous sea did not completely cover the entire area but was broken here and there by island masses in the form of an elongated archipelago. The presence of land plants in the Carboniferous of Pisco warrants the conclusion that a second island mass, possibly an island chain parallel to the first, extended along and west of the present shore.

CRETACEOUS

The Cretaceous formations are of very limited extent in the belt of country under consideration, in spite of their generally wide distribution in Peru. They are exposed distinctly only on the western border of the Cordillera and in special relations. In the gorge of Cotahuasi, over seven thousand feet deep, about two thousand feet of Cretaceous limestones are exposed. The series includes only a very resistant blue limestone and terminates abruptly along a well-marked and highly irregular erosion surface covered by almost a mile of volcanic material, chiefly lava flows. The character of the bottom of the section is likewise unknown, since it lies apparently far below the present level of erosion.

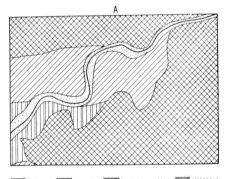

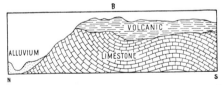

FIG. 166—Geologic sketch map and cross-section in the Cotahuasi Canyon at Cotahuasi. With a slight gap this figure continues Fig. 167 to the left. The section represents a spur of the main plateau about 1,500 feet high in the center of the map.

The Cretaceous limestones of the Cotahuasi Canyon are everywhere greatly and irregularly disturbed. Typical conditions are represented in the maps and sections, Figs. 166 and 167. They are penetrated and tilted by igneous masses, apparently the feeders of the great lava sheets that form the western summit of the Cordillera. From the restricted development of the limestones along a western border zone it might be inferred that they represent a very limited marine invasion. It is certainly clear that great deformative movements were in progress from at least late Palæozoic time since all the Palæozoic deposits are broken abruptly down in this direction, and, except for such isolated occurrences as the land Carboniferous at Pacasmayo, are not found anywhere in the coastal region today. The Cretaceous is not only limited within a relatively narrow shore zone, but also, like the Palæozoic, it is broken down toward the west. not reappearing from beneath the Tertiary cover of the desert

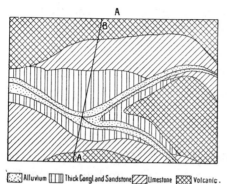

Fig. 167—Geologic sketch map and cross-section in the Cotahuasi Canyon at Taurisma, above Cotahuasi. The relations of limestone and lava flows in the center of the map and on a spur top near the canyon floor. Thousands of feet of lava extend upward from the flows that cap the limestone.

region or upon the granite-gneisses that form the foundation for all the known sedimentary strata of the immediate coast.

From these considerations I think we have a strong suggestion of the geologic date assignable to the development of the great fault that is the most strongly marked structural and physiographic feature of the west coast of South America. Since the development of this fault is so intimately related to the origin of the Pacific Ocean basin its study is of special importance. The points of chief interest may be summarized as follows:

(1) The character of the land Carboniferous implies a much greater extent of the land than is now visible.

(2) The progressive coarsening of the Carboniferous deposits westward and their land derivation, together with the great thickness of the series, point to an elevated land mass in process of

erosion west of the series as a whole, that is west of the present coast.

(3) The restricted development of the Cretaceous seas upon the western border of the Carboniferous, and the still more restricted development of the Tertiary deposits between the mountains and the present coast, point to increasing definition of the submarine scarp through the Mesozoic and the Tertiary.

(4) The Tertiary deposits are all clearly derived from the present mountains and have been washed seaward down slopes with geographic relations approximately like those of the present.

(5) From the great width, deep dissection, and subsequent

Clays and sands.
Red sandstone and shale.

Gray and yellow sandstone and shale.

Basal sandstone.
Volcanic agglomerate.
Volcanic flows.
Slaty schist.
Granite.

Fig. 168—Composite structure section representing the succession of rocks in the Urubamba Valley from Urubamba to Torontoy.

burial of the Tertiary terraces of the coast, it is clear that the greater part of the adjustment of the crust to which the bordering ocean basin is due was accomplished at least by mid-Tertiary time.

Aside from the fossiliferous limestones of known Cretaceous age there have been referred to the Cretaceous certain red sandstones and shales marked, especially in the central portions of the Cordillera, by the presence of large amounts of salt and gypsum. These beds were at first considered Permian, but Steinmann has since found at Potosí related and similar formations with Cretaceous fossils. In this connection it is also necessary to add that the great red sandstone series forming the eastern border of the Andes in Bolivia is of uncertain age and has likewise been re-

ferred to the Cretaceous, though the matter of its age has not yet
been definitely determined. In 1913 I found it appearing in northwestern Argentina in the Calchaquí Valley in a relation to the
main Andean mass, similar to that displayed farther north. It
contains fossils and its age was, therefore, readily determinable
there.[4]

In the Peruvian field the red beds of questionable age were not
examined in sufficient detail to make possible a definite age determination. They occur in a great and only moderately disturbed
series in the Anta basin north of Cuzco, but are there not fossiliferous. The northeastern side of the hill back of Puqura (of
the Anta basin: to be distinguished from Puquiura in the Vilcabamba Valley) is composed largely of rocks of this class. In a
few places their calcareous members have been weathered out in
such a manner as to show karst topography. Where they occur
on the well-drained brow of a bluff the caves are used in place
of houses by Indian farmers. The large and strikingly beautiful
Lake Huaipo, ten miles north of Anta, and several smaller, neighboring lakes, appear to have originated in solution depressions
formed in these beds.

The structural relation of the red sandstone series to the older
rocks is well displayed about half-way between Urubamba and
Ollantaytambo in the deep Urubamba Valley. The basal rocks are
slaty schist and granite succeeded by agglomerates and basalt porphyries upon whose eroded surfaces (Fig. 169) are gray to yellow cross-bedded sandstones. Within a few hundred feet of the
unconformity gypsum deposits begin to appear and increase in
number to such an extent that the resulting soil is in places rendered worthless. Copper-stained bands are also common near the
bottom of the series, but these are confined to the lower beds.
Higher up in the section, for example, just above the gorge between
Urubamba and Ollantaytambo, even-bedded sandstones occur
whose most prominent characteristic is the regular succession of

---

[4] See paper by H. S. Palmer, my assistant on the Expedition to the Central Andes,
1913, entitled: Geological Notes on the Andes of Northwestern Argentina, Am. Journ.
Sci., Vol. 38, 1914, pp. 309-330.

FIG. 169.

FIG. 170.

FIG. 169—The line of unconformity between the igneous basement rocks (agglomerates at this point) and the quartzites and sandstones of the Urubamba Valley,
between the town of Urubamba and Ollantaytambo.

FIG. 170—The inclined lower and horizontal upper sandstone on the southeastern
wall of the Majes Valley at Hacienda Cantas. The section is a half-mile high.

coarse and fine sandstone beds. Such alternations of character in sedimentary rocks are commonly marked by alternating shales and sandstones, but in this locality shales are practically absent. Toward the top of the section gypsum deposits again appear first as beds and later, as in the case of the hill-slope on the southern shore of Lake Huaipo, as veins and irregular masses of gypsum. The top of the deformed Cretaceous (?) is eroded and again covered unconformably by practically flat-lying Tertiary deposits.

TERTIARY

The Tertiary deposits of the region under discussion are limited to three regions: (1) the extreme eastern border of the main Cordillera, (2) intermontane basins, the largest and most important of which are (a) the Cuzco basin and (b) the Titicaca-Poopó basin on the Peruvian-Bolivian frontier, and (3) in the west-coast desert and in places upon the huge terraces that form a striking feature of the topography of the coast of Peru.

It has already been pointed out that the eastern border of the Cordillera is marked by a fault of great but undetermined throw, whose topographic importance may be estimated from the fact that even after prolonged erosion it stands nearly four thousand feet high. Cross-bedded and ripple-marked features and small lenses of conglomerate are common. The beds now dip at an angle approximately 20° to 50° northward at the base of the scarp, but have decreasing dip as they extend farther north and east. It is noteworthy that the deposits become distinctly conglomeratic as flatter dips are attained, and that there seems to have been a steady accumulation of detrital material from the mountains for a long period, since the deposits pass in unbroken succession from the highly indurated and massive beds of the mountain base to loose conglomerates that now weather down much like an ordinary gravel bank. In a few places just below the mouth of the Ticumpinea, logs about six inches in diameter were observed embeded in the deposits, but these belong distinctly to the upper horizons.

The border deposits, though they vary in dip from nearly flat to 50°, are everywhere somewhat inclined and now lie up to several hundred feet above the level of the Urubamba River. Their upper surface is moderately dissected, the degree of dissection being most pronounced where the dips are steepest and the height greatest. In fact, the attitude of the deposits and their progressive change in character point toward, if they do not actually prove, the steady and progressive character of the beds first deposited and their erosion and redeposition in beds now higher in the series.

Upon the eroded upper surfaces of the inclined border deposits, gravel beds have been laid which, from evidence discussed in a later paragraph, are without doubt referable to the Pleistocene. These in turn are now dissected. They do not extend to the highest summits of the deformed beds but are confined, so far as observations have gone, to elevations about one hundred feet above the river. From the evidence that the overlying horizontal beds are Pleistocene, the thick, inclined beds are referred to Tertiary age, though they are nowhere fossiliferous.

Observations along the Urubamba River were extended as far northward as the mouth of the Timpia, one of the larger tributaries. Upon returning from this point by land a wide view of the country was gained from the four-thousand-foot ridge of vertical Carboniferous limestone, in which it appeared that low and irregular strike ridges continue the features of the Tertiary displayed along the mountain front far northward as well as eastward, to a point where the higher ridges and low mountains of older rock again appear—the last outliers of the Andean system in Peru. Unfortunately time enough was not available for an extension of the trip to these localities whose geologic characters still remain entirely unknown. From the topographic aspects of the country, it is, however, reasonably certain that the whole intervening depression between these outlying ranges and the border of the main Cordillera, is filled with inclined and now dissected and partly covered Tertiary strata. The elevation of the upper surface does not, however, remain the same; it appears to decrease steadily and the youngest Tertiary strata disappear from view below the sediments of either the Pleistocene or the present river gravels. In the more central parts of the depression occupied by the Urubamba Valley, only knobs or ridges project here and there above the general level.

The Coastal Tertiary

The Tertiary deposits of the Peruvian desert region southwest of the Andes have many special features related to coastal deformation, changes of climate, and great Andean uplifts. They lie between the west coast of Peru at Camaná and the high, lava-covered country that forms the western border of the Andes and in places are over a mile thick. They are non-fossiliferous, cross-bedded, ripple-marked, and have abundant lenses of conglomerate of all sizes. The beds rest upon an irregular floor developed upon a varied mass of rocks. In some places the basement consists of old strata, strongly deformed and eroded. In other places it consists of a granite allied in character and probably in origin with the old granite-gneiss of the Coast Range toward the west. Elsewhere the rock is lava, evidently the earliest in the great series of volcanic flows that form this portion of the Andes.

The deposits on the western border of the Andes are excellently exposed in the Majes Valley, one of the most famous in Peru, though its fame rests rather upon the excellence and abundance of its vineyards and wines than its splendid geologic sections. Its head lies near the base of the snow-capped peaks of Coropuna; its mouth is at Camaná on the Pacific, a hundred miles north of Mollendo. It is both narrow and deep; one may ride across its floor anywhere in a half hour. In places it is a narrow canyon. Above Cantas it is sunk nearly a mile below the level of the desert upland through which it flows. Along its borders are exposed basal granites, old sedimentaries, and lavas; inter-bedded with it are other lavas that lie near the base of the great volcanic series; through it still project the old granites of the Coast Range; and upon it have been accumulated additional volcanic rocks, wind-blown deposits, and, finally, coarse wash formed during the glacial period. From both the variety of the formations,

the small amount of marginal dissection, and the excellent exposures made possible by the deep erosion and desert climate, the
Majes Valley is one of the most profitable places in Peru for
physiographic and geologic study.

The most complete succession of strata (Tertiary) occurs just
below Cantas on the trail to Jaguey (Fig. 171). Upon a floor of
granite-gneiss, and alternating beds of quartzite and shale belong-

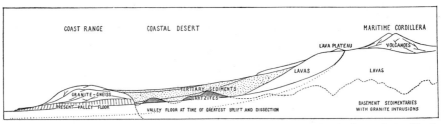

FIG. 171—Generalized sketch section to show the structural relations of the Maritime Cordillera, the desert pampas, and the Coast Range.

ing to an older series, are deposited heavy beds of red sandstone
with many conglomerate lenses. The sandstone strata are measurably deformed and their upper surfaces moderately dissected.
Upon them have been deposited unconformably a thicker series
of deposits, conglomerates, sandstones, and finer wind-blown material. The basal conglomerate is very coarse—much like beach
material in both structure and composition, and similar to that
along and south of the present coast at Camaná. Higher in the
section the material is prevailingly sandy and is deposited in
regular beds from a few inches to a few feet in thickness. Near
the top of the section are a few hundred feet of strata chiefly wind
deposited. Unconformably overlying the whole series and in
sharp contrast to the fine wind-blown stuff below it, is a third
series of coarse deposits about five hundred feet thick. The top-
most material, that forming the surface of the desert upland, consists of wind-blown sand now shifted by the wind and gathered
into sand dunes or irregular drifts, banks of white earth, "tierra
blanca," and a pebble pavement a few inches thick.

If the main facts of the above section are now summarized
they will facilitate an understanding of other sections about to be
described, inasmuch as the summary will in a measure anticipate

our conclusions concerning the origin of the deposits and their subsequent history. The sediments in the Majes Valley between Cantas and Jaguey consist of three series separated by two unconformities. The lowermost series is evenly bedded and rather uniform in composition and topographic expression, standing forth in huge cliffs several hundred feet high on the eastern side

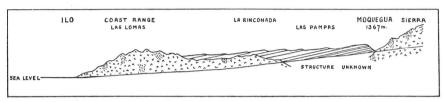

FIG. 172—Geologic relations of Coast Range, desert deposits, and Maritime Cordillera at Moquegua, Peru. After G. I. Adams; Bol. de Minas del Perú, Vol. 2, No. 4, 1906, p. 20.

of the valley. This lower series is overlain by a second series, which consists of coarse conglomerate grading into sand and ultimately into very fine fluffy wind-deposited sands and silts. The lower series is much more deformed than the upper, showing that the deforming movements of later geologic times have been much less intense than the earlier, as if there had been a fading out or weakening of the deforming agents. Finally there is a third series several hundred feet thick which forms the top of the section.

Three other sections may now be examined, one immediately below Cantas, one just above, and one opposite Aplao. The section below Cantas is shown in Fig. 173, and indicates a lower series of red sandstones crossed by vertical faults and unconformably overlain by nearly hori-

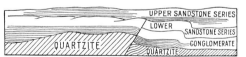

FIG. 173—Sketch section to show structural details on the walls of the Majes Valley near Aplao, looking south.

zontal conglomerates, sandstones, etc., and the whole faulted again with an inclined fault having a throw of nearly 25°. A white to gray sandstone unconformably overlying the red sandstone is shown interpolated between the lowermost and uppermost series, the only example of its kind, however. No important differences in lithographical character may be noted between these and the beds of the preceding section.

Again just above Cantas on the east side of the valley is a clean section exposing about two thousand feet of strata in a half mile of distance. The foundation rocks are old quartzites and shales in regularly alternating beds. Upon their uneven upper surfaces are several thousand feet of red sandstones and conglomerates, which are both folded and faulted with the underlying quartzites. Above the red sandstones is a thick series of gray sandstones and silts which makes the top of the section and unconformably overlies the earlier series.

A similar succession of strata was observed at Aplao, still farther up the Majes Valley, Fig. 174. A greatly deformed and metamorphosed older series is unconformably overlaid by a great

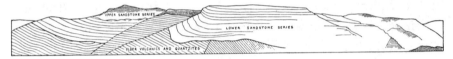

FIG. 174—The structural relations of the strata on the border of the Majes Valley at Aplao, looking west. Field sketch from opposite side of valley. Height of section about 3,000 feet; length about ten miles.

thickness of younger strata. The younger strata may be again divided into two series, a lower series consisting chiefly of red sandstones and an upper consisting of gray to yellow, and only locally red sands of finer texture and more uniform composition. The two are separated by an erosion surface and only the upper series is tilted regionally seaward with faint local deformation; the lower series is both folded and faulted with overthrusts aggregating several thousand feet of vertical and a half mile of horizontal displacement.

The above sections all lie on the eastern side of the Majes Valley. From the upper edge of the valley extensive views were gained of the strata on the opposite side, and two sections, though they were not examined at close range, are at least worth comparing with those already given. From the narrows below Cantas the structure appears as in Figs. 175-176, and shows a deforming movement succeeded by erosion in a lower series. The upper series of sedimentary rock has suffered but slight deformation. A still more highly deformed basal series occurs on the right of the section, presumably the older quartzites. At Huancarqui, opposite Aplao, an extensive view was gained of the western side

FIG. 175—Sketch section to show the structural details of the strata on the south wall of the Majes Valley near Cantas. The section is two miles long.

of the valley, but the lower Tertiary seems not to be represented here, as the upper undeformed series rests unconformably upon a tilted series of quartzites and slates. Farther up the Cantas valley (an hour's ride above Aplao) the Tertiary rests upon volcanic flows or older quartzites or the granite-gneiss exposed here and there along the valley floor.

In no part of the sedimentaries in the Majes Valley were fossils found, save in the now uplifted and dissected sands that overlie the upraised terraces along the coast immediately south of

FIG. 176—Composite geologic section to show the structural relations of the rocks on the western border of the Maritime Cordillera. The inclined strata at the right bottom represent older rocks; in places igneous, in other places sedimentary.

Camaná and also back of Mollendo. Like similar coastal deposits elsewhere along the Peruvian littoral, the terrace sands are of Pliocene or early Pleistocene age. The age of the deposits back of the Coast Range is clearly greater than that of the coastal deposits, (1) since they involve two unconformities, a mile or more of sediments, and now stand at least a thousand feet above the highest Pliocene (or Pleistocene) in the Camaná Valley, and (2) because the erosion history of the interior sediments may be correlated with the physiographic history of the coastal terraces and the correlation shows that uplift and dissection of the terraces and of the interior deposits went hand in hand, and that the deposits on the terraces may similarly be correlated with alluvial deposits in the valley.

We shall now see what further ground there is for the determination of the age of these sediments. Just below Chuquibamba, where they first appear, the sediments rest upon a floor of volcanic and older rock belonging to the great field now known from evidence in many localities to have been formed in the early Tertiary, and here known to be post-Cretaceous from the relations between Cretaceous limestones and volcanics in the Cotahuasi Valley (see p. 247). Although volcanic flows were noted interbedded with the desert deposits, these are few in number, insignificant in volume, and belong to the top of the volcanic series. The same may be said of the volcanic flows that locally overlie the desert deposits. We have then definite proof that the sandstones, conglomerates, and related formations of the Majes Valley and bordering uplands are older than the Pliocene or early Pleistocene and younger than the Cretaceous and the older Tertiary lavas. Hence it can scarcely be doubted that they represent a considerable part of the Tertiary period, especially in view of the long periods of accumulation which the thick sediments represent, and the additional long periods represented by the two well-marked unconformities between the three principal groups of strata.

If we now trace the physical history of the region we have first of all a deep depression between the granite range along the coast and the western flank of the Andes. Here and there, as in the Vitor, the Majes, and other valleys, there were gaps through the Coast Range. Nowhere did the relief of the coastal chain exceed 5,000 feet. The depression had been partly filled in early geologic (probably early Paleozoic) time by sediments later deformed and metamorphosed so that they are now quartzites and shales. The greater resistance of the granite of the Coast Range resulted in superior relief, while the older deformed sedimentaries were deeply eroded, with the result that by the beginning of the Tertiary the basin quality of the depression was again emphasized. All these facts are expressed graphically in Fig. 171. On the western flanks of the granite range no corresponding sedimentary deposits are found in this latitude. The sea thus appears to have stood farther west of the Coast Range in Paleozoic times than at present.

For the later history it is necessary to assemble the various Tertiary sections described on the preceding pages. First of all we recognize three quite distinct types of accumulations, for which

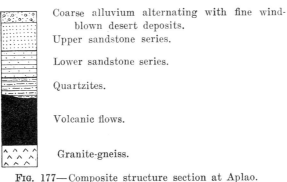

Coarse alluvium alternating with fine wind-
blown desert deposits.
Upper sandstone series.

Lower sandstone series.

Quartzites.

Volcanic flows.

Granite-gneiss.

FIG. 177—Composite structure section at Aplao.

we shall have to postulate three sets of conditions and possibly three separate agents. The first or lowermost consists of even-bedded deposits of red and gray sandstones, the former color predominating. The material is in general well-sorted save locally, where lenses and even thin beds of conglomerate have been developed. There is, however, about the whole series a uniformity and an orderliness in striking contrast to the coarse, cross-bedded, and irregular material above the unconformity. On their northeastern or inner margin the sandstones are notably coarser and thicker, a natural result of proximity to the mountains, the source of the material. The general absence of wind-blown deposits is marked; these occur entirely along the eastern and northern portions of the deposits and are recognized (1) by their peculiar cross-bedding, and (2) by the fact that the cross-bedding is directed northeastward in a direction contrary to the regional dip of the series, a condition attributable to the strong sea breezes that prevail every afternoon in this latitude.

The main body of the material is such as might be deposited on the wide flood plains of piedmont streams during a period of prolonged erosion on surrounding highlands that served as the feeding grounds of the streams. The alternations in the character of the deposits, alternations which, in a general view, give a banded appearance to the rock, are produced by successions of beds of fine and coarse material, though all of it is sandstone. Such successions are probably to be correlated with seasonal changes in the volume and load of the depositing streams.

To gain an idea of the conditions of deposition we may take the character of the sediments as described above, and from them draw deductions as to the agents concerned and the manner of their action.

We may also apply to the area the conclusions drawn from the study of similar deposits now in process of formation. We have between the coast ranges of northern Chile and the western flanks of the Cordillera Sillilica, probably the best example of piedmont accumulation in a dry climate that the west coast of South America affords.

Along the inner edge of the Desert of Tarapacá, roughly between the towns of Tarapacá and Quillagua, Chile, the piedmont gravels, sands, silts, and muds extend for over a hundred miles, flanking the western Andes and forming a transition belt between these mountains and the interior basins of the coast desert. The silts and muds constitute the outer fringe of the piedmont and are interrupted here and there where sands are blown upon them from the higher portions of the piedmont, or from the desert mountains and plains on the seaward side. Practically no rain falls upon the greater part of the desert and the only water it receives is that borne to it by the piedmont streams in the early summer, from the rains and melted snows of the high plateau and mountains to the eastward. These temporary streams spread upon the outer edge of the piedmont a wide sheet of mud and silt which then dries and becomes cracked, the curled and warped plates retaining their character until the next wet season or until covered with wind-blown sand. The wind-driven sand fills the cracks in the muds and is even drifted under the edges of the up-curled plates, filling the spaces completely. Over this combined fluvial and æolian deposit is spread the next layer of mud, which frequently is less extensive than the earlier deposits, thus giving abundant opportunity for the observation of the exact manner of burial of the older sand-covered stratum.

Now while the alternations are as marked in Peru as in Chile, it is noteworthy that the Tertiary material in Peru is not only coarse throughout, even to the farthest limits of the piedmont, but also that the alternating beds are thick. Moreover, there are only the most feeble evidences of wind action in the lowermost Tertiary series. I was prepared to find curled plates, wind-blown sands, and muds and silts, but they are almost wholly absent. It is, therefore, concluded that the dryness was far less extreme than it is today and that full streams of great competency flowed vigorously down from the mountains and carried their loads to the inner border of the Coast Range and in places to the sea.

The fact that the finer material is *sandy*, not clayey or silty, that it almost equals in thickness the coarser layers, and that its distribution appears to be co-extensive with the coarser, warrants the conclusion that it too was deposited by competent streams of a type far different from the withering streams associated with piedmont deposits in a thoroughly arid climate like that of today. Both in the second Tertiary series and on the present surface are such clear examples of deposits made in a drier climate as to leave little doubt that the earliest of the Tertiary strata of the Majes Valley were deposited in a time of far greater rainfall than the present. It is further concluded that there was increasing dryness, as shown by hundreds of feet of wind-blown sand near the top of the section. But the growing dryness was interrupted by at least one period of greater precipitation. Since that time there has been a return to the dry climate of a former epoch.

Uplift and erosion of the earliest of the Tertiary deposits of the Majes Valley is indicated in two ways: (1) by the deformed character of the beds, and (2) by the ensuing coarse deposits which were derived from the invigorated streams. Without strong deformations it would not be possible to assign the increased erosion so confidently to uplift; with the coarse deposits that succeed the unconformity we have evidence of accumulation under conditions of renewed uplift in the mountains and of full streams competent to remove the increasing load.

It is in the character of the sediments toward the top of the Tertiary that we have the clearest evidence of progressive desiccation of the climate of the region. The amount of wind-blown material steadily increases and the uppermost five hundred feet is composed predominantly, and in places exclusively, of this material. The evidences of wind action lie chiefly in the fine (in places fluffy) nature of the deposits, their uniform character, and in the tangency of the layers with respect to the surface on which they were deposited. There are three diagnostic structural features of great importance: the very steep dip of the fine laminae; the peculiar and harmonious blending of their contacts; the manner in which the highly inclined laminae cut off and succeed each other, whereby quite bewildering changes in the direction of dip of the inclined beds are brought about on any exposed plane. Some of these features require further discussion.

It is well known that the front of a sand dune generally consists of sand deposited on a slope inclined at the angle of repose, say between 30° and 35°, and rolled into place up the long back slope of the dune by the wind. It has not, however, been generally recognized that the angle of repose may be exceeded (a) when there exists a strong back eddy or (b) when the wind blows violently and for a short time in the opposite direction. In either case sand is carried up the short steep slope of the dune front and accumulated at an angle not infrequently running up to 43° and 48° and locally, and under the most favorable circumstances, in excess of 50°. The conditions under which these steep angles are attained are undoubtedly not universal, but they can be found in some parts of almost any desert in the world. They appear not to be present where the sand grains are of uniform size throughout, since that leads to rolling. They are found rather where there is a certain limited variation in size that promotes packing. Packing and the development of steep slopes are also facilitated in parts of the coastal desert of Peru by a cloud canopy that hangs over the desert in the early morning, that in the most favorable places moistens even the dune surfaces and that has least penetration on the steep semi-protected dune fronts. Sand later blown up the dune front or rolled down from the dune crest is encouraged to remain near the cornice on an abnormally steep slope by the attraction which the slightly moister sand has for the dry grains blown against it. Since dunes travel and since their front layers, formed on steep slopes, are cut off to the level of the surface in the rear of the dune, it follows that the steepest dips in exposed sections are almost always less than those in existing dunes. Exceptions to the rule will be noted in filled hollows not re-excavated until deeply covered by wind-blown material. These, re-exposed at the end of a long period of wind accumulation, may exhibit even the maximum dips of the dune cornices. Such will be conspicuously the case in sections in aggraded desert deposits. On the border of the Majes Valley, from 400 to 500 feet of wind-accumulated deposits may be observed, representing a long period of successive dune burials.

The peculiar blending of the contact lines of dune laminae, related to the tangency commonly noted in dune accumulations, is apparently due to the fact that the wind does not require a graded surface to work on, but blows uphill as well as down. It is present on both the back-slope and the front-slope deposits. Its finest expression appears to be in districts where the dune material was accumulated by a violent wind whose effects the less powerful winds could not destroy.

It is to the ability of the wind to transport material against, as well as with, gravity, that we owe the third distinct quality of dune material, the succession of flowing lines, in contrast to the succession of now flat-lying now steeply inclined beds characteristic of cross-bedded material deposited by water. One dune travels across the face of the country only to be succeeded by another.[5] Even if wind aggradation is in progress, the plain-like surface in the rear of a dune may be excavated to the level of steeply inclined

---

[5] The best photograph of this condition which I have yet seen is in W. Sievers, Süd- und Mittelamerika, second ed., 1914, Plate 15, p. 358.

beds upon whose truncated outcrop other inclined beds are laid, Fig. 178. The contrast to these conditions in the case of aggradation by water is so clearly and easily inferred that space will not be taken to point them out. It is also true as a corollary to the above that the greater part of a body of wind-drifted material will consist of cross-bedded layers, and not a series of evenly divided and alternating flat-lying and cross-bedded layers which result from deposition in active and variable currents of water.

The caution must of course be observed that wind action and water action may alternate in a desert region, as already described in Tarapacá in northern Chile, so that the whole of a deposit may exhibit an alternation of cross-bedded and flat-lying layers; but the former only are due to wind action, the latter to water action.

Finally it may be noted that the sudden, frequent, and diversified dips in the cross-bedding are peculiarly characteristic of wind action. Although one sees in a given cross-section dips apparently directed only toward the left or the right, excavation will supply a third dimension from which the true dips may be either observed or calculated. These show an almost infinite variety of directions of dip, even in restricted areas, a condition due to the following causes:

(1) the curved fronts of sand dunes, which produce dips concentric with respect to a point and ranging through 180° of arc; (2) the irregular character of sand dunes in many places, a condition due in turn to (a) the changeful character of the strong wind (often not the prevailing wind) to which the formation of the dunes is due, and (b) the influence of the local topography upon wind directions within short distances or upon winds of different directions in which a slight change in wind direction is followed by a large change in the local currents; (3) the fact that all combinations are possible between the erosion levels of the wind in successive generations of dunes blown across a given area, hence *any* condition at a given level in a dune may be combined with *any other* condition of a succeeding dune; (4) variations in the sizes of successive dunes will lead to further contrasts

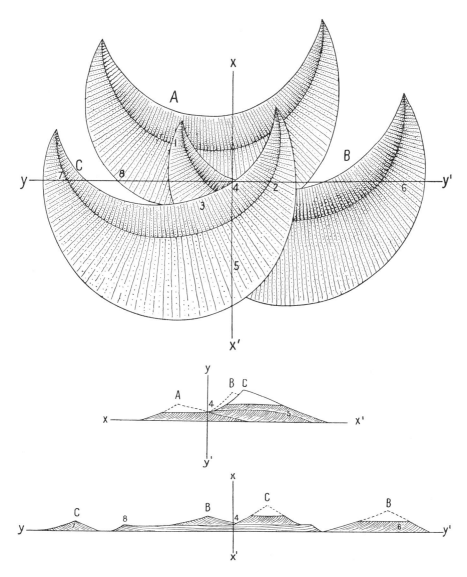

Fig. 178—Plan and cross-sections of superimposed sand dunes of conventional outline. In the sections, dune *A* is supposed to have left only a small basal portion to be covered by dune *B*. In the same way dune *C* has advanced to cover both *A* and *B*. The basal portions that have remained are exaggerated vertically in order to display the stratification. It is obviously not necessary that the dunes should all be of the same size and shape and advancing in the same direction in order to have the tangential relations here displayed. Nor need the aggrading material be derived from true dunes. The results would be the same in the case of sand *drifts* with their associated wind eddies. All bedded wind-blown deposits would have the same general relations. No two successive deposits, no matter from what direction the successive drifts or dunes travel, would exactly correspond in direction and amount of dip.

not only in the scale of the features but also in the direction and amount of the dips.

Finally, we may note that a section of dune deposits has a distinctive feature not exhibited by water deposits. If the foreset beds of a cross-bedded water deposit be exposed in a plane parallel to the strike of the beds, the beds will appear to be horizontal. They could not then be distinguished from the truly horizontal beds above and below them. But the conditions of wind deposition we have just noted, and chiefly the facts expressed by Fig. 178, make it impossible to select a position in which both tangency and irregular dips are not well developed in a wind deposit. I believe that we have in the foregoing facts and inferences a means for the definite separation of these two classes of deposits. Difficulties will arise only when there is a quick succession of wind and water action in time, or where the wind produces powerful and persistent effects without the actual formation of dunes.

The latest known deposits in the coastal region are found surmounting the terrace tops along the coast between Camaná and Quilca, where they form deposits several hundred feet thick in places. The age of these deposits is determined by fossil evidence, and is of extraordinary interest in the determination of the age of the great terraces upon which they lie. They consist of alternating beds of coarse and fine material, the coarser increasing in thickness and frequency toward the bottom of the section. It is also near the bottom of the section that fossils are now found; the higher members are locally saline and throughout there is a marked inclination of the beds toward the present shore. The deposits appear not to have been derived from the underlying granite-gneiss. They are distributed most abundantly near the mouths of the larger streams, as near the Vitor at Quilca, and the Majes at Camaná. Elsewhere the terrace summit is swept clean of waste, except where local clay deposits lie in the ravines, as back of Mollendo and where "tierras blancas" have been accumulated by the wind.

These coastal deposits were laid down upon a dissected terrace up to five miles in width. The degree of dissection is variable, and depends upon the relation of the through-flowing streams to the Coast Range. The Vitor and the Majes have cut down through the Coast Range, and locally removed the terrace; smaller streams rising on the flanks of the Coast Range either die out near the foot of the range or cross it in deep and narrow valleys. The present drainage on the seaward slopes of the Coast Range is entirely ineffective in reaching the sea, as was seen in 1911, the wettest season known on the coast in years and one of the wettest probably ever observed on this coast by man.

In consequence of their deposition on a terrace that ranges in elevation from zero to 1,500 feet above sea level, the deposits of the coast are very irregularly disposed. But in consequence of their great bulk they have a rather smooth upper surface, gradation having been carried to the point where the irregularities of the dissected terrace were smoothed out. Their general uniformity is broken where streams cross them, or where streams crossed them during the wetter Pleistocene. Their elevation, several hundred feet above sea level, is responsible for the deep dissection of their coastal margin, where great cliffs have been cut.

PLEISTOCENE

The broad regional uplift of the Peruvian Andes in late Tertiary and in Pleistocene times carried their summits above the level of perpetual snow. It is still an open question whether or not uplift was sufficiently great in the early Pleistocene to be influenced by the first glaciations of that period. As yet, there are evidences of only two glacial invasions, and both are considered late events on account of the freshness of their deposits and the related topographic forms. The coarse deposits—nearly 500 feet thick—that form the top of the desert section described above clearly indicate a wetter climate than prevailed during the deposition of the several hundred feet of wind-blown deposits beneath them. But if our interpretation be correct these deposits are of late Tertiary age, and their character and position are taken to indicate climatic changes in the Tertiary. They may have been the mild precursors of the greater climatic changes of glacial times. Certain it is that they are quite unlike the mass of the Tertiary deposits. On the other hand they are separated from the deposits of known glacial age by a time interval of great length—an epoch in which was cut a benched canyon nearly a mile deep and three miles wide. They must, therefore, have been formed when the Andes were thousands of feet lower and unable to nourish glaciers. It was only after the succeeding uplifts had raised the mountain crests well above the frost line that the records of oscillating climates were left in erratic deposits, troughed valleys, cliffed cirques and pinnacled divides.

The glacial forms are chiefly at the top of the country; the glacial deposits are chiefly in the deep valleys that were carved before the colder climate set in. The rock waste ground up by the ice was only a small part of that delivered to the streams in glacial times. Everywhere the wetter climate resulted in the partial stripping of the residual soil gathered upon the smooth mature slopes formed during the long Tertiary cycle of erosion. This moving sheet of waste as well as the rock fragments carried away from the glacier ends were strewn along the valley floors, forming a deep alluvial fill. Thereby the canyon floors were rendered habitable.

In the chapters on human geography we have already called attention to the importance of the U-shaped valleys carved by the glaciers. Their floors are broad and relatively smooth. Their walls restrain the live stock. They are sheltered though lofty. But all the human benefits conferred by ice action are insignificant beside those due to the general shedding of waste from the cold upper surfaces to the warm levels of the valley floors. The alluvium-filled valleys are the seats of dense populations. In the lowest of them tropical and sub-tropical products are raised, like sugar-cane and cotton, in a soil that once lay on the smooth upper slopes of mountain spurs or that was ground fine on the bed of an Alpine glacier.

The Pleistocene deposits fall into three well-defined groups: (1) glacial accumulations at the valley heads, (2) alluvial deposits

Fig. 179—Snow fields on the summit of the Cordillera Vilcapampa near Ollantay-tambo. A huge glacier once lay in the steep canyon in the background and descended to the notched terminal moraine at the canyon mouth. In places the glacier was over a thousand feet thick. From the terminal moraine an enormous alluvial fan extends forward to the camera and to the opposite wall of the Urubamba Valley. It is confluent with other fans of the same origin. See Fig. 180. In the foreground are flowers, shrubs, and cacti. A few miles below Urubamba at 11,500 feet.

FIG. 180.

FIG. 181.

FIG. 180—Urubamba Valley between Ollantaytambo and Torontoy, showing (1)
more moderate upper slopes and steeper lower slopes of the two-cycle mountain spurs;
(2) the extensive alluvial deposits of the valley, consisting chiefly of confluent alluvial
fans heading in the glaciated mountains on the left. See Fig. 179.

FIG. 181—Glacial features of the Central Ranges (see Fig. 204). Huge lateral
moraines built by ice streams tributary to the main valley north of Chuquibambilla.
That the tributaries persisted long after the main valley became free of ice is shown
by the descent of the lateral moraines over the steep border of the main valley and
down to the floor of it.

in the valleys, and (3) lacustrine deposits formed on the floors of temporary lakes in inclosed basins. Among these the most variable in form and composition are the true glacier-laid deposits at the valley heads. The most extensive are the fluvial deposits accumulated as valley fill throughout the entire Andean realm. Though important enough in some respects the lacustrine deposits are of small extent and of rather local significance. Practically none of them fall within the field of the present expedition; hence we shall describe only the first two classes.

The most important glacial deposits were accumulated in the eastern part of the Andes as a result of greater precipitation, a lower snowline, and catchment basins of larger area. In the Cordillera Vilcapampa glaciers once existed up to twelve and fifteen miles in length, and those several miles long were numerous both here and throughout the higher portions of the entire Cordillera, save in the belt of most intense volcanic action, which coincides with the driest part of the Andes, where the glaciers were either very short or wanting altogether.

Since vigorous glacial action results in general in the cleaning out of the valley heads, no deposits of consequence occur in these locations. Down valley, however, glacial deposits occur in the form of terminal moraines of recession and ground moraines. The general nature of these deposits is now so well known that detailed description seems quite unnecessary except in the case of unusual features.

It is noteworthy that the moraines decrease in size up valley since each valley had been largely cleaned out by ice action before the retreat of the glacier began. Each lowermost terminal moraine is fronted by a great mass of unsorted coarse bowldery material forming a fill in places several hundred feet thick, as below Choquetira and in the Vilcapampa Valley between Vilcabamba and Puquiura. This bowldery fill is quite distinct from the long, gently inclined, and stratified valley train below it, or the marked ridge-like moraine above it. It is in places a good half mile in length. Its origin is believed to be due to an overriding action beyond the last terminal moraine at a time when the ice was well charged with débris, an overriding not marked by morainal accumulations, chiefly because the ice did not maintain an extreme position for a long period.

In the vicinity of the terminal moraines the alluvial valley fill is often so coarse and so unorganized as to look like till in the cut banks along the streams, though its alluvial origin is always shown by the topographic form. This characteristic is of special geologic interest since the form may be concealed through deposition or destroyed by erosion, and no condition but the structure remain to indicate the manner of origin of the deposit. In such an event it would not be possible to distinguish between alluvium and till. The gravity of the distinction appears when it is known that such apparently unsorted alluvium may extend for several miles forward of a terminal moraine, in the shape of a wide-spreading alluvial fan apparently formed under conditions of extremely rapid aggradation. I suppose it would not be doubted in general that a section of such stony, bowldery, unsorted material two miles long would have other than a glacial origin, yet such may be the case. Indeed, if, as in the Urubamba Valley, a future section should run parallel to the valley across the heads of a great series of fans of similar composition, topographic form, and origin, it would be possible to see many miles of such material.

The depth of the alluvial valley fill due to tributary fan accumulation depends upon both the amount of the material and the form of the valley. Below Urubamba in the Urubamba Valley a fine series is displayed, as shown in Fig. 180. The fans head in valleys extending up to snow-covered summits upon whose flanks living glaciers are at work today. Their heads are now crowned by terminal moraines and both moraines and alluvial fans are in process of dissection. The height and extent of the moraines and the alluvial fans are in rough proportion and in turn reflect the height, elevation, and extent of the valley heads which served as fields of nourishment for the Pleistocene glaciers. Where the fans were deposited in narrow valleys the effect was to increase the thickness of the deposits at the expense of their area, to dam the drainage lines or displace them, and to so load the streams that they have not yet cleared their beds after thousands of years of work under torrential conditions.

Below Urubamba the alluvial fans entering the main valley from the east have pushed the river against its western valley wall, so that the river flows on one side against rock and on the other against a hundred feet of stratified material. In places, as at the head of the narrows on the valley trail to Ollantaytambo, a flood plain has been formed in front of the scarp cut into the alluvium, while the edge of the dissected alluvial fans has been sculptured into erosion forms resembling bad-lands topography. On the western side of the valley the alluvial fans are very small, since they are due to purely local accumulations of waste from the edge of the plateau. Glaciation has here displaced the river. Its effects will long be felt in the disproportionate erosion of the western wall of the valley.

By far the most interesting of the deposits of glacial time are those laid down on the valley floors in the form of an alluvial fill. Though such deposits have greater thickness as a rule near the nourishing moraines or bordering alluvial fans at the lower ends of the valleys, they are everywhere important in amount, distinctive in topographic form, and of amazingly wide extent. They reach far into and possibly across the Amazon basin, they form a distinct though

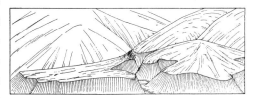

Fig. 189—Dissected alluvial fans on the border of the Urubamba Valley near Hacienda Chinche. A characteristic feature of the valleys of the Peruvian Andes below the zone of glaciation but within the limits of its aggraditional effects. Through alluviation the valleys and basins of the Andean Cordillera, and vast areas of the great Amazon plains east of it, felt the effects of the glacial conditions of a past age.

small piedmont fringe along the eastern base of the Andes, and they are universal throughout the Andean valleys. That a deposit of such volume—many times greater than all the material accumulated in the form of high-level alluvial fans or terminal moraines—should originate in a tropical land in a region that suffered but limited Alpine glaciation vastly increases its importance.

The fill is composed of both fine and coarse material laid down by water in steep valley floors to a depth of many feet. It breaks the steep slope of each valley, forming terraces with pronounced frontal scarps facing the river. On the raw bluffs at the scarps made by the encroaching stream good exposures are afforded. At Chinche in the Urubamba Valley above Santa Ana, the material is both sand and clay with an important amount of gravel laid down with steep valleyward inclination and under torrential conditions; so that within a given bed there may be an apparent absence of lamination. Almost identical conditions are exhibited frequently along the railway to Cuzco in the Vilcanota Valley. The material is mixed sand and gravel, here and there running to a bowldery or stony mass where accessions have been received from some source nearby. It is modified along its margin not only in topographic form but also in composition by small tributary alluvial fans, though these in general

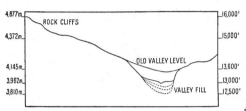

FIG. 183—Two-cycle slopes and alluvial fill between Huichihua and Chuquibambilla. The steep slopes on the inner valley border are in many places vertical and rock cliffs are everywhere abundant. Mature slopes have their greatest development here between 13,500 and 15,000 feet (4,110 to 4,570 m.). Steepest mature slopes run from 15° to 21°. Least steep are the almost level spur summits. The depths of the valley fill must be at least 300, and may possibly be 500 feet. The break between valley fill and steep slopes is most pronounced where the river runs along the valley wall or undercuts it; least pronounced where alluvial fans spread out from the head of some ravine. It is a bowldery, stony fill almost everywhere terraced and cultivated.

constitute but a small part of the total mass. At Cotahuasi, Fig. 29, there is a remarkable fill at least four hundred feet deep in many places where the river has exposed fine sections. The depth of the fill is, however, not determined by the height of the erosion bluffs cut into it, since the bed of the river is made of the same material. The rock floor of the valley is probably at least an additional hundred feet below the present level of the river.

Similar conditions are well displayed at Huadquiña, where a fine series of terraces at the lower end of the Torontoy Canyon break the descent of the environing slopes; also in the Urubamba

Valley below Rosalina, and again at the edge of the mountains at the Pongo de Mainique. It is exhibited most impressively in the Majes Valley, where the bordering slopes appear to be buried knee-deep in waste, and where from any reasonable downward extension of rock walls of the valley there would appear to be at least a half mile of it. It is doubtful and indeed improbable that the entire fill of the Majes Valley is glacial, for during the Pliocene or early Pleistocene there was a submergence which gave opportunity for the partial filling of the valley with non-glacial alluvium, upon which the glacial deposits were laid as upon a flat and extensive floor that gives an exaggerated impression of their depth. However, the head of the Majes Valley contains at least six hundred feet and probably as much as eight hundred feet of alluvium now in process of dissection, whose coarse texture and position indicates an origin under glacial conditions. The fact argues for the great thickness of the alluvial material of the lower valley, even granting a floor of Pliocene or early Pleistocene sediments. The best sections are to be found just below Chuquibamba and again about halfway between that city and Aplao, whereas the best display of the still even-floored parts of the valley are between Aplao and Cantas, where the braided river still deposits coarse gravels upon its wide flood plain.

CHAPTER XVI

GLACIAL FEATURES

THE SNOWLINE

SOUTH AMERICA is classical ground in the study of tropical snowlines. The African mountains that reach above the snowline in the equatorial belt—Ruwenzori, Kibo, and Kenia—have only been studied recently because they are remote from the sea and surrounded by bamboo jungle and heavy tropical forest. On the other hand, many of the tropical mountains of South America lie so near the west coast as to be visible from it and have been studied for over a hundred years. From the days of Humboldt (1800) and Boussingault (1825) down to the present, observations in the Andes have been made by an increasing number of scientific travelers. The result is a large body of data upon which comparative studies may now be profitably undertaken.

Like scattered geographic observations of many other kinds, the earlier studies on the snowline have increased in value with time, because the snowline is a function of climatic elements that are subject to periodic changes in intensity and cannot be understood by reference to a single observation. Since the discovery of physical proofs of climatic changes in short cycles, studies have been made to determine the direction and rate of change of the snowline the world over, with some very striking results.

It has been found [1] that the changes run in cycles of from thirty to thirty-five years in length and that the northern and southern hemispheres appear to be in opposite phase. For example, since 1885 the snowline in the southern hemisphere has been decreasing in elevation in nine out of twelve cases by the average amount of nine hundred feet. With but a single excep-

---

[1] Paschinger, Die Schneegrenze in verschiedenen Klimaten. Peter. Mitt. Erganz'heft, Nr. 173. 1912, pp. 92-93.

tion, the snowline in the northern hemisphere has been rising since 1890 with an average increase of five hundred feet in sixteen cases. To be sure, we must recognize that the observations upon which these conclusions rest have unequal value, due both to personal factors and to differences in instrumental methods, but that in spite of these tendencies toward inequality they should agree in establishing a general rise of the snowline in the northern hemisphere and an opposite effect in the southern is of the highest significance.

It must also be realized that snowline observations are altogether too meager and scattered in view of the abundant opportunities for making them, that they should be standardized, and that they must extend over a much longer period before they attain their full value in problems in climatic variations. Once the possible significance of snowline changes is appreciated the number and accuracy of observations on the elevation and local climatic relations of the snowline should rapidly increase.

In 1907 I made a number of observations on the height of the snowline in the Bolivian and Chilean Andes between latitudes 17° and 20° south, and in 1911 extended the work northward into the Peruvian Andes along the seventy-third meridian. It is proposed here to assemble these observations and, upon comparison with published data, to make a few interpretations.

From Central Lagunas, Chile, I went northeastward via Pica and the Huasco Basin to Llica, Bolivia, crossing the Sillilica Pass in May, 1907, at 15,750 feet (4,800 m.). Perpetual snow lay at an estimated height of 2,000-2,500 feet above the pass or 18,000 feet (5,490 m.) above the sea. Two weeks later the Huasco Basin, 14,050 feet (4,280 m.), was covered a half-foot deep with snow and a continuous snow mantle extended down to 13,000 feet. Light snows are reported from 12,000 feet, but they remain a few hours only and are restricted to the height of exceptionally severe winter seasons (June and early July). Three or four distant snow-capped peaks were observed and estimates made of the elevation of the snowline between the Cordillera Sillilica and Llica on the eastern border of the Maritime Cordillera. All observations agreed in giving an elevation much in excess of 17,000 feet. In general the values run from 18,000 to 19,000 feet (5,490 to 5,790 m.). Though the bases of these figures are estimates, it should be noted that a large part of the trail lies between 14,000 and 16,000 feet, passing mountains snow-free at least 2,000 to 3,000 feet higher, and that for general comparisons they have a distinct value.

In the Eastern Cordillera of Bolivia, snow was observed on the summit of the Tunari group of peaks northwest of Cochabamba. Steinmann, who visited the region in 1904, but did not reach the summit of the Tunari group of peaks, concludes that the limit of perpetual snow should be placed above the highest point, 17,300 (5,270 m.); but in July and August, 1907, I saw a rather extensive snow cover over at least the upper 1,000 feet, and what appeared to be a very small glacier. Certain it is that the Cochabamba Indians bring clear blue ice from the Tunari to the principal hotels, just as ice is brought to Cliza from the peaks above Arani. On these grounds I am inclined to place the snow-line at 17,000 feet (5,180 m.) near the eastern border of the Eastern Cordillera, latitude 17° S. At 13,000 feet, in July, 1907, snow occurred in patches only on the pass called Abre de Malaga, northeast of Colomi, 13,000 feet, and fell thickly while we were descending the northern slopes toward Corral, so that in the early morning it extended to the cold timber line at 10,000 feet. In a few hours, however, it had vanished from all but the higher and the shadier situations.

In the Vilcanota knot above the divide between the Titicaca and Vilcanota hydrographic systems, the elevation of the snow-line was 16,300+ feet (4,970 m.) in September, 1907. On the Cordillera Real of Bolivia it is 17,000 to 17,500 feet on the northeast, but falls to 16,000 feet on the southwest above La Paz. In the first week of July, 1911, snow fell on the streets of Cuzco (11,000 feet) and remained for over an hour. The heights north of San Geronimo (16,000 feet) miss the limit of perpetual snow and are snow-covered only a few months each year.

In taking observations on the snowline along the seventy-third meridian I was fortunate enough to have a topographer the heights of whose stations enabled me to correct the readings of my aneroid barometer whenever these were taken off the line of traverse. Furthermore, the greater height of the passes—15,000 to 17,600 feet—brought me more frequently above the snowline than had been the case in Bolivia and Chile. More detailed observations were made, therefore, not only upon the elevation of the snowline from range to range, but also upon the degree of canting of the snowline on a given range. Studies were also made on the effect of the outline of the valleys upon the extent of the glaciers, the influence on the position of the snowline of mass elevation, precipitation, and cloudiness.

Snow first appears at 14,500 feet (4,320 m.) on the eastern flanks of the Cordillera Vilcapampa, in 13° south latitude. East of this group of ridges and peaks as far as the extreme eastern border of the mountain belt, fifty miles distant, the elevations decrease rapidly to 10,000 feet and lower, with snow remaining on exceptionally high peaks from a few hours to a few months. In the winter season snow falls now and then as low as 11,500 feet, as in the valley below Vilcabamba pueblo in early September, 1911, though it vanishes like mist with the appearance of the sun or the warm up-valley winds from the forest. Storms gather daily about the mountain summits and replenish the perpetual snow above 15,000 feet. In the first pass above Puquiura we encountered heavy snow banks on the northeastern side a hundred feet below the pass (14,500 feet), but on the southwestern or leeward side it is five hundred feet lower. This distribution is explained by the lesser insolation on the southwestern side, the immediate drifting of the clouds from the windward to the leeward slopes, and to the mutual intensification of cause and effect by topographic changes such as the extension of collecting basins and the steeping of the slopes overlooking them with a corresponding increase in the duration of shade.

It is well known that with increase of elevation and therefore of the rarity of the air there is less absorption of the sun's radiant energy, and a corresponding increase in the degree of insolation. It follows, therefore, that at high altitudes the contrasts between sun and shade temperatures will increase. Frankland [2] has shown that the increase may run as high as 500 per cent between 100 to 10,000 feet above the sea. I have noted a fall of temperature of 15° F. in six minutes, due to the obscuring of the sun by cloud at an elevation of 16,000 feet above Huichihua in the Central Ranges of Peru. Since the sun shines approximately half the time in the snow-covered portions of the mountains and since the tropical Andes are of necessity snow-covered only at lofty elevations, this contrast between shade and sun temperatures is by far the most powerful factor influencing differences in elevation of the snowline in Peru.

To the drifting of the fallen snow is commonly ascribed a large portion of this contrast. I have yet to see any evidence of its action near the snowline, though I have often observed it, especially under a high wind in the early morning hours at considerable elevations above the snowline, as at the summits of lofty peaks. It appears that the lower ranges bearing but a limited amount of snow are not subject to drifting because of the wetness of the snow, and the fact that it is compacted by occasional rains and hail storms. Only the drier snow at higher elevations and under stronger winds can be effectively dislodged.

The effect of unequal distribution of precipitation on the windward and leeward slopes of a mountain range is in general to depress the snowline on the windward slopes where the greater amount falls, but this may be offset in high altitudes by temperature contrasts as in the westward trending Cordillera Vilcapampa, where north and south slopes are in opposition. If the Cordillera Vilcapampa ran north and south we should have the windward and leeward slopes equally exposed to the sun and the snowline would lie at a lower elevation on the eastern side. Among all the ranges the slopes have decreasing precipitation to the leeward, that is, westerly. The second and third passes, between Arma and Choquetira, are snow-free (though their elevations equal those of

---

[2] Hann, Handbook of Climatology, Part 1, trans. by Ward, 1903, p. 232.

the first pass) because they are to leeward of the border range, hence receive less precipitation. The depressive effect of increased precipitation on the snowline is represented by A-B, Fig. 184; in an individual range the effect of heavier precipitation may be off-set by temperature contrasts between shady and sunny slopes, as shown by the line a-b in the same figure.

The degree of canting of the snowline on opposite slopes of the Cordillera Vilcapampa varies between 5° and 12°, the higher value being represented four hours southwest of Arma on the Choquetira trail, looking northeast. A general view of the Cordillera looking east at this point (Fig. 186), shows the appearance of the snowline as one looks along the flanks of the range. In detail the snowline is fur-ther complicated by topog-

FIG. 184—To illustrate the canting of the snowline. *A-B* is the snowline depressed toward the north (right) in response to heavier precipitation. The line *a-b* represents a depression in the opposite direction due to the different degree of insolation on the northern (sunny) and southern (shady) slopes.

raphy and varying insolation, each spur having a snow-clad and snow-free aspect as shown in the last figure. The degree of difference on these minor slopes may even exceed the difference between opposite aspects of the range in which they occur.

To these diversifying influences must be added the effect of warm up-valley winds that precede the regular afternoon snow squalls and that melt the latest fall of snow to exceptionally high elevations on both the valley floor and the spurs against which they impinge. The influence of the warmer air current is notably confined to the heads of those master valleys that run down the wind, as in the valley heading at the first pass, Cordillera Vilca-pampa, and at the heads of the many valleys terminating at the passes of the Maritime Cordillera. Elsewhere the winds are dis-sipated in complex systems of minor valleys and their effect is too well distributed to be recognized.

It is clear from the conditions of the problem as outlined on preceding pages that the amount of canting may be expressed in feet of difference of the snowline on opposite sides of a range or in degrees. The former method has, heretofore, been employed. It is proposed that this method should be abolished and degrees substituted, on the following grounds: Let *A* and *B*, Fig. 190, represent two mountain masses of unequal area and unequal elevation. Let the opposite ends of the snowlines of both figures lie 1,000 feet apart as between the windward and leeward sides of a

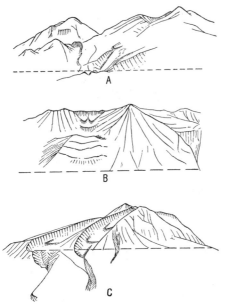

broad cordillera (A), or as between the relatively sunnier and relatively shadier slopes of individual mountains or narrow ranges in high latitudes or high altitudes (B). With increasing elevation there is increasing contrast between temperatures in sunshine and in shade, hence a greater degree of canting (B). Tending toward a still greater degree of contrast is the effect of the differences in the amounts of snowy precipitation, which are always more marked on an isolated and lofty mountain summit than upon a broad mountain mass (1) because in the former there is a very restricted area where snow may accumulate, and (2)

Fig. 185—Glacial features in the Peruvian Andes near Arequipa. Sketched from a railway train, July, 1911. The horizontal broken lines represent the lower limit of light snow during late June, 1911. There is a fine succession of moraines in U-shaped valleys in all the mountains of the Arequipa region. *A* represents a part of Chacchani northwest of Arequipa; *B* is looking south by east at the northwest end of Chachani near Pampa de Arrieros; *C* also shows the northwest end of Chacchani from a more distant point.

because with increase of elevation there is a rapid and differential decrease in both the rate of adiabatic cooling and the amount of water vapor; hence the snow-producing forces are more quickly dissipated.

Furthermore, the leeward side of a lofty mountain not only receives much less snow proportionally than the leeward side of

Fig. 186.

Fig. 187.

Fig. 186—Canted snowline in the Cordillera Vilcapampa between Arma and Choquetira. Looking east from 13,500 feet.

Fig. 187—Glacial topography between Lambrama and Antabamba in the Central Ranges. A recent fall of snow covers the foreground. The glaciers are now almost extinct and their action is confined to the deepening and steepening of the cirques at the valley heads.

Fig. 188.

Fig. 189.

Fig. 188—Asymmetrical peaks in the Central Ranges between Antabamba and Lambrama. The snow-filled hollows in the photograph face away from the sun—that is, south—and have retained snow since the glacial epoch; while the northern slopes are snow-free. There is no true glacial ice and the continued cirque recession is due to nivation.

Fig. 189—Glacial topography north of the divide on the seventy-third meridian, Maritime Cordillera. Looking downstream at an elevation of 16,500 feet (5,030 m.).

a lower mountain, but also loses it faster on account of the smaller extent of surface upon which it is disposed and the proportionally larger extent of counteractive, snow-free surface about it. Among the volcanoes of Ecuador are many that show differences of 500 feet in snowline elevation on windward and leeward (east) slopes and some, as for example Chimborazo, that exhibit differences of 1,000 feet. The latter figure also expresses

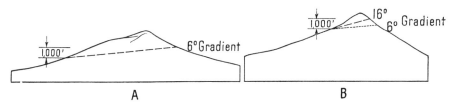

FIG. 190—To illustrate the difference in the degree of canting of the snowline on large and on small mountain masses.

the differences in the broad Cordillera Vilcapampa and in the Maritime Cordillera, though the *rate* of canting as expressed in degrees is much greater in the case of the western mountains.

The advantages of the proposed method of indicating the degree of canting of the snowline lie in the possibility thus afforded of ultimately separating and expressing quantitatively the various factors that affect the position of the line. In the Cordillera Vilcapampa, for example, the dominant canting force is the difference between sun and shade temperatures, while in the volcanoes of Ecuador, where *symmetrical volcanoes, almost on the equator, have equal insolation on all aspects* and the temperature contrasts are reduced to a minimum—the differences are owing chiefly to varying exposure to the winds. The elusive factors in the comparison are related to the differences in area and in elevation.

The value of arriving finally at close snowline analyses grows out of (1) the possibility of snowline changes in short cycles and (2) uncertainty of arriving by existing methods at the snowline of the glacial period, whose importance is fundamental in refined physiographic studies in glaciated regions with a complex topography. To show the application of the latter point we shall now attempt to determine the snowline of the glacial period in the belt of country along the route of the Expedition.

In the group of peaks shown in Fig. 188 between Lambrama and Antabamba, the elevation of the snowline varies from 16,000 to 17,000 feet (4,880-5,180 m.), depending on the topography and the exposure. The determination of the limit of perpetual snow was here, as elsewhere along the seventy-third meridian, based upon evidences of nivation. It will be observed in Fig. 191 that just under the snow banks to the left of the center are streams of rock waste which head in the snow. Their size is roughly proportional to the size of the snow banks, and, furthermore, they are not found on snow-free slopes. From these facts it is concluded that they represent the waste products of snow erosion or nivation, just as the hollows in which the snow lies represent the topographic products of nivation. On account of the seasonal and annual variation in precipitation and temperature—hence in the elevation of the snowline—it is often difficult to make a correct snowline observation based upon depth and *apparent* permanence. Different observers report great changes in the snowline in short intervals, changes not explained by instrumental variations, since they are referred to topographic features. It appears to be impossible to rely upon present records for small changes possibly related to minor climatic cycles because of a lack of standardization of observations.

Nothing in the world seems simpler at first sight than an observation on the elevation of the snowline. Yet it can be demonstrated that large numbers of observers have merely noted the position of temporary snow. It is strongly urged that evidences of nivation serve henceforth as proof of permanent snow and that photographic records be kept for comparison. In this way measurements of changes in the level of the snowline may be accurately made and the snow cover used as a climatic gauge.

Farther west in the Maritime Cordillera, the snowline rises to 18,000 feet on the northern slopes of the mountains and to 17,000 feet on the southern slopes. The top of the pass above Cotahuasi, 17,600 feet (5,360 m.), was snow-free in October, 1911, but the snow extended 500 feet lower on the southern slope. The degree of canting is extraordinary at this point, single volcanoes only 1,500 to 2,000 feet above the general level and with bases but a few miles in circumference exhibit a thousand feet of difference in the snowline upon northern and southern aspects. This is to be attributed no less to the extreme elevation of the snow (and, therefore, stronger contrasts of shade and sun temperatures) than to the extreme aridity of the region and the high daytime temperatures. The aridity is a factor, since heavy snowfall means a lengthening of the period of precipitation in which a cloud cover shuts out the sun and a shortening of the period of insolation and melting.

Contrasts between shade and sun temperatures increase with altitude but their effects also increase in *time*. Of two volcanoes of equal size and both 20,000 feet above sea level, that one will show the greater degree of canting that is longer exposed to the sun. The high daytime temperature is a factor, since it tends to remove the thinnest snow, which also falls in this case on the side receiving the greatest amount of heat from the sun. The high daytime temperature is phenomenal in this region, and is owing to the great extent of snow-free land at high elevations and yet below the snowline, and to the general absence of clouds and the thinness of vegetation.

On approach to the western coast the snowline descends again to 17,500 feet on Coropuna. There are three chief reasons for this condition. First, the well-watered Majes Valley is deeply incised almost to the foot of Coropuna, above Chuquibamba, and gives the daily strong sea breeze easy access to the mountain. Second, the Coast Range is not only low at the mouth of the Majes Valley, but also is cut squarely across by the valley itself, so that heavy fogs and cloud sweep inland nightly and at times completely cover both valley and desert for an hour after sunrise. Although these yield no moisture to the desert or the valley floor except such as is mechanically collected, yet they do increase the precipitation upon the higher elevations at the valley head.

A third factor is the size of Coropuna itself. The mountain

is not a simple volcano but a composite cone with five main summits reaching well above the snowline, the highest to an elevation of 21,703 feet (6,615 m.). It measures about 20 miles (32 km.) in circumference at the snowline and 45 miles (72 km.) at its base (measuring at the foot of the steeper portion), and stands upon a great tributary lava plateau from 15,000 to 17,000 feet above sea level. Compared with El Misti, at Arequipa, its volume is three times as great, its height two thousand feet more, and its access to ocean winds at least thirty per cent more favorable. El Misti, 19,200 feet (5,855 m.) has snow down as far as 16,000 feet in the wet season and rarely to 14,000 feet, though by sunset a fall of snow may almost disappear whose lower limit at sunrise was 16,000 feet. Snow may accumulate several thousand feet below the summit during the wet season, and in such quantities as to require almost the whole of the ensuing dry season (March to December) for its melting. Northward of El Misti is the massive and extended range, Chachani, 20,000 feet (6,100 m.) high; on the opposite side is the shorter range called Pichu-Pichu. Snow lies throughout the year on both these ranges, but in exceptional seasons it nearly disappears from Chachani and wholly disappears from Pichu-Pichu, so that the snowline then rises to 20,000 feet. It is considered that the mean of a series of years would give a value between 17,000 and 18,000 feet for the snowline on all the great mountains of the Arequipa region.[3] This would, however, include what is known to be temporary snow; the limit of "perpetual" snow, or the true snowline, appears to lie about 19,000 feet on Chachani and *above* El Misti, say 19,500 feet. It is also above the crest of Pichu-Pichu. The snowline, therefore, appears to rise a thousand feet from Coropuna to El Misti, owing chiefly to the poorer exposure of the latter to the sources of snowy precipitation.

It may also be noted that the effect of the easy access of the ocean winds in the Coropuna region is also seen in the increasing amount of vegetation which appears in the most favorable situa-

---

[3] S. I. Bailey, Peruvian Meteorology, 1888-1890. Ann. Astron. Observ. of Harvard Coll., Vol. 39, Pt. I, 1899, pp. 1-3.

tions. Thus, along the Salamanca trail only a few miles from the base of Coropuna are a few square kilometers of *quenigo* woodland generally found in the cloud belt at high altitudes; for example, at 14,000 feet above Lambrama and at 9,000 feet on the slope below Incahuasi, east of Pasaje. The greater part of the growth is disposed over hill slopes and on low ridges and valley walls. It is, therefore, clearly unrelated as a whole to the greater amount of ground-water with which a part is associated, as along the valley floors of the streams that head in the belt of perpetual snow. The appearance of this growth is striking after days of travel over the barren, clinkery lava plateau to eastward that has a less favorable exposure. The *quenigo* forest, so-called, is of the greatest economic value in a land so desolate as the vast arid and semi-arid mountain of western Peru. Every passing traveler lays in a stock of fire-wood as he rests his beasts at noonday; and long journeys are made to these curious woodlands from both Salamanca and Chuquibamba to gather fuel for the people of the towns.

NIVATION

The process of nivation, or snow erosion, does not always produce visible effects. It may be so feeble as to make no impression upon very resistant rock where the snow-fall is light and the declivity low. Ablation may in such a case account for almost the whole of the snow removed. On strong and topographically varied slopes where the snow is concentrated in headwater alcoves, there is a more pronounced downward movement of the snow masses with more prominent effects both of erosion beneath the snow and of accumulation at the border of the snow. In such cases the limit of perpetual snow may be almost as definitely known as the limit of a glacier. Like glaciers these more powerful snow masses change their limits in response to regional changes in precipitation, temperature, or both. It would at first sight appear impossible to distinguish between these changes through the results of nivation. Yet in at least a few cases it may be as readily determined as the past limits of glaciers are inferred from the terminal moraines, still intact, that cross the valley floors far below the present limits of the ice.

In discussing the process of nivation it is necessary to assume a sliding movement on the part of the snow, though it is a condition in Matthes' original problem in which the nivation idea was introduced that the snow masses remain stationary. It is believed, however, that Matthes' valuable observations and conclusions really involve but half the problem of nivation; or at the most but one of two phases of it. He has adequately shown the manner in which that phase of nivation is expressed which we find *at the border of the snow*. Of the action *beneath* the snow he says merely: "Owing to the frequent oscillations of the edge and the successive exposure of the different parts of the site to frost action, the area thus affected will have no well-defined boundaries. The more accentuated slopes will pass insensibly into the flatter ones, and the general tendency will be to give the drift site a cross section of smoothly curved outline and ordinarily concave."[4]

From observations on the effects of nivation in valleys, Matthes further concludes that "on a grade of about 12 per cent . . . névé must attain a thickness of at least 125 feet in order that it may have motion,"[5] though as a result of the different line of observations Hobbs concludes[6] that a somewhat greater thickness is required.

The snow cover in tropical mountains offers a number of solid advantages in this connection. Its limits, especially on the Cordillera Vilcapampa, on the eastern border of the Andes, are subject to *small seasonal oscillations* and the edge of the "perpetual" snow is easily determined. Furthermore, it is known from the comparatively "fixed quality of tropical climate," as Humboldt put it, that the variations of the snowline in a period of years do not exceed rather narrow limits. In mid-latitudes on the contrary there is an extraordinary shifting of the margin of the snow

[4] F. E. Matthes, Glacial Sculpture of the Bighorn Mountains, Wyoming, Twentieth Ann. Rept. U. S. Geol. Surv., 1899-1900, Pt. 2, p. 181.

[5] Idem, p. 190.

[6] W. H. Hobbs, Characteristics of Existing Glaciers, 1911, p. 22.

FIG. 191.

FIG. 192.

FIG. 191—The "pocked" surface characteristically developed in the zone of light nivation. Compare with Fig. 194, showing the effects of heavy nivation.

FIG. 192—Steep cirque walls and valleys head in the Central Ranges between Lambrama and Chuquibambilla. The snow is here a vigorous agent in transporting talus material and soil from all the upper slopes down to the foot of the cirque wall.

FIG. 193.

FIG. 194.

FIG. 193—Panta Mountain and its glacier system. The talus-covered mass in the center (B) is a terminal moraine topped by the dirt-stained glacier that descends from the crest. The separate glaciers were formerly united to form a huge ice tongue that truncated the lateral spurs and flattened the valley floor. One of its former stages is shown by the terminal moraine in the middle distance, breached by a stream, and impounding a lake not visible from this point of view.

FIG. 194—Recessed southern slopes of volcanoes whose northern slopes are practically without glacial modifications. Summit of the lava plateau, Maritime Cordillera, western Peru, between Antabamba and Cotahuasi.

cover, and a correspondingly wide distribution of the feeble effects of nivation.

Test cases are presented in Figs. 191, 192, and 193, Cordillera Vilcapampa, for the determination of the fact of the movement of the snow long before it has reached the thickness Matthes or Hobbs believes necessary for a movement of translation to begin. Fig. 191 shows snow masses occupying pockets on the slope of a ridge that was never covered with ice. Past glacial action with its complicating effects is, therefore, excluded and we have to deal with snow action pure and simple. The pre-glacial surface with smoothly contoured slopes is recessed in a noteworthy way from the ridge crest to the snowline of the glacial period at least a thousand feet lower. The recesses of the figure are peculiar in that not even the largest of them involve the entire surface from top to bottom; they are of small size and are scattered over the entire slope. This is believed to be due to the fact that they represent the limits of variations of the snowline in short cycles. Below them as far as the snowline of the glacial period are larger recesses, some of which are terminated by masses of waste as extensive as the neighboring moraines, but disposed in irregular scallops along the borders of the ridges or mountain slopes in which the recesses have been found.

The material accumulated at the lower limit of the snow cover of the glacial period was derived from two sources: (1) from slopes and cliffs overlooking the snow, (2) from beneath the snow by a process akin to ice plucking and abrasion. The first process is well known and resembles the shedding of waste upon a valley glacier or a névé field from the bordering cliffs and slopes. Material derived in this manner in many places rolls down a long incline of snow and comes to rest at the foot of it as a fringe of talus. The snow is in this case but a substitute for a normal mass of talus. The second process produces its most clearly recognizable effects on slopes exceeding a declivity of 20°; and upon 30° and 40° slopes its action is as well-defined as true glacial action which it imitates. It appears to operate in its simplest form as if independent of the mass of the snow, small and large snow

patches showing essentially the same results. This is the reverse
of Matthes' conclusion, since he says that though the minimum
thickness "must vary inversely with the percentage of the grade,"
"the influence of the grade is inconsiderable," and that the law
of variation must depend upon additional observation.[7]

Let us examine a number of details and the argument based
upon them and see if it is not possible to frame a satisfactory law
of variation.

In Fig. 193 the chief conditions of the problem are set forth.
Forward from the right-hand peak are snow masses descending
to the head of a talus (*A*) whose outlines are clearly defined by
freshly fallen snow. At (*B*) is a glacier whose tributaries descend
the middle and left slopes of the picture after making a descent
from slopes several thousand feet higher and not visible in this
view. The line beneath the glacier marks the top of the moraine
it has built up. Moraines farther down valley show a former
greater extent of the glacier. Clearly the talus material at (*A*)
was accumulated after the ice had retreated to its present position. It will be readily seen from an inspection of the photograph
that the total amount of material at (*A*) is an appreciable fraction
of that in the moraine. The ratio appears to be about 1:8 or 1:10.
I have estimated that the total area of snow-free surface about
the snowfields of the one is to that of the other as 2:3. The
gradients are roughly equivalent, but the volume of snow in the
one case is but a small fraction of that in the other. It will be
seen that the snow masses have recessed the mountain slopes at *A*
and formed deep hollows and that the hollowing action appears to
be most effective where the snow is thickest.

Summarizing, we note first, that the roughly equivalent factors
are gradient and amount of snow-free surface; second, that the
unequal factors are (a) accumulated waste, (b) degree of recessing, and (c) the degree of compacting of snow into ice and a corresponding difference in the character of the glacial agent, and
(d) the extent of the snow cover. The direct and important

---

[7] Op. cit., p. 286. Reference on p. 190.

relation of the first two unequal factors to the third scarcely need
be pointed out.

We have then an inequality in amount of accumulated material
to be explained by either an inequality in the extent of the snow
and therefore an inequality of snow action, or an inequality due
to the presence of ice in one valley and not in the other, or by
both. It is at once clear that if ice is absent above (*A*) and the
mountain slopes are recessed that snow action is responsible for
it. It is also recognized that whatever rate of denudation be assigned to the snow-free surfaces this rate must be exceeded by
the rate of snow action, else the inequalities of slope would be
decreased rather than increased. The accumulated material at
(*A*) is, therefore, partly but not chiefly due to denudation of snow-
free surfaces. It is due chiefly to *erosion* beneath the snow. Nor
can it be argued that the hollows now occupied by snow were
formed at some past time when ice not snow lay in them. They
are not ice-made hollows for they are on a steep spur above the
limits of ice action even in the glacial period. Any past action is,
therefore, represented here in *kind* by present action, though there
would be differences in *degree* because the heavier snows of the
past were displaced by the lighter snows of today.

While it appears that the case presents clear proof of degradation by snow it is not so clear how these results were accomplished.
Real abrasion on a large scale as in bowlder-shod glaciers is
ruled out, since glacial striæ are wholly absent from nivated surfaces according to both Matthes' observations and my own. Yet
all nivated surfaces have very distinctive qualities, delicately organized slopes which show a marked change from any original
condition related to water-carving. In the absence of striæ, the
general absence of all but a thin coating of waste *even in rock hollows,* and the accumulation of waste up to bowlders in size at the
lower edge of the nivated zone, I conclude that compacted snow
or névé of sufficient thickness and gradient may actually pluck
rock outcrops in the same manner though not at the rate which
ice exhibits. That the products of nivation may be bowlders as
well as fine mud would seem clearly to follow increase in effective-

ness, due to increase in amount of the accumulated snow; that bowlders are actually transported by snow is also shown by their presence on the lower margins of nivated tracts.

Our argument may be made clearer by reference to the observed action of snow in a particular valley. Snow is shed from the higher, steeper slopes to the lower slopes and eventually accumulates to a marked degree on the bottoms of the depressions, whence it is avalanched down valley over a series of irregular steps on the valley floor. An avalanche takes place through the breaking of a section of snow just as an iceberg breaks off the end of a tide-water glacier. Evidently there must be pressure from behind which crowds the snow forward and precipitates it to a lower level.

As a snow mass falls it not only becomes more consolidated, beginning at the plane of impact, but also gives a shock to the mass upon which it falls that either starts it in motion or accelerates its rate of motion. The action must therefore be accompanied by a drag upon the floor and if the rock be close-jointed and the blocks, defined by the joint planes, small enough, they will be transported. Since snow is not so compact as ice and permits included blocks easily to adjust themselves to new resistances, we should expect the detached blocks included in the snow to change their position constantly and to form irregular scratches, but not parallel striæ of the sort confidently attributed to stone-shod ice.

It is to the plasticity of snow that we may look for an explanation of the smooth-contoured appearance of the landscape in the foreground of Fig. 135. The smoothly curved lines are best developed where the entire surface was covered with snow, as in mid-elevations in the larger snowfields. At higher elevations, where the relief is sharper, the snow is shed from the steeper declivities and collected in the minor basins and valley heads, where its action tends to smooth a floor of limited area, while snow-free surfaces retain all their original irregularities of form or are actually sharpened.

The degree of effectiveness of snow and névé action may be estimated from the reversed slopes now marked by ponds or small marshy tracts scattered throughout the former névé fields, and the many niched hollows. They are developed above Pampaconas in an admirable manner, though their most perfect and general development is in the summit belt of the Cordillera Vilcapampa between Arma and Choquetira, Fig. 135. It is notable in *all* cases where nivation was associated with the work of valley glaciers that the rounded nivated slopes break rather sharply with the steep slopes that define an inner valley, whose form takes on the flat floor and under-cut marginal walls normal to valley glaciation.

A classification of numerous observations in the Cordillera Vilcapampa and in the Maritime Cordillera between Lambrama and Antabamba may now be presented as the basis for a tentative expression of the law of variation respecting snow motion. The statement of the law should be prefaced by the remark that thorough checking is required under a wider range of conditions before we accept the law as final. Near the lower border of the snow where rain and hail and alternate freezing and thawing take place, the snow is compacted even though but fifteen to twenty feet thick, and appears to have a down-grade movement and to exercise a slight drag upon its floor when the gradient does not fall below 20°. Distinct evidences of nivation were observed on slopes with a declivity of 5° near summit areas of past glacial action, where the snow did not have an opportunity to be alternately frozen and thawed.

The *thickness* of the former snow cover could, however, not be accurately determined, but was estimated from the topographic surroundings to have been at least several hundred feet. Upon a 40° slope a snow mass 50 feet thick was observed to be breaking off at a cliff-face along the entire cross-section as if impelled forward by thrust, and to be carrying a small amount of waste —enough distinctly to discolor the lowermost layers—which was shed upon the snowy masses below. With increase in the degree of compactness of the snow at successively lower elevations along a line of snow discharge, gradients down to 25° were still observed to carry strongly crevassed, waste-laden snow down to the melting border. It appeared from the clear evidences of vigorous action—the accumulation of waste, the strong crevassing, the stream-like character of the discharging snow, and the pronounced topographic depression in which it lay—that much flatter gradients would serve, possibly not more than 15°, for a snow mass 150 feet wide, 30 to 40 feet thick, and serving as the outlet for a set of tributary slopes about a square mile in area and with declivities ranging from small precipices to slopes of 30°.

We may say, therefore, that the factors affecting the rate of motion are (1) thickness, (2) degree of compactness, (3) diurnal temperature changes, and (4) gradient. Among these, diurnal temperature changes operate indirectly by making the snow more compact and also by inducing motion directly. At higher elevations above the snowline, temperature changes play a decreasingly important part. The thickness required varies inversely as the gradient, and upon a 20° slope is 20 feet for wet and compact snow subjected to alternate freezing and thawing. For dry snow masses above the zone of effective diurnal temperature changes, an increasing gradient is required. With a gradient of 40°, less than 50 feet of snow will move *en masse* if moderately compacted under its own weight; if further compacted by impact of falling masses from above, the required thickness may diminish to 40 feet and the required declivity to 15°. The gradient may decrease to 0° or actually be reversed and motion still continue provided the compacting snow approach true névé or even glacier ice as a limit.

From the sharp topographic break between the truly glaciated portions of the valley in regions subjected to temporary glaciation, it is concluded that the eroding power of the moving mass is suddenly increased at the point where névé is finally transformed into true ice. This transformation must be assumed to take place suddenly to account for so sudden a change of function as the topographic break requires. Below the point at which the transformation occurs the motion takes place under a new set of conditions whose laws have already been formulated by students of glaciology.

The foregoing readings of gradient and depth of snow are

typical of a large number which were made in the Peruvian Andes and which have served as the basis of Fig. 195. It will be observed that between 15° and 20° there is a marked change of function and again between +5° and —5° declivity, giving a double reversed curve. The meaning of the change between 15° and 20° is inferred to be that, with gradients over 20°, snow cannot wholly resist

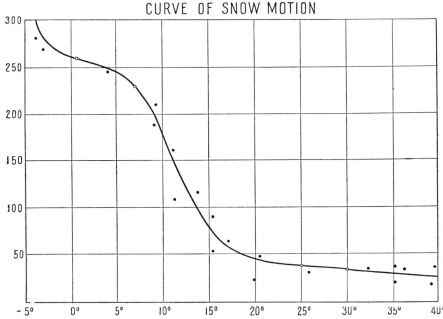

FIG. 195—Curve of snow motion. Based on many observations of snow motion to show minimum thickness of snow required to move on a given gradient. Figures on the left represent thickness of snow in feet. The degrees represent the gradient of the surface. The gradients have been run in sequence down to 0° for the sake of completing the accompanying discussion. Obviously no glacially unmodified valley in a region of mountainous relief would start with so low a gradient, though glacial action would soon bring it into existence. Between +5° and —5° the curve is based on the gradients of nivated surfaces.

gravity in the presence of diurnal temperature changes across the freezing point and occasional snow or hail storms. With increase of thickness compacting appears to progress so rapidly as to permit the transfer of thrust for short distances before absorption of thrust takes place in the displaced snow. At 250 feet thorough compacting appears to take place, enabling the snow to move out under its own weight on even the faintest slopes; while, with a thickness still greater, the resulting névé may actually be forced up slight inclines whose declivity appears to approach 5° as a limit. I have nowhere been able to find in truly nivated areas reversed curves exceeding 5°, though it should be added that depressions whose leeward slopes were reversed to 2° and 3° are fairly common. If the curve were continued we should undoubtedly find it again turning to the left at the point where the thickness of the snow results in the transformation of snow to ice. From the sharp topographic break observed to occur in a narrow belt between the névé and the ice, it is inferred that the erosive power of the névé is to that of the ice as 2:4 or 1:5 *for equal areas;* and that reversed slopes of a declivity of 10° to 15° may be formed by glaciers is well known. Precisely what thickness of snow or névé is necessary and what physical conditions effect its transformation into ice are problems not included in the main theme of this chapter.

It is important that the proposed curve of snow motion under minimum conditions be tested under a large variety of circumstances. It may possibly be found that each climatic region requires its special modifications. In tropical mountains the sudden alternations of freezing and thawing may effect such a high degree of compactness in the snow that lower minimum gradients are required than in the case of mid-latitude mountains where the perpetual snow of the high and cold situations is compacted through its own weight. Observations of the character introduced here are still unattainable, however. It is hoped that they will rapidly increase as their significance becomes apparent; and that they have high significance the striking nature of the curve of motion seems clearly to establish.

BERGSCHRUNDS AND CIRQUES

The facts brought out by the curve of snow-motion (Fig. 195) have an immediate bearing on the development of cirques, whose precise mode of origin and development have long been in doubt. Without reviewing the arguments upon which the various hypotheses rest, we shall begin at once with the strongest explanation—W. D. Johnson's famous bergschrund hypothesis. The critical condition of this hypothesis is the diurnal migration across the freezing point of the air temperature at the bottom of the schrund. Alternate freezing and thawing of the water in the joints of the rock to which the schrund leads, exercise a quarrying effect upon the rock and, since this effect is assumed to take place at the foot of the cirque, the result is a steady retreat of the steep cirque wall through basal sapping.

While Johnson's hypothesis has gained wide acceptance and is by many regarded as the final solution of the cirque problem it has several weaknesses in its present form. In fact, I believe it is but one of two factors of equal importance. In the first place, as A. C. Andrews [8] has pointed out, it is extremely improbable that the bergschrund of glacial times under the conditions of a greater volume of snow could have penetrated to bedrock at the base of the cirque where the present change of slope takes place. In the second place, the assumption is untenable that the bergschrund in all cases reaches to or anywhere near the foot of the cirque wall. A third condition outside the hypothesis and contradictory to it is the absence of a bergschrund in snowfields at many valleys heads where cirques are well developed!

Johnson himself called attention to the slender basis of observation upon which his conclusions rest. In spite of his own caution with respect to the use of his meager data, his hypothesis has been applied in an entirely too confident manner to all kinds of cirques under all kinds of conditions. Though Johnson descended an open bergschrund to a rock floor upon which ice rested, his observations raise a number of proper questions as to the application of these valuable data: How long are bergschrunds open? How often are they open? Do they everywhere open to the foot of the cirque wall? Are they present for even a part of the year in all well-developed cirques? Let us suppose that it is possible to find many cirques filled with snow, not ice, surrounded by truly precipitous walls and with an absence of berg-

---

[8] Corrosion of Gravity Streams with Application of the Ice Flood Hypothesis, Journ. and Proc. of the Royal Society of N. S. Wales, Vol. 43, 1909, p. 286.

schrunds, how shall we explain the topographic depressions excavated underneath the snow? If cirque formation can be shown to take place without concentrated frost action at the foot of the bergschrund, then is the bergschrund not a secondary rather than a primary factor? And must we not further conclude that when present it but hastens an action which is common to all snow-covered recesses?

It is a pleasure to say that we may soon have a restatement of the cirque problem from the father of the bergschrund idea. The

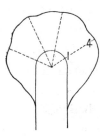

Fig. 196—Relation of cirque wall to trough's end at the head of a glaciated valley. The ratio of the inner to the outer radius is 1:4.

argument in this chapter was presented orally to him after he had remarked that he was glad to know that some one was finding fault with his hypothesis. "For," he said, with admirable spirit, " I am about to make a most violent attack upon the so-called Johnson hypothesis." I wish to say frankly that while he regards the following argument as a valid addition to the problem, he does not think that it solves the problem. There are many of us who will read his new explanation with the deepest interest.

We shall begin with the familiar fact that many valleys, now without perpetual snow, formerly contained glaciers from 500 to 1,000 feet thick and that their snowfields were of wide extent and great depth. At the head of a given valley where the snow is crowded into a small cross-section it is compacted and suffers a reduction in its volume. At first nine times the volume of ice, the gradually compacting névé approaches the volume of ice as a limit. At the foot of the cirque wall we may fairly assume in the absence of direct observations, a volume reduction of one-half due to compacting. But this is offset in the case of a well-developed cirque by volume increases due to the convergence of the snow from the surrounding slopes, as shown in Fig. 196. Taking a typical cirque from a point above Vilcabamba pueblo I find that the radius of the trough's end is to the radius of the upper wall of the cirque as 1:4; and since the corresponding surfaces are to one another as the squares of their similar dimensions we have 1:4 or 1:16 as the ratio of their snow areas. If no compacting took place, then to accommodate all the snow in the glacial trough would require an increase in thickness in the ratio of 1:4. If the snow were compacted to half its original volume then the ratio would be 1:2. Now, since the volume ratio of ice to

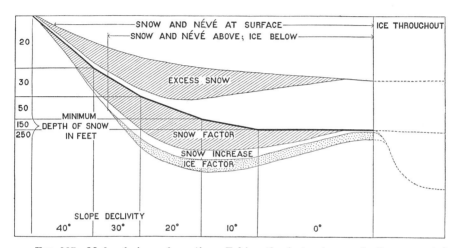

FIG. 197—Mode of cirque formation. Taking the facts of snow depth represented in the curve, Fig. 195, and transposing them over a profile (the heavy line) which ranges from 0° declivity to 50°, we find that the greatest excess of snow occurs roughly in the center. Here ice will first form at the bottom of the snow in the advancing hemicycle of glaciation, and here it will linger longest in the hemicycle of retreat. Here also there will be the greatest mass of névé. All of these factors are self-stimulating and will increase in time until the floor of the cirque is flattened or depressed sufficiently to offset through uphill ice-flow the augmented forces of erosion. The effects of self-stimulation are shown by "snow increase"; the ice shoe at the bottom of the cirque is expressed by "ice factor." The form accompanying both these terms is merely suggestive. The top of "excess snow" has a gradient characteristic of the surface of snow fields. A preglacial gradient of 0° is not permissible, but I have introduced it to complete the discussion in the text and to illustrate the flat floor of a cirque. A bergschrund is not required for any stage of this process, though the process is hastened wherever bergschrunds exist.

snow is 1:9 and the thickness of the ice down valley is, say 400 feet, the equivalent of loose snow at the foot of the cirque must be more than 1:4 over 1:9 or more than two and one-quarter times thicker, or 400 feet thick; and would give a pressure of (900 ÷ 10) × 62.5 pounds, or 5,625 pounds, or a little less than three tons per square foot. Since a pressure of 2,500 pounds per square foot will convert snow into ice at freezing temperature, it is clear that ice and not snow was the state at the bottom of the mass in glacial times. Further, between the surface of the snow and the surface of the bottom layer of the ice there must have been every gradation between loose snow and firm ice, with the result that a thickness much less than 900 feet must be assumed. Precisely what thickness would be found at the foot of the cirque wall is unknown. But granting a thickness of 400 feet of ice an additional 300 feet for névé and snow would raise the total to 700 feet.

The application of the facts in the above paragraph is clearly seen when we refer to Fig. 197. The curve of snow motion of Fig. 195 is applied to an unglaciated mountain valley. Taking a normal snow surface and filling the valley head it is seen that the excess of snow depth over the amount required to give motion is a measure at various points in the valley head and at different gradients of the erosive force of the snow. It is strikingly concentrated on the 15°-20° gradient which is precisely where the so-called process of basal sapping is most marked. If long continued the process will lead to the developing of a typical cirque for it is a process that is self-stimulating. The more the valley is changed in form the more it tends to change still further in form because of deepening snowfields until cliffed pinnacles and matterhorns result.

By further reference to the figure it is clear that a schrund 350 feet deep could not exist on a cirque wall with a declivity of even 20° without being closed by flow, unless we grant *more rapid flow* below the crevasse. In the case of a glacier flowing over a nearly flat bed away from the cirque it is difficult to conceive of a rate of flow greater than that of snow and névé on the steep lower portion of the cirque wall, when movement on that gradient *begins* with snow but 20 feet thick.

In contrast to this is the view that the schrund line should lie well up the cirque wall where the snow is comparatively thin and where there is an approach to the lower limits of movement. The schrund would appear to open where the bottom material changes its form, i.e., where it first has its motion accelerated by transformation into névé. In this view the schrund opens not at the foot of the cirque wall but well above it as in Fig. 198, in which C represents snow from top to bottom; B, névé; and A, ice. The required conditions are then (1) that the steepening of the cirque wall from x to y should be effected by sapping originated at y through the agencies outlined by Johnson; (2) that the steepening from x to y should be effected by sapping originated at x through the change of the agent from névé to ice with a sudden change of function; (3) and that the essential unity of the wall x-y-z be maintained through the erosive power of the névé, which would tend to offset the formation of a shelf along a horizontal plane passed through y. The last-named process not only appears entirely reasonable from the conditions of gradient and depth outlined on pp. 296 to 298, but also meets the actual field conditions in all the cases examined in the Peruvian Andes. This brings up the second and third of our main considerations, that the bergschrund does not always or even in many cases reach the foot of the cirque wall, and that cirques exist in many cases where bergschrunds are totally absent.

It is a striking fact that frost action at the bottom of the bergschrund has been assumed to be the only effective sapping force, in spite of the common observation that bergschrunds lie in general well toward the upper limits of snowfields—so far, in fact, that their bottoms in general occur several hundred feet above the cirque floors. Is the cirque under these circumstances a result of the schrund or is the schrund a result of the cirque? *In what class of cirques do schrunds develop?* If cirque development in its early stages is not marked by the development of bergschrunds, then are bergschrunds an *essential* feature of cirques in their later stages, however much the sapping process may be hastened by schrund formation?

Our questions are answered at once by the indisputable facts that many schrunds occur well toward the upper limit of snow, and that many cirques exist whose snowfields are not at all broken by schrunds. It was with great surprise that I first noted the bergschrunds of the Central Andes, especially after becoming

familiar with Johnson's apparently complete proof of their
genetic relation to the cirques. But it was less surprising to dis-
cover the position of the few observed—high up on the cirque
walls and always near the upper limit of the snowfields.

A third fact from regions once glaciated but now snow-free
also combined with the two preceding facts in weakening the wholesale application of Johnson's hypothesis. In many headwater
basins the cirque whose wall at a distance seemed a unit was really
broken into two unequal portions; a lower, much grooved and
rounded portion and an upper unglaciated, steep-walled portion.
This condition was most puzzling in view of the accepted explanation of cirque formation, and it was not until the two first-named
facts and the applications of the curves of snow motion were
noted that the meaning of the break on the cirque became clear.

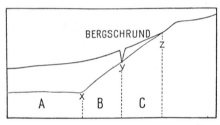

FIG. 198—The development of cirques.
See text, p. 299, and Fig. 199.

Referring to Fig. 198 we see at
once that the break occurs at y
and means that under favorable
topographic and geologic conditions sapping at y takes place
faster than at x and that the retreat of y-z is faster than x-y.
It will be clear that when these
conditions are reversed or sapping at x and at y are equal a
single wall will result. On reference to the literature I find that
Gilbert recently noted this feature and called it the *schrundline*.[9]
He believes that it marks the base of the bergschrund *at a late
stage in the excavation of the cirque basin*. He notes further that
the lower less-steep slope is glacially scoured and that it forms
"a sort of shoulder or terrace."

If all the structural and topographic conditions were known in
a great variety of gathering basins we should undoubtedly find
in them, and not in special forms of ice erosion, an explanation
of the various forms assumed by cirques. The limitations inherent in a high-altitude field and a limited snow cover prevented

[9] G. K. Gilbert, Systematic Asymmetry of Crest Lines in the High Sierra of
California. Jour. Geol., Vol. 12, 1904, p. 582.

me from solving the problem, but it offered sufficient evidence at least to indicate the probable lines of approach to a solution. For example it is noteworthy that in *all* the cases examined the schrundline was better developed the further glacial erosion had advanced. So constantly did this generalization check up, that if at a distance a short valley was observed to end in a cirque, I knew at once and long before I came to the valley head that a shoulder below the schrundline did not exist. At the time this observation was made its significance was a mystery, but it represents a condition so constant that it forms one of the striking features of the glacial forms in the headwater region.

The meaning of this feature is represented in Fig. 199, in which three successive stages in cirque development are shown. In *A,* as displayed in small valleys or mountainside alcoves which were but temporarily occupied by snow and ice, or as in all higher valleys during the earlier stages of the advancing hemicycle of glaciation, snow collects, a short glacier forms,

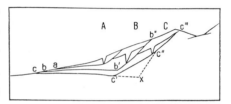

Fig. 199—Further stages in the development of cirques. See p. 299 and Fig. 198.

and a bergschrund develops. As a result of the concentrated frost action at the base of the bergschrund a rapid deepening and steepening takes place at *a*. As long as the depth of snow (or snow and névé) is slight the bergschrund may remain open. But its existence at this particular point is endangered as the cirque grows, since the increasing steepness of the slope results in more rapid snow movement. Greater depth of snow goes hand in hand with increasing steepness and thus favors the formation of névé and even ice at the bottom of the moving mass and a constantly accelerated rate of motion. At the same time the bergschrund should appear higher up for an independent reason, namely, that it tends to form between a mass of slight movement and one of greater movement, which change of function, as already pointed out, would appear to be controlled by change from snow to névé or ice on the part of the bottom material.

The first stages in the upward migration of the bergschrund will not effect a marked change from the original profile, since the converging slopes, the great thickness of névé and ice at this point, and the steep gradient all favor powerful erosion. When, however, stage C is reached, and the bergschrund has retreated to c'', a broader terrace results below the schrundline, the gradient is decreased, the ice and névé (since they represent a constant discharge) are spread over a greater area, hence are thinner, and we have the cirque taking on a compound character with a lower, less steep and an upper, precipitous section.

It is clear that a closely jointed and fragile rock might be quarried by moving ice at c'-c'' and the cirque wall extended unbroken to x; it is equally clear that a homogeneous, unjointed granite would offer no opportunities for glacial plucking and would powerfully resist the much slower process of abrasion. Thus Gilbert[10] observed the schrundline in the granites of the Sierra Nevada, which are "in large part structureless" and my own observations show the schrundline well developed in the open-jointed granites of the Cordillera Vilcapampa and wholly absent in the volcanoes of the Maritime Cordillera, where ashes and cinders, the late products of volcanic action, form the easily eroded walls of the steep cones. Somewhere between these extremes— lack of a variety of observations prevents our saying where—the resistance and the internal structure of the rock will just permit a cirque wall to extend from x to c''' of Fig. 199.

A common feature of cirques that finds an explanation in the proposed hypothesis is the notch that commonly occurs at some point where a convergence of slopes above the main cirque wall concentrates snow discharge. It is proposed to call this type the notched cirque. It is highly significant that these notches are commonly marked by even steeper descents at the point of discharge into the main cirque than the remaining portion of the cirque wall, even when the discharge was from a very small basin and in the form of snow or at the most névé. The excess of discharge at a point on the basin rim ought to produce the form

---

[10] Op. cit., p. 300; reference on p. 582.

we find there under the conditions of snow motion outlined in earlier paragraphs. It is also noteworthy that it is at such a point of concentrated discharge that crevasses no sooner open than they are closed by the advancing snow masses. To my mind the whole action is eminently representative of the action taking place elsewhere along the cirque wall on a smaller scale.

What seems a good test of the explanation of cirques here proposed was made in those localities in the Maritime Cordillera, where large snowbanks but not glaciers affect the form of the catchment basins. A typical case is shown in Fig. 201. As in many other cases we have here a great lava plateau broken frequently by volcanic cones of variable composition. Some are of lava, others consist of ashes, still others of tuff and lava and ashes. At lower elevations on the east, as at 16,000 feet between Antabamba and Huancarama, evidences of long and powerful glaciers are both numerous and convincing. But as we rise still higher the glaciated topography is buried progressively deeper under the varying products of volcanic action, until finally at the summit of the lava fields all evidences of glaciation disappear in the greater part of the country between Huancarama and the main divide. Nevertheless, the summit forms are in many cases as significantly altered as if they had been molded by ice. Precipitous cirque walls surround a snow-filled amphitheater, and the process of deepening goes forward under one's eyes. No moraines block the basin outlets, no U-shaped valleys lead forward from them. We have here to do with post-glacial action pure and simple, the volcanoes having been formed since the close of the Pleistocene.

Likewise in the pass on the main divide, the perpetual snow has begun the recessing of the very recent volcanoes bordering the pass. The products of snow action, muds and sands up to very coarse gravel, glaciated in texture with an intermingling of blocks up to six inches in diameter in the steeper places, are collected into considerable masses at the snowline, where they form broad sheets of waste so boggy as to be impassable except by carefully selected routes. No ice action whatever is visible below the snowline and the snow itself, though wet and compact, is not underlain by ice. Yet the process of hollowing goes forward visibly and in time will produce serrate forms. In neither case is there the faintest sign of a bergschrund; the gradients seem so well adjusted to the thickness and rate of movement of the snow from point to point that the marginal crack found in many snowfields is absent.

The absence of bergschrunds is also noteworthy in many localities where formerly glaciation took place. This is notoriously the case in the summit zone of the Cordillera Vilcapampa, where the accumulating snows of the steep cirque walls tumble down hundreds of feet to gather into prodigious snowbanks or to form névé fields or glaciers. From the converging walls the snowfalls keep up an intermittent bombardment of the lower central snow masses. It is safe to say that if by magic a bergschrund could be opened on the instant, it would be closed almost immediately by the impetus supplied by the falling snow masses. The explanation appears to be that the thicker snow and névé concentrated at the bottom of the cirque results in a corresponding concentration of action and effect; and cirque development goes on without reference to a bergschrund. The chief attraction of the bergschrund hypothesis lies in the concentration of action at the foot of the cirque wall. But in the thickening of the snow far beyond the minimum thickness required for motion at the base of the cirque wall and its change of function with transformation into névé, we need invoke no other agent. If a bergschrund forms, its action may take place at the foot of the cirque wall or high up on the wall, and yet *sapping at the foot of the wall* continue.

From which we conclude (1) that where frost action occurs at the bottom of a bergschrund opening to the foot of the cirque wall it aids in the retreat of the wall; (2) that a sapping action takes place at this point whether or not a bergschrund exists and that bergschrund action is not a *necessary* part of cirque formation; (3) that when a more or less persistent bergschrund opens on the cirque wall above its foot it tends to develop a schrundline with a marked terrace below it; (4) that schrundlines are best developed in the mature stages of topographic development in the glacial cycle; (5) that the varying rates of snow, névé, and ice motion at a valley head are the *persistent* features to which we must look for topographic variations; (6) that the hypothesis here proposed is applicable to all cases whether they involve the presence of snow or névé or ice or any combination of these, and whether bergschrunds are present or not; and (7) at the same time affords a reasonable explanation for such variations in forms as the compound cirque with its schrundline and terrace, the unbroken cirque wall, the notched cirque, and the recessed, snow-covered mountain slopes unaffected by ice.

ASYMMETRICAL CREST LINES AND ABNORMAL VALLEY PROFILES IN THE CENTRAL ANDES

To prove that under similar conditions glacial erosion may be greater than subaërial denudation quantitative terms must be sought. Only these will carry conviction to the minds of many opponents of the theory that ice is a vigorous agent of erosion. Gilbert first showed in the Sierra Nevada that headwater glaciers eroded more rapidly than nonglacial agents under comparable topographic and structural conditions.[11] Oddly enough none of the supporters of opposing theories have replied to his arguments; instead they have sought evidence from other regions to show that ice cannot erode rock to an important degree. In this chapter evidence from the Central Andes, obtained in 1907 and 1911, will be given to show the correctness of Gilbert's proposition.

The data will be more easily understood if Gilbert's argument is first outlined. On the lower slopes of the glaciated Sierra Nevada asymmetry of form resulted from the presence of ice on one side of each ridge and its absence on the other (Fig. 200). The glaciers of these lower ridges were the feeblest in the entire region and were formed on slopes of small extent; they were also short-lived, since they could have existed only when glacial conditions had reached a maximum. Let the broken line in the upper

---

[11] Op. cit., p. 300; see pp. 579-588 and Fig. 8.

part of the figure represent the preglacial surface and the solid line beneath it the present surface. It will not matter what value we give the space between the two lines on the left to express non-glacial erosion, since had there been no glaciers it would be the same on both sides of the ridge. The feeble glacier occupying the right-hand slope was able in a very brief period to erode a depression far deeper than the normal agents of denudation were able to erode in a much longer period, i.e., during all of interglacial and postglacial time. Gilbert concludes: "The visible ice-made hollows, therefore, represent the local excess of glacial over nonglacial conditions."

In the Central Andes are many volcanic peaks and ridges formed since the last glacial epoch and upon them a remarkable

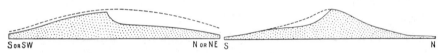

FIG. 200—Diagrammatic cross-section of a ridge glaciated on one side only; with hypothetical profile (broken line) of preglacial surface.

FIG. 201—Postglacial volcano recessed on shady southern side by the process of nivation. Absolute elevation 18,000 feet (5,490 m.), latitude 14° S., Maritime Cordillera, Peru.

asymmetry has been developed. Looking southward one may see a smoothly curved, snow-free, northward-facing slope rising to a crest line which appears as regular as the slope leading to it. Looking northward one may see by contrast (Fig. 194) sharp ridges, whose lower crests are serrate, separated by deeply recessed, snow-filled mountain hollows. Below this highly dissected zone the slopes are smooth. The smooth slope represents the work of water; the irregular slopes are the work of snow and ice. The relation of the north and south slopes is diagrammatically shown in Fig. 201.

To demonstrate the erosive effects of snow and ice it must be shown: (1) that the initial slopes of the volcanoes are of postglacial age; (2) that the asymmetry is not structural; (3) that the snow-free slopes have not had special protection, as through a more abundant plant cover, more favorable soil texture, or otherwise.

Proof of the postglacial origin of the volcanoes studied in this connection is afforded: (1) by the relation of the flows and the ash and cinder beds about the bases of the cones to the glacial topography; (2) by the complete absence of glacial phenomena below the present snowline. Ascending a marginal valley (Fig. 202), one comes to its head, where two tributaries, with hanging relations to the main valley, come down from a maze of lesser valleys and irregular slopes. Glacial features of a familiar sort are everywhere in evidence until we come to the valley heads. Cirques, reversed grades, lakes, and striæ are on every hand. But at altitudes above 17,200 feet, recent volcanic deposits have over large areas entirely obscured the older glacial topography. The glacier which occupied the valley of Fig. 202 was more than one-quarter of a mile wide, the visible portion of its valley is now over six miles long, but the extreme head of its left-hand tributary is so concealed by volcanic material that the original length of the glacier cannot be determined. It was at least ten miles long. From this point southward to the border of the Maritime Cordillera no evidence of past glaciation was observed, save at Solimana and Coropuna, where slight changes in the positions of the glaciers have resulted in the development of terminal moraines a little below the present limits of the ice.

From the wide distribution of glacial features along the northeastern border of the Maritime Cordillera and the general absence of such features in the higher country farther south, it is concluded that the last stages of volcanic activity were completed in postglacial time. It is equally certain, however, that the earlier and greater part of the volcanic material was ejected before glaciation set in, as shown by the great depth of the canyons (over 5,000 feet) cut into the lava flows, as contrasted with the relatively slight filling of coarse material which was accumulated on their floors in the glacial period and is now in process of dissection. Physiographic studies throughout the Central Andes demonstrate both the general distribution of this fill and its glacial origin.

So recent are some of the smaller peaks set upon the lava

plateau that forms the greater part of the Maritime Cordillera, that the snows massed on their shadier slopes have not yet effected any important topographic changes. The symmetrical peaks of this class are in a few cases so very recent that they are entirely uneroded. Lava flows and beds of tuff appear to have originated but yesterday, and shallow lava-dammed lakes retain their original shore relations. In a few places an older topography, glacially modified, may still be seen showing through a veneer of recent ash and cinder deposits, clear evidence that the loftier parts of the lava plateau were glaciated before the last volcanic eruption.

The asymmetry of the peaks and ridges in the Maritime Cordillera cannot be ascribed to the manner of eruption, since the contrast in declivity and form is persistently between northern and southern slopes. Strong and persistent winds from a given direction undoubtedly influence the form of volcanoes to at least a perceptible degree. In the case in hand the ejectamenta are ashes, cinders, and the like, which are blown into the air and have at least a small component of motion down the wind during both their ascent and descent. The *prevailing* winds of the high plateaus are, however, easterly and the strongest winds are from the west and blow daily, generally in the late afternoon. Both wind directions are at right angles to the line of asymmetry, and we must, therefore, rule out the winds as a factor in effecting the slope contrasts which these mountains display.

It remains to be seen what influence a covering of vegetation on the northern slopes might have in protecting them from erosion. The northern slopes in this latitude (14° S.) receive a much greater quantity of heat than the southern slopes. Above 18,000 feet (5,490 m.) snow occurs on the shady southern slopes, but is at least a thousand feet higher on the northern slopes. It is therefore absent from the northern side of all but the highest peaks. Thus vegetation on the northern slopes is not limited by snow. Bunch grass—the characteristic *ichu* of the mountain shepherds—scattered spears of smaller grasses, large ground mosses called *yareta,* and lichens extend to the snowline. This vegetation, however, is so scattered and thin above 17,500 feet (5,330 m.) that it exercises no retarding influence on the run-off. Far more important is the porous nature of the volcanic material, which allows the rainfall to be absorbed rapidly and to appear in springs on the lower slopes, where sheets of lava direct it to the surface.

The asymmetry of the north and south slopes is not, then, the result of preglacial erosion, of structural conditions, or of special protection of the northern slopes from erosion. It must be concluded, therefore, that it is due to the only remaining factor— snow distribution. The southern slopes are snow-clad, the northern are snow-free—in harmony with the line of asymmetry. The distribution of the snow is due to the contrasts between shade and sun temperatures, which find their best expression in high altitudes and on single peaks of small extent. Frankland's observations with a black-bulb thermometer *in vacuo* show an increase in shade and sun temperatures contrasts of over 40° between sea level and an elevation of 10,000 feet. Violle's experiments show an increase of 26 per cent in the intensity of solar radiation between 200 feet and 16,000 feet elevation. Many other observations up to 16,000 feet show a rapid increase in the difference between sun and shade temperatures with increasing elevation. In the region herein described where the snowline is between 18,000 and 19,000 feet (5,490 to 5,790 m.) these contrasts are still further heightened, especially since the semi-arid climate and the consequent long duration of sunshine and low relative humidity afford the fullest play to the contrasting forces. The coefficient of absorption of radiant energy by water vapor is 1,900 times that of air, hence the lower the humidity the more the radiant energy expended upon the exposed surface and the greater the sun and shade contrasts. The effect of these temperature contrasts is seen in a canting of the snowline on individual volcanoes amounting to 1,500 feet in extreme instances. The average may be placed at 1,000 feet.

The minimum conditions of snow motion and the bearing of the conclusions upon the formation of cirques have been described in the chapters immediately preceding. It is concluded that snow moves upon 20° slopes if the snow is at least forty feet deep, and that through its motion under more favorable conditions of greater depth and gradient and the indirect effects of border melting there is developed a hollow occupied by the snow. Actual ice is not considered to be a necessary condition of either movement or erosion. We may at once accept the conclusion that the invariable association of the cirques and steepened profiles with snowfields proves that snow is the predominant modifying agent.

An argument for glacial erosion based on profiles and steep cirque walls in a volcanic region has peculiar appropriateness in view of the well-known symmetrical form of the typical volcano. Instead of varied forms in a region of complex structure long eroded before the appearance of the ice, we have here simple forms which immediately after their development were occupied by snow. *Ever since their completion these cones have been eroded by snow on one side and by water on the other.* If snow cannot move and if it protects the surface it covers, then this surface should be uneroded. All such surfaces should stand higher than the slopes on the opposite aspect eroded by water. But these assumptions are contrary to fact. The slopes underneath the snow are deeply recessed; so deeply eroded indeed, that they are bordered by steep cliffs or cirque walls. The products of erosion also are to some extent displayed about the border of the snow cover. In strong contrast the snow-free slopes are so slightly modified that little of their original symmetry is lost—only a few low hills and shallow valleys have been formed.

The measure of the excess of snow erosion over water erosion is therefore the difference between a northern or water-formed and a southern or snow-formed profile, Fig. 200. This difference is also shown in Fig. 201 and from it and the restored initial profiles we conclude that the rate of water erosion is to that of nivation as 1:3. This ratio has been derived from numerous observations on cones so recently formed that the interfluves without question are still intact.

Thus far only those volcanoes have been considered which

have been modified by nivation. There are, however, many volcanoes which have been eroded by ice as well as by snow and
water. It will be seen at once that where a great area of snow is
tributary to a single valley, the snow becomes compacted into
névé and ice, and that it then erodes at a much faster rate. Also
a new force—plucking—is
called into action when ice is
present, and this greatly accelerates the rate of erosion.
While it lies outside the
limits of my subject to determine quantitatively the
ratio between water and ice
action, it is worth pointing
out that by this method a
ratio much in excess of 1:3
is determined, which even in
this rough form is of considerable interest in view of
the arguments based on the
protecting influence of both
ice and snow. I have, in-
deed, avoided the question
of ice erosion up to this
point and limited myself to
those volcanoes which have

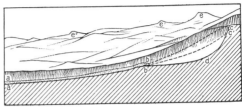

Fig. 202—Graphic representation of
amount of glacial erosion during the glacial
period. In the background are mature slopes
surmounted by recessed asymmetrical peaks.
The river entrenched itself below the mature
slopes before it began to aggrade, and, when aggradation set in, had cut its valley floor to
a'-b'-c. By aggradation the valley floor was
raised to a-b while ice occupied the valley head.
By degradation the river has again barely
lowered its channel to a'-b', the ice has disappeared, and the depression of the profile represents the amount of glacial erosion.

a'-b'-c = preglacial profile.
a-b-d-c = present profile.
b'-d-c-b = total ice erosion in the glacial
        period.
a-b = surface of an alluvial valley fill
        due to excessive erosion at valley
        head.
b-b' = terminal moraine.
d-c = cirque wall.
e, e' e'' = asymmetrical summits.

been modified by nivation only, since the result is more striking
in view of the all but general absence of data relating to this form
of erosion.

If we now turn to the valley profiles of the glaciated portions
of the Peruvian Andes, we shall see the excess of ice over water
erosion expressed in a manner equally convincing. To a thoughtful person it is one of the most remarkable features of any glaciated region that the flattest profiles, the marshiest valley flats,
and the most strongly meandering stretches of the streams should
occur near the heads of the valleys. The mountain shepherds

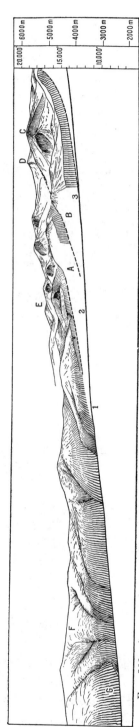

FIG. 203—A composite sketch to represent general conditions in the Peruvian Andes. In order to have the actual facts represented the profiles of this figure were taken from the accompanying topographic sheets. The main depression on the right and the corresponding depression of the tributary profiles bear out most strikingly the conclusions concerning the erosive power of the ice. At A and B the spurs have been cut off to exhibit the profiles of tributary valleys. At 2 and 3 were tributary glaciers of such size that they entered the main valley at grade. Lesser tributaries had floors elevated above those they joined and now have a hanging character, as just above 2. D is a matterhorn; C is deeply recessed by cirques; E represents a peak just below the limit of glaciation. At F are the undissected post-mature slopes of an earlier cycle of erosion. G lies on the steep lower slopes formed during the canyon cycle of erosion. The down-cutting of the stream in the canyon cycle was generally checked by glaciation and was superseded by aggradation.

recognize this condition and drive their flocks up from the warmer valley into the mountain recesses, confident that both distance and elevation will be offset by the extensive pastures of the finest *ichu* grass. Indeed, to be near the grazing grounds of sheep and llamas which are their principal means of subsistence, the Indians have built their huts at the extraordinarily lofty elevations of 16,000 to 17,000 feet.

An examination of a large number of these valleys and the plotting of their gradients discloses the striking fact that the heads of the valleys were deeply sunk into the mountains. It is thus possible by restoring the preglacial profiles to measure with considerable certainty the excess of ice over water erosion.

The results are graphically expressed in Fig. 202. It will be seen that until glacial conditions intervened the stream was flowing on a rock floor. During the whole of glacial time it was aggrading its rock floor below b' and forming a deep valley fill. A return to warmer and drier conditions led to the dissection of the fill and this is now in progress. The stream has not yet reached its preglacial profile, but it has almost reached it. We may, therefore, say that the preglacial valley profile below b' fixes the position of the present profile just as surely as if the stream had been magically halted in its work at the beginning of the period of glaciation. There, b'-d-c-b represents the amount of ice erosion. To be sure the line b-c is inference, but it is reasonable inference and, whatever position is assigned to it, it cannot be coincident with b'-d, nor can it be anywhere near it. The break in the valley profile at b' is always marked by a terminal moraine, regardless of the character of the rock. This is not an accidental but a causal association. It proves the power of the ice to erode. In glacial times it eroded the quantity b-c-d-b'. This is not an excess of ice over water erosion, but an absolute measure of ice erosion, since a'-b' has remained intact. The only possible error arises from the position assigned b-c, and even if we lower it to b-c' (for which we have no warrant but extreme conservatism) we shall still have left b'-c'-d-b as a striking value for rock erosion (plucking and abrasion) by a valley glacier.

A larger diagram, Fig. 203, represents in fuller detail the topographic history of the Andes of southern Peru and the relative importance of glaciation. The broad spurs with grass-covered tops that end in steep scarps are in wonderful contrast to the serrate profiles and truncated spurs that lie within the zone of past glaciation. In the one case we have minute irregularities on a canyon wall of great dimensions; in the other, more even walls that define a glacial trough with a flat floor. Before glaciation on a larger scale had set in the right-hand section of the diagram had a greater relief. It was a residual portion of the mountain and therefore had greater height also. Glaciers formed upon it in the Ice Age and glaciation intensified the contrast between it and the left-hand section; not so much by intensifying the relief as by diversifying the topographic forms.

APPENDIX A

SURVEY METHODS EMPLOYED IN THE CONSTRUCTION OF THE SEVEN ACCOMPANYING TOPOGRAPHIC SHEETS

BY KAI HENDRIKSEN, TOPOGRAPHER

THE main part of the topographical outfit consisted of (1) a 4-inch theodolite, Buff and Buff, the upper part detachable, (2) an 18 x 24 inch plane-table with Johnson tripod and micro-meteralidade. These instruments were courteously loaned the expedition by the U. S. Coast and Geodetic Survey and the U. S. Geological Survey respectively.

The method of survey planned was a combination of graphic triangulation and traverse with the micro-meteralidade. All directions were plotted on the plane-table which, was oriented by backsight; distances were determined by the micro-meteralidade or triangulation, or both combined; and elevations were obtained by vertical angles. Finally, astronomical observations, usually to the sun, were taken at intervals of about 60 miles for latitude and azimuth to check the triangulation. No observations were made for differences in longitude because this would probably not have given any reliable result, considering the time and instruments at our disposal. Because the survey was to follow very closely the seventy-third meridian west of Greenwich, directions and distances, checked by latitude and azimuth observations, undoubtedly afforded far better means of determining the longitude than time observations. In other words, the time observations made in connection with azimuth observations were not used for computing longitudinal differences. Absolute longitude was taken from existing observations of principal places.

Principal topographical points were located by from two to four intersections from the triangulation and plane-table stations; and elevations were determined by vertical angle measurements. Whenever practicable, the contours were sketched in the field; the details of the topography otherwise depend upon a great number of photographs taken by Professor Bowman from critical stations or other points which it was possible to locate on the maps.

CROSS-SECTION MAP FROM ABANCAY TO CAMANÁ AT THE PACIFIC OCEAN

Seven sheets. Scale, 1 : 125,000; contour interval, 200 feet. Datum is mean sea level. Astronomical control: 5 latitude and 5 azimuth observations as indicated on the accompanying topographic sheets.

On September 10th, returning from a reconnaissance survey of the Pampaconas River, I joined Professor Bowman's party, Dr. Erving acting as my assistant. We crossed the Cordillera Vilcapampa and the Canyon of the Apurimac and after a week's rest at Abancay started the topographic work near Hacienda San Gabriel south of Abancay. Working up the deep valley of Lambrama, observations for latitude and azimuth were made midway between Hacienda Matara and Caypi.

On October 4th we made our camp in newly fallen snow surrounded by beautiful glacial scenery. The next day on the high plateau, we passed sharp-crested glaciated peaks; a heavy thunder and hail storm broke out while I occupied the station at the pass, the storm continuing all the afternoon—a frequent occurrence. The camp was made 6 miles farther on, and the next morning I returned to finish the latter station. I succeeded in sketching the detailed topography just south of the pass, but shortly after noon, a furious storm arose similar to the one the day before, and made further topographic work impossible; to get connection farther on I patiently kept my eye to the eye-piece for more than an hour after the storm had started, and was fortunate to catch the station ahead in a single glimpse. I had a similar experience some days later at station 16,079, Antabamba Quadrangle, on the rim of the high-level puna, the storm preventing all topographic work and barely allowing a single moment in which to catch a dim sight of the signals ahead while I kept my eye steadily at the telescope to be ready for a favorable break in the heavy clouds and hail.

At Antabamba we got a new set of Indian carriers, who had orders to accompany us to Cotahuasi, the next sub-prefectura. Raimondi's map indicates the distance between the two cities to be 35 miles, but although nothing definite was stated, we found out in Antabamba that the distance was considerably longer, and moreover that the entire route lay at a high altitude.

From the second day out of Antabamba until Huaynacotas was in sight in the Cotahuasi Canyon, a distance of 50 miles, the route lay at an altitude of from 16,000 to 17,630 feet, taking in 5 successive camps at an altitude from 15,500 to 17,000 feet; 12 successive stations had the following altitudes:

16,379 feet
16,852 "
17,104 "
17,559 "
17,675 " —highest station occupied.
17,608 "
17,633 "
16,305 "
17,630 "
17,128 "
16,794 "
16,260 "

The occupation of these high stations necessitated a great deal of climbing, doubly hard in this rarefied air, and often on volcanoes with a surface consisting of bowlders and ash and in the face of violent hailstorms that made extremely difficult the task of connecting up observations at successive stations.

At Cotahuasi a new pack-train was organized, and on October 25th I ventured to return alone to the high altitudes in order to continue the topography at the station at 17,633 feet on the summit of the Maritime Cordillera. Dr. Erving was obliged to leave on October 18th and Professor Bowman left a week later in order to carry out his plans for a physiographic study of the coast between Camaná and Mollendo. Philippi Angulo, a native of Taurisma, a town above Cotahuasi, acted as majordomo on this journey. Knowing the trail and the camp sites, I was able to pick out the stations ahead myself, and made good progress, returning to Cotahuasi on October 29th, three or four days earlier than planned. From Cotahuasi to the coast I had the assistance of Mr. Watkins. The most trying part of the last section of high altitude country was the great Pampa Colorada, crowned by the snow-capped peaks of Solimana and Coropuna, reaching heights of 20,730 and 21,703 feet respectively. The passing of this pampa took seven days and we arrived at Chuquibamba on November 9th. Two circumstances made the work on this stretch peculiarly difficult—the scarcity of camping places and the high temperature in the middle of the day, which heated the rarefied air to a degree that made long-distance shots very strenuous work for the eyes. Although our base signals were stone piles higher than a man, I was often forced to keep my eye to the telescope for hours to catch a glimpse of the signals; lack of time did not allow me to stop the telescope work in the hottest part of the day.

The top of Coropuna was intersected from the four stations: 16,344, 15,545, 16,168, and 16,664 feet elevation, the intersections giving a very small triangular error. The elevation of Mount Coropuna's high peak as computed from these 4 stations is:

> 21,696 feet
> 21,746 "
> 21,714 "
> 21,657 "
> ———
>
> Mean elevation 21,703 feet above sea level.

The elevation of Coropuna as derived from these four stations has thus a mean error of 18 feet (method of least squares) while the elevation of each of the four stations as carried up from mean sea level through 25 stations—vertical angles being observed in both directions—has an esti-

mated mean error of 30 feet. The result of this is a mean error of 35 feet
in Coropuna's elevation above mean sea level.

The latitude is 15° 31' 00" S.; the longitude is 72° 42' 40" W. of Greenwich, the checking of these two determinations giving a result unexpectedly
close.

On November 11th azimuth and latitude observations were taken at
Chuquibamba and two days later we arrived at Aplao in the bottom of the
splendid Majes Valley. In the northern part of this valley I was prevented
from doing any plane-table work in the afternoons of four successive days.
A strong gale set in each noon raising a regular sandstorm, that made
seeing almost impossible, and blowing with such a velocity that it was
impossible to set up the plane-table.

From Hacienda Cantas to Camaná we had to pass the western desert
for a distance of 45 miles. We were told that on the entire distance there
was only one camping place. This was at Jaguey de Majes, where there
was a brook with just enough water for the animals but no fodder. Thus
we faced the necessity of carrying water for ten men and fodder for 14
animals in excess of the usual cargo; and we were unable to foretell how
many days the topography over the hot desert would require.

Although plane-table work in the desert was impossible at all except in
the earliest and latest hours of the day, we made regular progress. We
camped three nights at Jaguey and arrived on the fourth day at Las
Lomas.

The next morning, on November 23rd, at an elevation of 2178 feet near
the crest of the Coast Range, we were repaid for two months of laborious
work by a glorious view of the Pacific Ocean and of the city of Camaná with
her olive gardens in the midst of the desert sand.

The next day I observed latitude and azimuth at Camaná and in the
night my companion and assistant Mr. Watkins and I returned across the
desert to the railroad at Vitor.

CONCLUSIONS

The planned methods were followed very closely. In two cases only
the plane-table had to be oriented by the magnetic needle, the backsights
not being obtainable because of the impossibility of locating the last station, passing Indians having removed the signals.

In one case only the distance between two stations had to be determined by graphic triangulation exclusively, the base signals having been
destroyed. Otherwise graphic triangulation was used as a check on
distances.

Vertical angles were always measured in both directions with the
exception of the above-mentioned cases.

Observations for azimuth were always taken to the sun before and after noon. The direction used in the azimuth observation was also taken with the prismatic compass. The mean of the magnetic declination thus found is: East 8° 30' plus.

Observations for latitude were taken to the sun by the method of circum-meridian altitudes, except at the town of Vilcabamba where star observations were taken.

As a matter of course, observations to the sun are not so exact as star observations, especially in low latitudes where one can expect to observe the near zenith. However, working in high altitudes for long periods, moving camp every day and often arriving at camp 2 to 4 hours after sunset, I found it essential to have undisturbed rest at night. It was beyond my capacity to spend an hour or two of the night in finding the meridian and in making the observation. Furthermore, the astronomic observations were to check the topography mainly, the latter being the most exact method with the outfit at hand.

The following table contains the comparisons between the latitude stations as located on the map and by observation:

	Map	Observation
Camaná Quadrangle S	16° 37' 34"	16° 37' 34" [1]
Coropuna, station 9,691S	15° 48' 30"	(15° 51' 44")
Cotahuasi, " 12,588S	15° 11' 40"	15° 12' 30"
La Cumbre, " 16,852S	14° 28' 10"	14° 29' 46"
Lambrama, " 8,341S	13° 43' 18"	13° 43' 14"

The other observations, with the exception of the one on the Coropuna Quadrangle, check probably as well as can be expected with the small and light outfit which we used, and under the exceptionally hard conditions of work. The observation on the Coropuna Quadrangle just south of Chuquibamba is, however, too much out. An explanation for this is that the meridian zenith distance was 1° 23' 12" only (in this case the exact formula was used in computing). Of course, an error or an accumulation of errors might have been made in the distances taken by the micrometer-alidade, but the first cause of error mentioned is the more probable, and this is indicated also by the fact that the location on the top of Mount Coropuna checks closely with the one determined in an entirely independent way by the railroad engineers.

For the cross-section map from Abancay to Camaná, the following statistics are desirable:

[1] The observation at Camaná checks very closely with a Peruvian observation the value of which is S. 16° 37' 00".

Micrometer traverse and graphic triangulation, with contours, field scale 1 : 90,000.

Total time required, days.................................... 40.5

Average distance per days in miles........................... 7.5

Average number of plane-table stations occupied per day....... 1.5

Average area per day in square miles......................... 38.

Located points per square mile............................... 0.25

Approximate elevations in excess of above, per square mile...... 0.25

Highest station occupied, feet above sea level.................17,675.

Highest point located, feet above sea level...................21,703.

APPENDIX B

FOSSIL DETERMINATIONS

A FEW fossil collections were gathered in order that age determinations might be made. With the following identifications I have included a few fossils (I and II) collected by W. R. Rumbold and put into my hands in 1907. The Silurian is from a Bolivian locality south of La Paz but in the great belt of shales, slates, and schists which forms one of the oldest sedimentary series in the Eastern Andes of Peru as well as Bolivia. While no fossils were found in this series in Peru the rocks are provisionally referred to the Silurian. Fossil-bearing Carboniferous overlies them but no other indication of their age was obtained save their general position in the belt of schists already mentioned. I am indebted to Professor Charles Schuchert of Yale University for the following determinations.

I. *Silurian*

San Roque Mine, southwest slope of Santa Vela Cruz, Canton Ichocu, Province Inquisivi, Bolivia.

Sent by William R. Rumbold in 1907.

Climacograptus?

Pholidops trombetana Clarke?

Chonetes striatellus (Dalman).

Atrypa marginalis (Dalman)?

Cœlospira n. sp.

Ctenodonta, 2 or more species.

Hyolithes.

Klœdenia.

Calymene?

Dalmanites, a large species with a terminal tail spine.

Acidaspis.

These fossils indicate unmistakably Silurian and probably Middle Silurian. As all are from blue-black shales, brachiopods are the rarer fossils, while bivalves and trilobites are the common forms. The faunal aspect does not suggest relationship with that of Brazil as described by J. M. Clarke and not at all with that of North America. I believe this is the first time that Silurian fossils have been discovered in the high Andes.

II. *Lower Devonian*

Near north end of Lake Titicaca.

Leptocœlia flabellites (Conrad), very common.

Atrypa reticularis (Linnæus)?

This is a part of the well-known and widely distributed Lower Devonian fauna of the southern hemisphere.

III. *Upper Carboniferous*

All of the Upper Carboniferous lots of fossils represent the well-known South American fauna first noted by d'Orbigny in 1842, and later added to by Orville Derby. The time represented is the equivalent of the Pennsylvanian of North America.

Huascatay between Pasaje and Huancarama.

Crinoidal limestone.

Trepostomata Bryozoa.

Polypora. Common.

Streptorhynchus hallianus Derby. Common.

Chonetes glaber Geinitz. Rare.

Productus humboldti d'Orb. Rare.

"   *cora* d'Orb. Rare.

"   *chandlessii* Derby.

"   sp. undet. Common.

"   sp. undet.   "

Spirifer condor d'Orb. Common.

Hustedia mormoni (Marcou). Rare.

Seminula argentea (Shepard).   "

Pampaconas, Pampaconas valley near Vilcabamba.

Lophophyllum?

Rhombopora, etc.

Productus.

Camarophoria. Common.

Spirifer condor d'Orb.

Hustedia mormoni (Marcou).

Euomphalus. Large form.

Pongo de Mainique. Extreme eastern edge of Peruvian Cordillera.

Lophophyllum.

Productus chandlessii Derby.

"   *cora* d'Orb.

Orthotetes correanus (Derby).

Spirifer condor d'Orb.

River bowlders and stones of Urubamba river, just beyond eastern edge of Cordillera at mouth of Ticumpinea river. (Detached and transported by stream action from the Upper Carboniferous at Pongo de Mainique.)

Mostly Trepostomata Bryozoa.

Many *Productus* spines.

Productus cora d'Orb.

Camarophoria. Same as at Pampaconos.

Productus sp. undet.

Cotahuasi A.

Lophophyllum.

Productus peruvianus d'Orb.

"   sp. undet.

Camarophoria.

Pugnax near *utah* (Marcou).

Seminula argentea (Shepard)?

Cotahuasi B.

Productus cora d'Orb.

      "   near *semireticulatus* (Martin).

IV. *Comanchian or Lower Cretaceous*

Near Chuquibambilla.

Pecten near *quadricostatus* Sowerby.

Undet. bivalves and gastropods.

The echinid *Laganum? colombianum* d'Orb. A clypeasterid.

This Lower Cretaceous locality is evidently of the same horizon as that of Colombia illustrated by d'Orbigny in 1842 and described on pages 63-105.

APPENDIX C

KEY TO PLACE NAMES

Abancay, town, lat. 12° 35′, Figs. 20, 204.

Abra Tocate, pass, between Yavero and Urubamba valleys, leaving latter at Rosalina, (Fig. 8). *See also* Fig. 55.

Anta, town, lat. 13° 30′, Fig. 20.

Antabamba, town, lat. 14° 20′, Figs. 20, 204.

Aplao, town, lat. 16°, Figs. 20, 204.

Apurimac, river, Fig. 20.

Arequipa, town, lat. 16° 30′, Fig. 66.

Arica, town, northern Chile, lat. 18° 30′.

Arma, river, tributary of Apurimac, lat. 13° 25′, (Fig. 20); tributary of Ocoña, lat. 15° 30′, (Fig. 20).

Arma, village, lat. 13° 15′, Fig. 20. *See also* Fig. 140.

Auquibamba, hacienda, lat. 13° 40′, Fig. 204.

Callao, town, lat. 12°, Fig. 66.

Camaná, town, lat. 16° 40′, Figs. 20, 66, 204.

Camisea, river, tributary of Urubamba entering from right, lat. 11° 15′.

Camp 13, lat. 14° 30′.

Cantas, hacienda, lat. 16° 15′, Fig. 204.

Caraveli, town, lat. 16°, Fig. 66.

Catacaos, town, lat. 5° 30′, Fig. 66.

Caylloma, town and mines, lat. 15° 30′, Fig. 66.

Caypi, village, lat. 13° 45′.

Central Ranges, lat. 14°, Fig. 20. *See also* Fig. 157.

Cerro Azul, town, lat. 13°, Fig. 66.

Chachani, mt., overlooking Arequipa, lat. 16° 30′, (Fig. 66).

Chaupimayu, river, tributary of Urubamba entering at Sahuayaco, *q.v.*

Chili, river, tributary of Vitor River, lat. 16° 30′, (Fig. 66).

Chinche, hacienda, Urubamba Valley above Santa Ana, lat. 13°, (Fig. 20).

Chira, river, lat. 5°, Fig. 66.

Choclococha, lake, lat. 13° 30′, Figs. 66, 68.

Choqquequirau, ruins, canyon of Apurimac above junction of Pachachaca River, lat. 13° 25′, (Fig. 20).

Choquetira, village, lat. 13° 20′, Fig. 20. *See also* Fig. 136.

Chosica, village, lat. 12°, Fig. 66.

Chuquibamba, town, lat. 15° 50′, Figs. 20, 204.

Chuquibambilla, village, lat. 14°, Figs. 20, 204.

Chuquito, pass, Cordillera Vilcapampa between Arma and Vilcabamba valleys, lat. 13° 10′, (Fig. 20). *See also* Fig. 139.

Coast Range, Figs. 66, 204.

Cochabamba, city, Bolivia, lat. 17° 20′, long. 66° 20′.

Colorada, pampa, lat. 15° 30′, Fig. 204.

Colpani, village, lower end of Canyon of Torontoy (Urubamba River), lat. 13° 10′. *See* Fig. 158.

Copacavana, village, Bolivia, lat. 16° 10′, long. 69° 10′.

Coribeni, river, lat. 12° 40′, Fig. 8.

Coropuna, mt., lat. 15° 30′, Figs. 20, 204.

Corralpata, village, Apurimac Valley near Incahuasi.

Cosos, village, lat. 16°, Fig. 204.

Cotabambas, town, Apurimac Valley, lat. 13° 45′, (Fig. 20).

Cotahuasi, town, lat. 15° 10′, Figs. 20, 204.

Cuzco, city, lat. 13° 30′, Fig. 20.

Echarati, hacienda, on the Urubamba River between Santa Ana and Rosalina, lat. 12° 40′. *See* inset map, Fig. 8, *and also* Fig. 54.

Huadquiña, hacienda, Urubamba River above junction with Vilcabamba, lat. 13° 10′, (Fig. 20). *See also* Fig. 158.

Huadquirca, village, lat. 14° 15′, Figs. 20, 204.

Huaipo, lake, north of Anta, lat. 13° 25′, (Fig. 20).

Huambo, village, left bank Pachachaca River between Huancarama and Pasaje, lat. 13° 35', (Fig. 20).
Huancarama, town, lat. 13° 40', Fig. 20.
Huancarqui, village, lat. 16° 5', Fig. 204.
Huascatay, village, left bank of Apurimac above Pasaje, lat. 13° 30', (Fig. 20).
Huaynacotas, village, lat. 15° 10', Fig. 204.
Huichihua, village, lat. 14° 10', Fig. 204.

(Tablazo de) Ica, plateau, lat. 14°–15° 30', Fig. 66.
Ica, town, lat. 14°, Figs. 66, 67.
Incahuasi, village, lat. 13° 20', Fig. 20.
Iquique, town, northern Chile, lat. 20° 15'.
(Pampa de) Islay, south of Vitor River, (Fig. 66).

Jaguey, village, Pampa de Sihuas, q.v.

La Joya, pampa, station on Mollendo-Puno R.R., 16° 40', (Fig. 66).
Lambrama, village, lat. 12° 50', Fig. 20.
Lima, city, lat. 12°, Fig. 66.

Machu Picchu, ruins, gorge of Torontoy, q.v., lat. 13° 10'.
Majes, river, Fig. 204.
Manugali, river, tributary of Urubamba entering from left above Puviriari River, lat. 12° 20', (Fig. 8).
Maritime Cordillera, Fig. 204.
Matara, village, lat. 14° 20', Fig. 204.
(El) Misti, mt., lat. 16° 30', Fig. 66.
Mollendo, town, lat. 17°, Fig. 66.
Moquegua, town, lat. 17°, Fig. 66.
Morococha, mines, lat. 11° 45', Fig. 66.
Mulanquiato, settlement, lat. 12° 10', Fig. 8.

Occobamba, river, uniting with Yanatili, q.v.
Ocoña, river, lat. 15°–16° 30', Figs. 20, 66.
Ollantaytambo, village, Urubamba River below Urubamba town, lat. 13° 15', (Fig. 20), and see inset map, Fig. 8.

Pabellon, hacienda, Urubamba River above Rosalina, (Fig. 20). See also Fig. 55.
Pacasmayo, town, lat. 7° 30', Fig. 66.
Pachatusca (Pachatusun), mt., overlooking Cuzco to northeast, lat. 13° 30'.
Pachitea, river, tributary of Ucayali entering from left, lat. 8° 50'.

Paita, town, lat. 5°, Fig. 66.
Pampacolca, village, south of Coropuna, q.v.
Pampaconas, river, known in lower course as Cosireni, tributary of Urubamba River, (Fig. 8). Source in Cordillera Vilcapampa west of Vilcabamba.
Pampas, river, tributary of Apurimac entering from left, lat. 13° 20'.
Panta, mt., Cordillera Vilcapampa, northwest of Arma, lat. 13° 15', (Fig. 20). See also Fig. 136.
Panticalla, pass, Urubamba Valley above Torontoy, lat. 13° 10'.
Pasaje, hacienda and ferry, lat. 13° 30', Fig. 20.
Paucartambo (Yavero), river, q.v.
Paucartambo, town, head of Paucartambo (Yavero) River, lat. 13° 20', long. 71° 40'. Inset map, Fig. 8.
Pichu-Pichu, mt., overlooking Arequipa, lat. 16°, (Fig. 66).
Pilcopata, river, tributary of Upper Madre de Dios east of Paucartambo, lat. 13°.
Piñi-piñi, river, tributary of Upper Madre de Dios east of Paucartambo, lat. 13°.
Pisco, town, lat. 14°, Fig. 66.
Piura, river, lat. 5°–6°, Fig. 66.
Piura, town, lat. 5° 30', Fig. 66.
Pomareni, river, lat. 12°, Fig. 8.
Pongo de Mainique, rapids, lat. 12°, Fig. 8.
Pucamoco, hacienda, Urubamba River, between Santa Ana and Rosalina, (Fig. 20).
Puquiura, village, lat. 13° 5', Fig. 20. See also Fig. 158. Distinguish Puqura in Anta basin near Cuzco.
Puqura, village, Anta basin, east of Anta, lat. 13° 30', (Fig. 20).

Quilca, town, lat. 16° 40', Fig. 66.
Quillagua, village, northern Chile, lat. 21° 30', long. 69° 35'.

Rosalina, settlement, lat. 12° 35', Fig. 8. See also Fig. 20.

Sahuayaco, hacienda, Urubamba Valley above Rosalina, (Fig. 20). See also Fig. 55.
Salamanca, town, lat. 15° 30', Fig. 20.
Salaverry, town, lat. 8°, Fig. 66.
Salcantay, mt., lat. 13° 20', Fig. 20.

San Miguel, bridge, canyon of Torontoy near Machu Picchu, lat. 13° 10'.

Santa Ana, hacienda, lat. 12° 50', Fig. 20.

Santa Ana, river, name applied to the Urubamba in the region about hacienda Santa Ana.

Santa Lucia, mines, lat. 16°, Fig. 66.

Santo Anato, hacienda, La Sama's hut, 12° 35', Fig. 8.

Sihuas, Pampa de, lat. 16° 30', Fig. 204.

Sillilica, Cordillera, east of Iquique, northern Chile.

Sintulini, rapids of Urubamba River above junction of Pomareni, lat. 12° 10', (Fig. 8).

Sirialo, river, lat. 12° 40', Fig. 8.

Soiroccocha, mt., Cordillera Vilcapampa north of Arma, lat. 13° 15', (Fig. 20).

Solimana, mt., lat. 15° 20', Fig. 204.

Soray, mt., Cordillera Vilcapampa, southeast of Mt. Salcantay, lat. 13° 20', (Fig. 20).

Sotospampa, village, near Lambrama, lat. 13° 50', (Fig. 204).

Sullana, town, Chira River, lat. 5°, (Fig. 66).

Taurisma, village, lat. 15° 10', Fig. 204.

Ticumpinea, river, tributary of Urubamba entering from right below Pongo de Mainique, lat. 11° 50', (Fig. 8).

Timpia, river, tributary of Urubamba entering from right, lat. 11° 45'.

Tono, river, tributary of Upper Madre de Dios, east of Paucartambo, lat. 13°.

Torontoy, canyon of the Urubamba between the villages of Torontoy and Colpani, lat. 13° 10'–13° 15'.

Torontoy, village at the head of the canyon of the same name, lat. 13° 15'. *See* inset map, Fig. 8.

Tumbez, town, lat. 4° 30', Fig. 66.

Tunari, Cerro de, mt., northwest of Cochabamba, *q.v.*

Urubamba, river, Fig. 20.

Urubamba, town, lat. 13° 20', Fig. 20.

Vilcabamba, river, tributary of Urubamba River entering from left above Santa Ana, lat. 13°, Fig. 8. *See also* Fig. 158.

Vilcabamba, village, lat. 13° 5', Fig. 20. *See also* Fig. 158.

Vilcanota, Cordillera, southern Peru.

Vilcanota, river, name applied to Urubamba above lat. of Cuzco, 13° 30', (Fig. 20).

Vilcapampa, Cordillera, lat. 13° 20', Fig. 20.

Vilque, town, southern Peru, lat. 15° 50', long. 70° 30'.

Vitor, pampa, lat. 16° 30', Fig. 66.

Vitor, river, Fig. 66.

Yanahuara, pass, between Urubamba and Yanatili valleys, lat. 13° 10'.

Yanatili, river, tributary of Urubamba entering from right above Rosalina, (Fig. 20). *See also* Fig. 55.

Yavero (Paucartambo), river, tributary of Urubamba entering from right, lat. 12° 10', Fig. 8.

Yavero, settlement, at junction of Yavero and Urubamba rivers, lat. 12° 10', Fig. 8.

Yunguyo, town, southern Peru, lat. 16° 20', long. 69° 10'.

Yuyato, river, lat. 12° 5', Fig. 8.

INDEX

DAT